Brief Menu

P9-DII-773

*How can I write a
stronger thesis?
See 1c or 6c.*

*What's the difference
between* affect *and*
effect? *See 19.*

How do periods and commas work with quotation marks? See 34d.

How should I format my essay? See 51 (MLA) or 53 (APA).

Where can I see model citations? See 50 (MLA) or 52 (APA).

THE
BEDFORD
Handbook

Eleventh Edition

Diana Hacker

Nancy Sommers
Harvard University

bedford/st.martin's
Macmillan Learning

Boston | New York

For Bedford/St. Martin's

Vice President, Editorial, Macmillan Learning Humanities: Edwin Hill
Executive Program Director for English: Leasa Burton
Executive Program Manager: Stacey Purviance
Director of Content Development, Humanities: Jane Knetzger
Senior Executive Editor: Michelle M. Clark
Associate Editor: Melissa Rostek
Assistant Editor: Aislyn Fredsall
Senior Content Project Manager: Gregory Erb
Senior Workflow Project Supervisors: Joe Ford and Paul Rohloff
Production Supervisor: Robin Besofsky
Senior Media Project Manager: Allison Hart
Senior Media Editor: Barbara G. Flanagan
Marketing Manager: Vivian Garcia
Copyeditor: Lifland et al., Bookmakers
Composition: Lumina Datamatics, Inc.
Text Permissions Editor: Kalina Ingham
Text Permissions Researcher: Elaine Kosta, Lumina Datamatics, Inc.
Photo Permissions Editor: Angela Boehler
Photo Researcher: Krystyna Borgen
Director of Design, Content Management: Diana Blume
Text Design: Claire Seng-Niemoeller
Cover Design: William Boardman
Printing and Binding: LSC Communications

3   4   5   6   24   23   22   21   20

For information, write: Bedford/St. Martin's, 75 Arlington Street, Boston, MA 02116

ISBN 978-1-319-36108-2 (Student Edition, APA Update)
ISBN 978-1-319-26361-4 (Instructor's Edition)

Acknowledgments

Text acknowledgments and copyrights appear at the back of the book on page 420, which constitute an extension of the copyright page. Art acknowledgments and copyrights appear on the same page as the art selections they cover.

Preface for instructors

Dear Colleagues:

Welcome to the eleventh edition of *The Bedford Handbook*. For this edition, I set the goal of creating a concise, affordable handbook. To do so, I did what I tell my students to do: revise with a purpose and seek feedback along the way. My purpose was clear — take a "less is more" approach to streamline the content. And I sought to learn from our Editorial Advisory Board, a talented team of writing faculty (see p. vii). *The Bedford Handbook* you hold in your hands has been reimagined for your students, at roughly half the size and half the cost of the previous edition, with everything your students need to become confident, successful college writers.

It sounds easy enough, almost like a mantra: look closely at each word, sentence, and section, then decide whether it is essential. Of course, some sections were easy to cut. Others, less so. For example, lengthy instruction about brainstorming and freewriting seemed nonessential — as did information about how to manage computer files. And multiple pages of instruction about taking notes could effectively be reduced, I discovered, to a practical "how to" page on taking notes responsibly.

It was time, in the eleventh edition, to rethink everything. This "less is more" approach gave me an opportunity to look squarely at each handbook section, thinking about what college writers need to know about quoting, summarizing, and paraphrasing sources, for example, or about building paragraphs and punctuating sentences. I wanted to find the essence of each grammar and research lesson and convey these lessons in practical, straightforward language. I wanted the handbook to answer students' big questions about constructing a thesis statement and writing persuasive arguments. Along the way, I learned (again) a central lesson we offer our students about the power of language: choose specific words and make each word count.

> It was time, in the eleventh edition, to rethink everything.

As I worked with our wonderful Editorial Advisory Board, I asked questions about their student writers' challenges and about the handbook sections their students find most useful. We weighed each decision

about what to cut, preserve, and add. Our reviewers suggested we combine instruction on analyzing traditional and multimodal texts, and they
welcomed our streamlined coverage of citing and integrating sources in MLA and APA styles. Removing
redundancies and combining instruction made space
for new features, such as instruction on detecting false
and misleading sources and on paraphrasing and integrating sources — key research skills. Reviewers were
firm about preserving what they called "one of *The
Bedford Handbook*'s great strengths," the practice exercises throughout
the handbook. You'll find these exercises in the eleventh edition as useful
as ever.

No extra
explanations;
nothing to skip
over; just the
essentials.

One of our reviewers asked, "Classroom time is short over a semester, so why have extra explanations in the text that we skip over?" I heard
these words in my head as I revised. No extra explanations; nothing to
skip over; just the essentials. A smaller, briefer handbook offers many
advantages, with its affordable price and ease of use. *The Bedford Handbook*, reaching back to the roots of composition handbooks, is designed to
save students time and help them find answers quickly, so that everything
they need to become successful college writers is at their fingertips.

I am eager to share this new edition with you.

Nancy Sommers

Nancy Sommers
nancy_sommers@harvard.edu

Meet our Editorial Advisory Board

The following fellow teachers of writing worked with us to reimagine *The Bedford Handbook* as a leaner resource for composition essentials. Students across the country will benefit from their expertise in the classroom and their passion for fostering writers' skills and habits.

A careful reader and experienced teacher, **Chuck Baker**, Academic Program Director for English at **Greenville Technical College**, inspired us to rethink the organization of the chapters on the writing process. See especially the new placement of the paragraph coverage in Part 1.

Jacob Blevins, English department chair at **Sam Houston State University**, firmly believes that college-level research should go beyond reporting. He helped us shape the kinds of examples we use to teach students how to evaluate sources and integrate them as they write.

Christine Peters Cucciarre is Director of Composition at the **University of Delaware**. Her candid feedback guided us as we simplified the research coverage. She also found the new sentence guides—fill-in models to help students write with an academic voice (see 49c)—"tremendously helpful."

With her students always in mind, **Monica Dimauro**, professor of English at **Florida State College at Jacksonville**, thanked us for leading with the term "academic writing" and confirmed that our new side-by-side presentation of MLA and APA (see 47–49) would work well in her courses.

Javier Dueñas is an assistant professor of English and Communications at **Miami Dade College, North Campus**. Javier's detailed comments on the text were integral to the reimagined grammar coverage. He appreciates how the new edition "distills this content down to the essentials" with briefer, more direct explanations.

We were grateful for the expertise of **Africa Fine**, associate professor of English and Literature at **Palm Beach State College**, who helped us think through the challenges students face when writing with sources—most notably, how to express their own ideas in relation to the ideas of others.

Megan Fischer is a composition instructor at **Angelina College**. Her numerous comments on early manuscript helped shape the reorganized writing chapters. She is a fan of the new research chapters (see Part 9) and thinks "they provide clear, useful guidelines that demystify the research process for students."

Bill Leach is the Online Liberal Arts Program chair and an English professor at the **Florida Institute of Technology**. He is passionate about handbook use in his course and believes that the new edition has "targeted the essential material that we can cover in the classroom setting." He gave thoughtful suggestions that strengthened the content throughout the handbook.

Because grammar instruction is part of the mission of the writing program at her school, we appreciated comments from **Jeannine Morgan**, chair of the Communications department at **St. Johns River State College**, that were specifically related to content for multilingual writers. The condensed material in section 29 supports students' development, according to Jeannine, and "focus[es] on the most common areas of difficulty [her] students tend to have."

Anthony Podlaski is an assistant professor of English at **Hudson Valley Community College** and an experienced user of LaunchPad. He notes that he "depend[s] on *The Bedford Handbook* for coverage of clear sentences, word choice, style, and grammar." His feedback, especially on sections such as the new Glossary of Usage (see 19), helped strengthen this edition.

See page xiv for a list of additional reviewers.

Welcome to the Eleventh Edition

What's new?

A portable, more affordable handbook means that students are more likely to have their help with them when they come to class, visit the writing center, and sit down to draft and revise. The new edition focuses on *essential skills and habits* students need to be successful college writers. With the help of a ten-member Editorial Advisory Board—writing teachers from two- and four-year colleges—we have made the content substantially more concise, reaching back to the roots of traditional coverage in composition handbooks. What's more, a significantly lower price will appeal to your students—and the high value gets even higher when you choose to use an e-book, create a custom edition, or package the book with one or more supplements.

Better navigational aids help students locate useful content quickly.

- **A new *How to use this book* page**, developed after usability research with students from two- and four-year colleges, orients students to the major avenues for finding help.

- **Chapter previews** point to boxes, checklists, examples, and other key content that students need to find fast.

- **Lists of documentation models** appear at the beginning of the documentation chapters to minimize page flipping.

New help designed for beginning academic writers leads students to develop important academic skills and habits.

- ***How-to pages on paraphrasing sources and identifying false and misleading information*** guide students as they begin to work with sources. (See pp. 273 and 291.)

- New ***sentence guides*** help students with the most basic academic scenario: presenting and responding to the views of others. Fill-in sentence starters (see 49c) provide useful models for participating in academic discourse and writing research essays.

- Newly reorganized and ***focused help for research writers*** teaches key skills such as integrating sources and avoiding plagiarism.

Meet the most practical handbook ever.

How to solve five common problems with thesis statements   9–10

How to write helpful peer review comments   29

How to improve your writing with an editing log   32

How to read like a writer   40

How to draft an analytical thesis statement   43★

How to write an analytical essay   47–48★

How to draft a thesis statement for an argument   65★

How to write an argument essay   74–75★

How to enter a research conversation   260★

How to go beyond a Google search   265

NEW How to take notes responsibly   269

How to avoid plagiarizing from the web   271

NEW How to detect false and misleading sources   273

How to write an annotated bibliography   278–279★

How to be a responsible research writer   285

NEW How to paraphrase effectively   291–292

How to answer the basic question "Who is the author?"   324

How to cite a source reposted from another source   344

★Video versions of some How-to boxes are included in LaunchPad Solo for Hacker Handbooks.

A complete series of resources for developing college writers

- *A Student's Companion to Hacker Handbooks*, a new supplemental workbook for students in paired or co-requisite sections, provides a wide range of activities to help students practice the skills and habits they need to be successful academic writers. Designed specifically to help underprepared students succeed in a first-year writing course, it includes coverage of important college success strategies and a variety of activities and templates to help students improve their reading and writing performance. Graphic organizers help visual learners, exercises on thesis statements and topic sentences help writers with little academic writing experience, and grammar and research exercises help strengthen students' work at the sentence level.

- *Developmental Exercises for Hacker Handbooks* offers a "grammar intensive" with 175 exercises that can be done right in the book, providing additional practice with all of the topics in the handbook. Exercise formats range from sentence sets to brief essays, and selections are thematically linked so that students can correct errors in realistic contexts.

- *Working with Sources: Exercises for Hacker Handbooks* provides low-stakes practice with foundational documentation skills, offering roughly 20 exercises per style (MLA and APA). Topics include integrating sources, avoiding plagiarism, and identifying citation elements. Visual exercises help students identify publication information on title pages and on websites.

Visit the catalog page for *The Bedford Handbook* to see a complete list of supplements and media. Go to macmillanlearning.com.

What hasn't changed?

The Bedford Handbook, Eleventh Edition, still includes **writing guides** for common assignments, because you told us how useful these are in your courses. The new edition still emphasizes **critical reading and academic writing.** We know how much you value the practice **exercises**

and activities that help with grammar, style, and punctuation topics, so we have retained exercises both in the print book and online. The coverage of **MLA style** is still as robust as ever. You'll find **professional support** in our online English Community (community.macmillan.com), where you can follow our Bits Blog for teaching ideas, download professional resources, and access *Teaching with Hacker Handbooks*. Finally, know that you can still rely on **outstanding service** from your Bedford/St. Martin's sales, marketing, and editorial teams — because we're as passionately committed to the discipline as ever.

Custom options

Whether you have high or low enrollments, you can **tailor content to your needs** and help your students make the most of their handbook. Visit macmillanlearning.com/curriculumsolutions to learn more about building your own handbook.

- **ForeWords for English.** Developed especially for writing courses, our ForeWords English program is custom content made simple. Choose from a library of the most commonly requested content in easy-to-use chapters (12–16 pages each) to help you build the best possible text. ForeWords includes chapters on time management, business writing, and proposal writing, sentence templates for academic writing, and more—all easy to add to your custom edition of *The Bedford Handbook*. (Minimum enrollment is 200 copies.)

- **Original material.** Many schools choose to add original school-specific or program-specific content to create a custom edition that reflects their goals and expectations. You can easily add course outcomes, a common syllabus, information about the writing center, sample student writing, a custom cover, and more. (Minimum enrollment is 200 copies.)

- **Bedford Select Handbooks.** With very low minimums (25 copies), you can build your own composition resource from archived Hacker Handbooks content. Students pay only for the chapters you choose, and the process is a snap for instructors.

Acknowledgments

I am grateful for the expertise, enthusiasm, and classroom experience
that so many individuals brought to the eleventh edition.

Reviewers

Natalie Belcher, Delaware State University; Shane Bradley, Erskine
College; Kenneth Brosky, University of Wisconsin–Rock County; Heather
Chacon, Greensboro College; Robin Colby, Meredith College; Nicole A.
Cosentino, University at Albany; Howard Cox, Angelina College; Brock
Dethier, Utah State University; Layla Dowlatshahi, Normandale Com-
munity College; Gwyn Enright, San Diego City College; Sallyanne H.
Fitzgerald, Polk State College; Wendy L. Grosskopf, Bemidji State Univer-
sity; Mickey Hall, Volunteer State Community College; Melody Hargraves,
St. Johns River State College; Joel B. Henderson, Chattanooga State Com-
munity College; Marie Hendry, State College of Florida–Venice; Jamie
Henthorn, Catawba College; Max Hohner, Eastern Washington Univer-
sity; Kimberley M. Holloway, King University; John F. Jebb, University of
Delaware; Laura Jeffries, Florida State College at Jacksonville; Heather
Keller-Giltner, John Wood Community College; Laura La Flair, Belmont
Abbey College; Jennifer Laufenberg, Bossier Parish Community College;
Elizabeth McDowell, University of Delaware; Rebecca V. Mills, California
State Polytechnic University, Pomona; Carmen Mise, Miami Dade
College–North Campus; Loren Mitchell, Hawaii Community College;
Jill Morris, Frostburg State University; Tracy Ann Morse, East Carolina
University; Van Piercy, Lone Star College–Tomball; Dan Portincaso,
Waubonsee Community College; Daniel Powell, Florida State College
at Jacksonville; Kevin M. Rulo, The Catholic University of America; Ed
Sams, San Jose State University; Susan Slavicz, Florida State College at
Jacksonville; Amy D. Stackhouse, Iona College; David Stivers, Savannah
College of Art and Design; James D. Suderman, Northwest Florida State
College; Nancy Wilson, Texas State University.

   I would like to acknowledge the generous contributions of our
Editorial Advisory Board and their important role in developing this
edition of *The Bedford Handbook*. Their smart, insightful questions
and critiques showed us where we met our goals and where we missed
the mark. Their close reading of the manuscript and their thoughtful,

practical suggestions helped us achieve our mission—to find the essential handbook instruction students need to become successful college writers. See pages vii–ix to read about our Editorial Advisory Board.

Contributors

I am grateful for contributions from the following individuals, all fellow teachers of writing: Margaret Price, associate professor of English at The Ohio State University, and Rosalie Roberts, adjunct instructor of English at Clark College, for helping me to think about new content on pronouns, gender, and audience awareness; and Sylvia Basile of Midlands Technical College, Sandra Chumchal of Blinn College, and Sarah Gottschall and Paul Madachy of Prince George's Community College, for contributing material on integrating sources, reading strategies, avoiding plagiarism, and audience, respectively, to *A Student's Companion to Hacker Handbooks*, an exciting new tool for ALP and co-requisite sections of composition.

Students

I extend my gratitude to the following students for letting us adapt their work as models throughout the handbook: Sophie Harba, Sam Jacobs, Emilia Sanchez, and April Bo Wang.

Bedford/St. Martin's and beyond

A handbook is a collaborative writing project, and it is my pleasure to acknowledge the enormously talented Bedford/St. Martin's editorial team, whose focus on students informs each new feature of *The Bedford Handbook*. Edwin Hill, vice president for humanities editorial, and Leasa Burton, executive program director for English, generously offer their deep knowledge of the field of composition. Stacey Purviance, executive program manager, brings her creative energy and enormous talents to *The Bedford Handbook*. I am grateful for her dedication to the handbook and for her commitment to designing new ways to pair print and digital content. Many thanks to Bedford colleagues Joy Fisher Williams and Vivian Garcia, who, like me, spend many hours on the road and in faculty offices, for their treasured advice. Doug Silver, product manager for English, helps us to reimagine writers' and teachers' opportunities with digital tools.

Michelle Clark, senior executive editor, is the editor every author dreams of having. She manages to be exacting and endearing all at once — a treasured friend and colleague and an endless source of creativity. Michelle combines imagination with practicality and hard work with good cheer. Melissa Rostek, associate editor, brings fresh ideas, bold questions, and excellent editorial instincts to our collaboration. I am grateful for her steady, judicious thinking as we debated cutting and condensing various sections; I am fortunate to work with such a talented editor. Barbara Flanagan, senior media editor, sets the bar high for all of us and we scramble to live up to her expectations. Barbara brings unrivaled expertise in documentation and manages content development for LaunchPad Solo for Hacker Handbooks. It is a pleasure to work with Barbara and to benefit from her wisdom and good sense on important details. Thanks also to Aislyn Fredsall, editorial assistant, for overseeing the review and permissions processes.

Many thanks to the media production team for delivering engaging handbook tools, including new e-books, for students in the digital age. Thanks also to Gregory Erb, senior content project manager, for a careful eye and smart management of production; to Sally Lifland, copyeditor, for thoroughness and attention to detail; to Claire Seng-Niemoeller, who kept our design clean, simple, and elegant; and to Billy Boardman, senior design manager, who has introduced a striking new cover.

Last, but never least, I offer thanks to my own students who, over many years, have shaped my teaching and helped me understand their challenges. Thanks to my friends and colleagues Jenny Doggett, Joan Feinberg, Suzanne Lane, Maxine Rodburg, Laura Saltz, and Kerry Walk for sustaining conversations about the teaching of writing. And thanks to my family: to Joshua Alper, an attentive reader of life and literature, for his steadfastness across the drafts; to my parents, Walter and Louise Sommers, who encouraged me to write and set me forth on a career of writing and teaching; to my extended family, Ron, Charles Mary, Alexander, Demian, Devin, Liz, Kate, Sam, Terry, Steve, and Yuval, for their good humor and good cheer; and to Rachel and Curran, Alexandra and Brian, world-class listeners, witty and wise beyond measure, always generous with their instruction and inspiration in all things that matter. They share my thrill when they hold this handbook in their hands. And to my grandchildren, Lailah and Oren, thanks for the joy and sweetness you bring to life.

Nancy Sommers

Contents

10 Add needed words. 87

10a Add words needed to complete compound structures. 87
10b Add the word *that* where needed for clarity. 87
10c Add words needed to make comparisons logical and complete. 88

11 Untangle mixed constructions. 89

11a Untangle the grammatical structure. 89
11b Straighten out the logical connections. 90
11c Avoid *is when, is where,* and *reason . . . is because* constructions. 91

12 Repair misplaced and dangling modifiers. 92

12a Put limiting modifiers in front of the words they modify. 92
12b Place phrases and clauses so that readers can see at a glance what they modify. 93
12c Avoid split infinitives when they are awkward. 93
12d Repair dangling modifiers. 94

13 Eliminate distracting shifts. 96

13a Make the point of view consistent in person and number. 96
13b Maintain consistent verb tenses. 97

14 Emphasize key ideas. 98

14a Coordinate equal ideas; subordinate minor ideas. 98
14b Combine choppy sentences. 100
14c Avoid ineffective or excessive coordination. 102
14d Do not subordinate major ideas. 103

15 Provide some variety. 104

15a Vary your sentence openings. 104
15b Use a variety of sentence structures. 105
15c Try inverting sentences occasionally. 106

A Process for Writing

Welcome to *The Bedford Handbook.* One of the pleasures of college writing is exploring ideas and discovering what you think about a subject.

You may find that the process leads you in unexpected directions. The more you read about a topic, the more questions you formulate, and new questions may lead you to challenge your initial assumptions. It is in the process of writing and thinking in depth about ideas that you learn what's interesting in a subject and why you care about it.

1 Exploring, planning, and drafting

Academic writing is a process of figuring out what you think and exploring questions to which you don't have answers. Since it's not possible to think about everything all at once, start by assessing your writing situation and composing a piece of writing in stages — planning, drafting, revising, and editing.

1a Assess your writing situation.

Before composing a first draft, spend time asking questions about your writing situation. The key elements include your subject, purpose, audience, and genre.

Subject

Frequently your subject will be given to you. When you are free to choose what to write about, select subjects that interest or puzzle you. Writing about a subject that you care about enables you to write with more authority and confidence.

Purpose

All writing has a purpose or reason—to inform, to analyze, to persuade, to call readers to action, and so on. The wording of an assignment may suggest its purpose. You may need to ask yourself "What do I want to accomplish?" and "What do I want to communicate to my audience?"

Audience

Take time to consider the interests and expectations of your readers. What do they know or believe about your subject? What information do they need to be able to understand your ideas? What kind of response do you want from your audience? Make choices that show respect for your readers' values and perspectives.

Genre

Pay attention to the genre, or type of writing, assigned. Each genre is a category of writing meant for a specific purpose and audience, with its own set of agreed-upon expectations and conventions for style, structure, and format. Genres include essays, lab reports, business memos, research proposals, and position papers.

Considering audience when writing an email message

When you write an email message to an instructor, a classmate, or a potential employer, respect your audience by using a concise subject line, keeping paragraphs brief, proofreading for errors, and paying attention to your tone. If you include someone else's words, let your reader know the source.

EXERCISE 1–1   Narrow the following subjects into topics that would be manageable for an essay of two to five pages. For each of the five narrowed topics, suggest a purpose and an audience.

1. The minimum wage
2. Immigration
3. Cyberbullying
4. The cost of a college education
5. Internet privacy

Checklist for assessing your writing situation

Subject

- Assigned or free choice?
- Why is your subject worth writing about?
- What questions will you explore?
- Do you need to narrow your subject to a more specific topic?

Purpose and audience

- Why are you writing: To inform readers? To persuade them? To call them to action? Some combination of purposes?
- What are the most effective strategies for achieving your purpose?
- Who are your readers? How well informed are they about the subject?
- What information do readers need to be able to understand your ideas?
- Will readers resist your ideas? What objections will you need to anticipate and counter?

Genre (type of document)

- What genre is required: Essay? Letter? Report? Proposal? Something else?
- Expectations for the genre? For example, what type of evidence is typically used?
- Does the genre require a specific format or organization?

Length and format

- Length requirements?
- Format requirements?
- Documentation requirements? MLA, APA, or *Chicago*?
- Do you have guidelines or examples to consult?

Deadlines

- Rough draft due date? Final due date?
- How to submit writing: print, post, email, or share?

1b Explore your subject.

Experiment with strategies for exploring your subject and discovering your purpose. The following strategies will help you generate ideas.

Talking and listening

Talking about your ideas can help you develop your thoughts and discover what your listeners find interesting, what they are curious about, and where they disagree with you. If you are writing an argument, you can try it out on listeners with other points of view to help you learn about counterarguments.

Reading and annotating texts

Reading is an important way to deepen your understanding of a topic, learn from the insights and research of others, and expand your perspective. Annotating (making notes on) a text encourages you to read actively — to highlight key concepts, to note possible contradictions in an argument, or to raise questions for further research and investigation.

Asking questions

Asking questions is a productive way to get started on a writing project. You might try asking *Who? What? When? Where? Why?* and *How?* to investigate your subject and discover important facts.

Brainstorming and freewriting

Brainstorming and freewriting are good ways to figure out what you know and what questions you have. Write quickly and freely, without pausing to think about word choice, to discover what questions are on your mind and what directions you might pursue.

Keeping a journal

A journal is a collection of informal or exploratory writing. You might pose questions, comment on an interesting idea from one of your classes, or keep a list of thoughts that occur to you while reading. You might imagine a conversation between yourself and your readers or stage a debate to understand opposing positions.

Blogging

Although a blog is a type of journal, it is a public rather than a private writing space. In a blog, you can explore an idea for a paper by writing posts from different angles. Since most blogs allow commenting, you can start a conversation by inviting readers to give you feedback in the form of questions, counterarguments, or links to other sources on a topic.

1c Draft and revise a working thesis statement.

For many types of writing, you will be able to assert your central idea in a sentence or two. Such a statement, which ordinarily appears at the end of your introduction, is called a *thesis statement*.

Understanding what makes an effective thesis statement

An effective thesis statement is a central idea that conveys your purpose, or reason for writing, and that requires support.

To be effective, a thesis statement should

- state a position that needs to be supported
- use concrete language and be sharply focused
- let your readers know what to expect
- be appropriate for the length requirements of the assignment, not too broad or too narrow
- stand up to the "So what?" question (see p. 8)

Drafting a working thesis statement

As you explore your topic, you will begin to see possible ways to focus your material.

You'll find that the process of answering a question you have posed or taking a position on a debatable topic will focus your thinking and lead you to develop a working thesis. Here, for example, are one student's efforts to pose a question and draft a working thesis for an essay in his ethics course.

QUESTION

Should athletes who enhance their performance through biotechnology be banned from athletic competition?

WORKING THESIS

Athletes who boost their performance through biotechnology should be banned from athletic competition.

The working thesis offers a useful place to start writing, a way to limit the topic and focus a first draft; but it doesn't respond to readers who will ask "Why?" and "So what?" The student has taken a position—athletes who use performance enhancers should be banned—but he hasn't explained *why* these athletes should be banned. To fully answer his own question, he might push his own thinking with the word *because*.

STRONGER WORKING THESIS

Athletes who boost their performance through biotechnology should be banned from competition *because* biotechnology gives athletes an unfair advantage and disrupts the sense of fair play.

Revising a working thesis statement

As you move toward a clearer and more specific position you want to take, you'll start to see ways to revise your working thesis. As your ideas change, your working thesis will change, too. You may find that the evidence you have collected supports a different thesis, or you may find that your position has changed as you have learned more about your topic. One effective way to keep audience and purpose in mind is to put your thesis to the "So what?" test on the next page.

> ### Putting your working thesis to the "So what?" test
>
> Use the following questions to help you revise your working thesis statement.
>
> - Why would readers want to read an essay with this thesis?
> - How would you respond to a reader who hears your thesis and asks "So what?" or "Why does it matter?"
> - Will any readers disagree with this thesis? If so, how might you revise your thesis?
> - Is the thesis too obvious? If you cannot come up with counterpositions that oppose your own, consider revising your thesis.

1d Draft a plan.

Listing and organizing supporting ideas, whether informally or formally, will help you develop your thesis. An informal outline can be drafted and revised quickly to help you figure out a tentative structure.

Here is one student's informal outline:

Working thesis: Animal testing should be banned because it is bad science and doesn't contribute to biomedical advances.

- Most animals don't serve as good models for the human body.
- Drug therapies can have vastly different effects on different species—92 percent of all drugs shown to be effective in animal tests fail in human trials.
- Some of the largest biomedical discoveries were made without the use of animal testing.
- The most effective biomedical research methods—tissue engineering and computer modeling—don't use animals.
- Animal studies are not scientifically necessary.

A formal outline may be useful later in the writing process, after you have written a rough draft, to help you see the logic and organization of your draft and to help you identify any gaps.

Solve five common problems with thesis statements

Revising a working thesis is easier if you have a method or an approach. The following problem/solution approach can help you recognize and solve common thesis problems.

1 Common problem: The thesis is a statement of fact.

Solution: Enter a debate by posing a question about your topic that has more than one possible answer. For example: Should the polygraph be used by private employers? Your thesis should be your answer to the question.

Working thesis: *The first polygraph was developed by Dr. John Larson in 1921.*

Revised: *Because the polygraph has not been proved reliable, even under controlled conditions, its use by private employers should be banned.*

2 Common problem: The thesis is a question.

Solution: Take a position on your topic by answering the question you have posed. Your thesis statement should be your answer to the question.

Working thesis: *Would President John F. Kennedy have continued to escalate the war in Vietnam if he had lived?*

Revised: *Although President John F. Kennedy sent the first American troops to Vietnam before he died, an analysis of his foreign policy suggests that he would not have escalated the war had he lived.*

→

9

3 Common problem: **The thesis is too broad.**

Solution: Focus on a subtopic of your original topic. Once you have chosen a subtopic, take a position in an ongoing debate and pose a question that has more than one answer. For example: Should people be tested for genetic diseases? Your thesis should be your answer to the question.

Working thesis: *Mapping the human genome has many implications for health and science.*

Revised: *Now that scientists can detect genetic predisposition for specific diseases, policymakers should establish clear guidelines about whom to test and under what circumstances.*

4 Common problem: **The thesis is too narrow.**

Solution: Identify challenging questions that readers might ask about your topic. Then pose a question that has more than one answer. For example: Do the risks of genetic testing outweigh its usefulness? Your thesis should be your answer to the question.

Working thesis: *A person who carries a genetic mutation linked to a particular disease might or might not develop that disease.*

Revised: *Avoiding genetic testing is a smart course of action because of both its emotional risks and its medical limitations.*

5 Common problem: **The thesis is vague.**

Solution: Focus your thesis with concrete language and clues about where the essay is headed. Pose a question about the topic that has more than one answer. For example: How does the physical structure of the Vietnam Veterans Memorial shape the experience of the visitors? Your thesis—your answer to the question—should use specific language.

Working thesis: *The Vietnam Veterans Memorial is an interesting structure.*

Revised: *By inviting visitors to see their own reflections in the wall, the Vietnam Veterans Memorial creates a link between the present and the past.*

EXERCISE 1–2   In each of the following pairs, which sentence might work well as a thesis for a short paper? What is the problem with the other one? Is it too factual? Too broad? Too vague? Use the problem/solution approach from pages 9–10 to evaluate each thesis.

1. a. Many drivers use their cell phones irresponsibly while driving.

    b. Current state laws are inadequate to punish drivers who use their cell phones irresponsibly to text, read email, or perform other distracting activities.

2. a. Although Facebook was designed to help college students keep in touch, it actually keeps them apart by discouraging face-to-face inter-actions and creating an illusion of intimacy.

    b. Facebook was designed to make it easier for people to keep in touch.

3. a. As we search to define the intelligence of animals, we run the risk of imposing our own understanding of intelligence on animals.

    b. How does the field of animal psychology help humans define intelligence?

4. a. The high cost of college needs to be reduced because it affects stu-dents and their families.

    b. To reduce the high cost of college, more students should be offered opportunities for dual-enrollment courses and a three-year college degree.

5. a. Opioid addiction affects people of all ages and from every socioeco-nomic group.

    b. The most effective way of treating opioid addiction is with combination therapies; often a single therapy is not enough.

1e Draft an introduction.

Your introduction will usually be a paragraph of 50 to 150 words (in a longer paper, it may be more than one paragraph). A common strategy is to open with a few sentences that engage readers, establish your purpose for writing, and state your thesis. Each sentence leading to your thesis should spark the interest of readers, drawing them into the world of your essay and showing them why your essay is worth reading.

> ### Strategies for drafting an introduction
>
> Whether you are composing a traditional essay or a work such as a slide presentation or a video, the following strategies can hook readers:
>
> - Offer a surprising statistic or an unusual fact
> - Ask a question
> - Introduce a quotation
> - Provide historical background
> - Define a key term or concept
> - Point out a problem, contradiction, or dilemma
> - Use a vivid example or image

In the following introduction, which opens with an engaging question, the thesis is highlighted.

Writer asks question to engage readers.

Shows two sides of the debate.

Thesis answers question and offers writer's position.

Should the government enact laws to regulate healthy eating choices? Many Americans would answer an emphatic "No," arguing that what and how much we eat should be left to individual choice rather than unreasonable laws. Others might argue that it would be unreasonable for the government not to enact legislation, given the rise of chronic diseases that result from harmful diets. In this debate, both the definition of reasonable regulations and the role of government to legislate food choices are at stake. In the name of public health and safety, state governments have the responsibility to shape health policies and to regulate healthy eating choices, especially since doing so offers a potentially large social benefit for a relatively small cost.

—Sophie Harba, student

TIP: For more examples of effective introductions, see pages 44, 51, and 69.

> **For Multilingual Writers**
>
> If you come from a culture that prefers an indirect approach in writing, you may feel that asserting a thesis in your introduction sounds unrefined or even rude. In the United States, however, readers appreciate a direct approach and expect, in your introduction, to see a clear thesis stating your position on the topic.

1f Draft the body.

As you draft the body of your essay, you might naturally ask: What should I say? How will I write an entire essay on my topic? Since the body of your essay develops support for your thesis, you will find the process easier if you have a working thesis to guide the drafting process. As you draft, keep asking questions: What does my thesis promise readers? What is my position on the topic? How will I support my position? Keep anticipating what information your readers will need to be able to understand your ideas. Remember that first drafts aren't finished drafts. They are just *first,* a place to begin. Find your momentum and keep writing.

If your thesis suggests a plan (see 1d) or if you have sketched a preliminary outline, try to organize your paragraphs accordingly. Draft the body of your essay by writing at least one paragraph about each supporting point you listed in the planning stage.

If you decide that some support for your thesis could come from one or more visuals, such as a table or infographic, keep in mind that the visual should support your writing, not substitute for it. See the student paper in 51b; the writer uses a graph to help develop her point.

For more detailed help with drafting and developing paragraphs, see section 2.

USING SOURCES RESPONSIBLY: As you draft, keep notes about sources you read and consult. If you quote, paraphrase, or summarize a source, include a citation, even in your draft (see 45 and 48). You will save time and avoid plagiarism if you do so.

> ### Strategies for drafting a conclusion
>
> In addition to echoing your main idea, a conclusion might do any of the following:
> - Briefly summarize your essay's key points
> - Return to the hook used in the introduction
> - Propose a course of action
> - Offer a recommendation
> - Suggest the topic's wider significance or implications

1g Draft a conclusion.

A conclusion completes an essay, reminding readers of the essay's main idea without repeating it. By the end of the essay, readers should already understand your main point, so concluding paragraphs are often relatively short. Avoid introducing new ideas at the end of an essay.

For examples of effective conclusions, see pages 46, 53, and 72.

2 Building effective paragraphs

▸ Writing focused and unified paragraphs, 16
▸ Common transitions, 20

A paragraph is a group of sentences that focuses on one main point or example. Except for special-purpose paragraphs, such as introductions and conclusions (see 1e and 1g), body paragraphs develop and support an essay's main point, or thesis. Aim for paragraphs that are well developed, organized, coherent, and neither too long nor too short for easy reading.

2a Focus on a main point.

An effective paragraph is unified around a main point. The point should be clear to readers, and all sentences in the paragraph should relate to it.

Stating the main point in a topic sentence

A clear topic sentence, a one-sentence summary of the paragraph's main point, acts as a signpost pointing in two directions: backward toward the thesis of the essay and forward toward the body of the paragraph.

Usually the topic sentence comes first in the paragraph.

> All living creatures manage some form of communication. The dance patterns of bees in their hive help to point the way to distant flower fields or announce successful foraging. Male stickleback fish regularly swim upside-down to indicate outrage in a courtship contest. Male deer and lemurs mark territorial ownership by rubbing their own body secretions on boundary stones or trees. Everyone has seen a frightened dog put his tail between his legs and run in panic. We, too, use gestures, expressions, postures, and movement to give our words point.
>
> —Olivia Vlahos, *Human Beginnings*

In college writing, topic sentences are often necessary for advancing or clarifying lines of an argument and introducing evidence from a source. In the following paragraph on the effects of the 2010 oil spill in the Gulf of Mexico, the writer uses a topic sentence to state that the extent of the threat is unknown, before quoting three sources that illustrate her point.

> To date, the full ramifications [of the oil spill] remain a question mark. An August report from the National Oceanic and Atmospheric Administration estimated that 75 percent of the oil had "either evaporated or been burned, skimmed, recovered from the wellhead, or dispersed." However, Woods Hole Oceanographic Institution researchers reported that a 1.2-mile-wide, 650-foot-high plume caused by the

spill "had and will persist for some time." And University of Georgia scientists concluded that almost 80 percent of the released oil hadn't been recovered and "remains a threat to the ecosystem."

— Michele Berger, "Volunteer Army"

Sticking to the point

Sentences that do not support the topic sentence destroy the unity of a paragraph. In the following paragraph describing the inadequate facilities in a high school, the information about the chemistry instructor is clearly off the point.

> As the result of tax cuts, the educational facilities of Lincoln High School have reached an all-time low. Some of the books date back to 1990 and have long since shed their covers. The few computers in working order must share one printer. The lack of lab equipment makes it necessary for four or five students to work at one table, with most watching rather than performing experiments. Also, the chemistry instructor left to have a baby at the beginning of the semester, and most of the students don't like the substitute. As for the furniture, many of the upright chairs have become recliners, and the desk legs are so unbalanced that they play seesaw on the floor.

Writing focused and unified paragraphs

A strong paragraph supports a thesis, opens with a topic sentence, focuses on and develops a main point, and holds together as a unit. As you build and revise your paragraphs, ask these questions:

- Does each paragraph support the thesis?
- Does each paragraph open with a clear topic sentence?
- Does each paragraph focus on a main point and develop the point?
- Is each paragraph organized and coherent?
- Is each paragraph the right length for its topic?

EXERCISE 2–1   Underline the topic sentence in the following paragraph and cross out sentences that do not support the main idea.

Quilt making has served as an important means of social, political, and artistic expression for women. In the nineteenth century, quilting circles provided one of the few opportunities for women to forge social bonds outside of their families. Once a week or more, they came together to sew as well as trade small talk, advice, and news. They used dyed cotton fabrics much like the fabrics quilters use today; surprisingly, quilters' basic materials haven't changed that much over the years. Sometimes the women joined their efforts in support of a political cause, making quilts that would be raffled to raise money for temperance societies, hospitals for sick and wounded soldiers, and the fight against slavery. Quilt making also afforded women a means of artistic expression at a time when they had few other creative outlets. Within their socially acceptable roles as homemakers, many quilters subtly pushed back at the restrictions placed on them by experimenting with color, design, and technique.

2b Make paragraphs coherent.

When sentences and paragraphs flow from one to another without discernible bumps, gaps, or shifts, they are said to be coherent. Coherence can be improved by strengthening the ties between old information and new. A number of techniques for strengthening those ties are detailed in this section.

Linking ideas clearly

Readers expect to learn a paragraph's main point in a topic sentence early in the paragraph. Then, as they move into the body of the paragraph, they expect to encounter specific details, facts, or examples that support the topic sentence—either directly or indirectly.

If a sentence does not support the topic sentence directly, readers expect it to support another sentence in the paragraph and therefore to support the topic sentence indirectly. The following paragraph begins with a topic sentence. The highlighted sentences are direct supports, and the rest of the sentences are indirect supports.

Topic sentence provides a preview of the paragraph.

Highlighted sentences answer the question "Why is the classroom not practical?"

> Though the open-space classroom works for many children, it is not practical for my son, David. First, David is hyperactive. When he was placed in an open-space classroom, he became distracted and confused. He was tempted to watch the movement going on around him instead of concentrating on his own work. Second, David has a tendency to transpose letters and numbers, a tendency that can be overcome only by individual attention from the instructor. In the open classroom he was moved from teacher to teacher, with each one responsible for a different subject. No single teacher worked with David long enough to diagnose the problem, let alone help him with it. Finally, David is not a highly motivated learner. In the open classroom, he was graded "at his own level," not by criteria for a certain grade. He could receive a B in reading and still be a grade level behind, because he was doing satisfactory work "at his own level."
>
> —Margaret Smith, student

Repeating key words

Repetition of key words is an important technique for gaining coherence. To prevent repetitions from becoming dull, you can use variations of a key word (*hike, hiker, hiking*), pronouns referring to the word (*gamblers ... they*), and synonyms (*run, spring, race, dash*). In the following paragraph describing plots among indentured servants in the seventeenth century, historian Richard Hofstadter binds sentences together by repeating the key word *plots* and echoing it with a variety of synonyms.

> Plots hatched by several servants to run away together occurred mostly in the plantation colonies, and the few recorded servant uprisings were entirely limited to those colonies. Virginia had been forced from its very earliest years to take stringent steps against mutinous plots,

and severe punishments for such behavior were recorded. Most servant plots occurred in the seventeenth century: a contemplated uprising was nipped in the bud in York County in 1661; apparently led by some left-wing offshoots of the Great Rebellion, servants plotted an insurrection in Gloucester County in 1663, and four leaders were condemned and executed; some discontented servants apparently joined Bacon's Rebellion in the 1670's.

—Richard Hofstadter, *America at 1750*

Providing transitions

Transitions are bridges between what has been read and what is about to be read. They help readers move from sentence to sentence; they also alert readers to more global connections of ideas—those between paragraphs or even larger blocks of text.

Sentence-level transitions   Certain words and phrases signal connections between (or within) sentences. Frequently used transitions are included in the chart on page 20.

In the following paragraph, taken from an article about how Amazon has changed our consumption habits, Joshua Rothman uses transitions to guide readers from one idea to the next.

It hasn't always been obvious that Amazon would transform the feeling of everyday life. At first, the company looked like a bookstore; next, it became a mass retailer; later, for somewhat obscure reasons, it transformed into a television and movie studio. It seemed to be growing horizontally, by learning to sell new kinds of products. But Amazon wasn't just getting wider; it was getting deeper, too. It wasn't just selling products but inventing a new method of selling; behind the scenes, it was using technology to vertically integrate nearly the entire process of consumption.

—Joshua Rothman, "What Amazon's
Purchase of Whole Foods Really Means"

> **Common transitions**
>
> | | |
> |---|---|
> | TO SHOW ADDITION | and, also, besides, further, furthermore, in addition, moreover, next, too, first, second |
> | TO GIVE EXAMPLES | for example, for instance, to illustrate, in fact, specifically |
> | TO COMPARE | also, in the same manner, similarly, likewise |
> | TO CONTRAST | but, however, on the other hand, in contrast, nevertheless, still, even though, on the contrary, yet, although |
> | TO SUMMARIZE OR CONCLUDE | in short, in summary, in conclusion, to sum up, therefore |
> | TO SHOW TIME | after, as, before, next, during, later, finally, meanwhile, then, when, while, immediately |
> | TO SHOW PLACE OR DIRECTION | above, below, beyond, nearby, opposite, close, to the left |
> | TO INDICATE LOGICAL RELATIONSHIP | if, so, therefore, consequently, thus, as a result, for this reason, because, since |

Paragraph-level transitions   Paragraph-level transitions usually link the *first* sentence of a new paragraph with the *first* sentence of the previous paragraph. In other words, the topic sentences signal global connections.

Look for opportunities to echo the subject of a previous paragraph (as summed up in its topic sentence) in the topic sentence of the next one. In his essay "Little Green Lies," Jonathan H. Adler uses this paragraph-level transition strategy to link topic sentences.

> Consider aseptic packaging, the synthetic packaging for the "juice boxes" so many children bring to school with their lunch. One criticism of aseptic packaging is that it is nearly impossible to recycle, yet on almost every other count, aseptic packaging is environmentally preferable to the packaging alternatives. Not only do aseptic containers not require refrigeration to keep their contents from spoiling, but their manufacture requires less than one-10th the energy of making glass bottles.

What is true for juice boxes is also true for other forms of synthetic packaging. The use of polystyrene, which is commonly (and mistakenly) referred to as "Styrofoam," can reduce food waste dramatically due to its insulating properties. (Thanks to these properties, polystyrene cups are much preferred over paper for that morning cup of coffee.) Polystyrene also requires significantly fewer resources to produce than its paper counterpart.

—Jonathan H. Adler, "Little Green Lies"

2c Choose a suitable strategy for developing paragraphs.

Although paragraphs and essays may be developed in any number of ways, certain methods of organization occur frequently, either alone or in combination: illustrations, narration, description, process, comparison and contrast, analogy, cause and effect, classification, and definition. These strategies for developing paragraphs have different uses, depending on the writer's subject and purpose.

Illustrations

Illustrations are extended examples and can be a vivid and effective means of developing a point. The writer of the following paragraph uses illustrations to support his point that Harriet Tubman was a genius at eluding her pursuers.

Part of [Harriet Tubman's] strategy of conducting was, as in all battle-field operations, the knowledge of how and when to retreat. Numerous allusions have been made to her moves when she suspected that she was in danger. When she feared the party was closely pursued, she would take it for a time on a train southward bound. No one seeing Negroes going in this direction would for an instant suppose them to be fugitives. Once on her return she was at a railroad station. She saw some men reading a poster and she heard one of them reading it aloud. It was a description of her, offering a reward for her capture. She took a south-bound train to avert suspicion. At another time when Harriet heard men talking about her, she pretended to read a book which she carried. One man remarked, "This can't be the woman. The one we want can't read or write." Harriet devoutly hoped the book was right side up.

—Earl Conrad, *Harriet Tubman*

Narration

A paragraph of narration tells a story or part of a story. Narrative paragraphs are usually arranged in chronological order, but they may also contain flashbacks, interruptions that take the story back to an earlier time. The following paragraph recounts an author's experiences in the African wild.

One evening when I was wading in the shallows of the lake to pass a rocky outcrop, I suddenly stopped dead as I saw the sinuous black body of a snake in the water. It was all of six feet long, and from the slight hood and the dark stripes at the back of the neck I knew it to be a Storm's water cobra—a deadly reptile for the bite of which there was, at that time, no serum. As I stared at it an incoming wave gently deposited part of its body on one of my feet. I remained motionless, not even breathing, until the wave rolled back into the lake, drawing the snake with it. Then I leaped out of the water as fast as I could, my heart hammering.

—Jane Goodall, *In the Shadow of Man*

Description

A descriptive paragraph sketches a portrait of a person, place, or thing by using concrete and specific details that appeal to one or more of our senses—sight, sound, smell, taste, and touch. Consider, for example, the following description of the grasshopper invasions that devastated the midwestern landscape in the United States in the late 1860s.

They came like dive bombers out of the west. They came by the millions with the rustle of their wings roaring overhead. They came in waves, like the rolls of the sea, descending with a terrifying speed, breaking now and again like a mighty surf. They came with the force of a williwaw and they formed a huge, ominous, dark brown cloud that eclipsed the sun. They dipped and touched earth, hitting objects and people like hailstones. But they were not hail. These were *live* demons. They popped, snapped, crackled, and roared. They were dark brown, an inch or longer in length, plump in the middle and tapered at the ends. They had transparent wings, slender legs, and two black eyes that flashed with a fierce intelligence.

—Eugene Boe, "Pioneers to Eternity"

Process

A process paragraph is structured in chronological order. A writer may choose this pattern either to describe how something is made or done or to explain to readers, step by step, how to do something. Here is a paragraph explaining how to perform a "roll cast," a fly-fishing technique.

Begin by taking up a suitable stance, with one foot slightly in front of the other and the rod pointing down the line. Then begin a smooth, steady draw, raising your rod hand to just above shoulder height and lifting the rod to the 10:30 or 11:00 position. This steady draw allows a loop of line to form between the rod top and the water. While the line is still moving, raise the rod slightly, then punch it rapidly forward and down. The rod is now flexed and under maximum compression, and the line follows its path, bellying out slightly behind you and coming off the water close to your feet. As you power the rod down through the 3:00 position, the belly of line will roll forward. Follow through smoothly so that the line unfolds and straightens above the water.

—*The Dorling Kindersley Encyclopedia of Fishing*

Comparison and contrast

To compare two subjects is to draw attention to their similarities, although the word *compare* also has a broader meaning that includes a consideration of differences. To contrast is to focus only on differences.

Whether a paragraph stresses similarities or differences, it may be patterned in one of two ways. The two subjects may be presented one at a time, as in the following paragraph of contrast.

So Grant and Lee were in complete contrast, representing two dia-
metrically opposed elements in American life. Grant was the modern
man emerging; beyond him, ready to come on the stage, was the great
age of steel and machinery, of crowded cities and a restless, burgeoning
vitality. Lee might have ridden down from the old age of chivalry, lance
in hand, silken banner fluttering over his head. Each man was the perfect
champion of his cause, drawing both his strengths and his weaknesses
from the people he led.
> —Bruce Catton, "Grant and Lee: A Study in Contrasts"

Alternatively, a paragraph may proceed point by point, treating the
two subjects together, one aspect at a time. The following paragraph
uses the point-by-point method to compare speeches given by Abraham
Lincoln in 1860 and Barack Obama in 2008.

Two men, two speeches. The men, both lawyers, both from Illinois,
were seeking the presidency, despite what seemed their crippling
connection with extremists. Each was young by modern standards for
a president. Abraham Lincoln had turned fifty-one just five days before
delivering his speech. Barack Obama was forty-six when he gave his.
Their political experience was mainly provincial, in the Illinois legislature
for both of them, and they had received little exposure at the national
level—two years in the House of Representatives for Lincoln, four years
in the Senate for Obama. Yet each was seeking his party's nomination
against a New York senator of longer standing and greater prior
reputation—Lincoln against Senator William Seward, Obama against
Senator Hillary Clinton.
> —Garry Wills, "Two Speeches on Race"

Analogy

Analogies draw comparisons between items that appear to have little in
common. Writers use analogies to make something abstract or unfamiliar
easier to grasp or to provoke fresh thoughts about a common subject.
In the following paragraph, physician Lewis Thomas draws an analogy
between the behavior of ants and that of humans.

Ants are so much like human beings as to be an embarrassment. They farm fungi, raise aphids as livestock, launch armies into wars, use chemical sprays to alarm and confuse enemies, capture slaves. The families of weaver ants engage in child labor, holding their larvae like shuttles to spin out the thread that sews the leaves together for their fungus gardens. They exchange information ceaselessly. They do everything but watch television.

—Lewis Thomas, "On Societies as Organisms"

Cause and effect

A paragraph may move from cause to effects or from an effect to its causes. The topic sentence in the following paragraph mentions an effect; the rest of the paragraph lists several causes.

The fantastic water clarity of the Mount Gambier sinkholes results from several factors. The holes are fed from aquifers holding rainwater that fell decades — even centuries — ago, and that has been filtered through miles of limestone. The high level of calcium that limestone adds causes the silty detritus from dead plants and animals to cling together and settle quickly to the bottom. Abundant bottom vegetation in the shallow sinkholes also helps bind the silt. And the rapid turnover of water prohibits stagnation.

—Hillary Hauser, "Exploring a Sunken Realm in Australia"

In the following paragraph, the topic sentence identifies a cause; the rest of the paragraph lists the effects.

The rise of rail transport in the nineteenth century forever changed American farming—for better and for worse. Farmers who once raised crops and livestock to sustain just their own families could now make a profit by selling their goods in towns and cities miles away. These new markets improved the living standard of struggling farm families and encouraged them to seek out innovations that would increase their profits. On the downside, the competition fostered by the new markets sometimes created hostility among neighboring farm families where there had once been a spirit of cooperation. Those farmers who couldn't compete with their neighbors left farming forever, facing poverty worse than they had ever known.

—Chris Mileski, student

Classification

Classification is the grouping of items into categories according to some consistent principle. The principle of classification that a writer chooses ultimately depends on the writer's purpose. The following paragraph classifies species of electric fish.

> Scientists sort electric fishes into three categories. The first comprises the strongly electric species like the marine electric rays or the freshwater African electric catfish and South American electric eel. Known since the dawn of history, these deliver a punch strong enough to stun a human. In recent years, biologists have focused on a second category: weakly electric fish in the South American and African rivers that use tiny voltages for communication and navigation. The third group contains sharks, nonelectric rays, and catfish, which do not emit a field but possess sensors that enable them to detect the minute amounts of electricity that leak out of other organisms.
>
> —Anne and Jack Rudloe, "Electric Warfare:
> The Fish That Kill with Thunderbolts"

Definition

A definition puts a word or concept into a general class and then provides enough details to distinguish it from others in the same class. In the following paragraph, the writer defines *crowdsourcing* as a savvy business practice.

> Despite the jargony name, crowdsourcing is a very real and important business idea. Definitions and terms vary, but the basic idea is to tap into the collective intelligence of the public at large to complete business-related tasks that a company would normally either perform itself or outsource to a third-party provider. Yet free labor is only a narrow part of crowdsourcing's appeal. More importantly, it enables managers to expand the size of their talent pool while also gaining deeper insight into what customers really want.
>
> —Jennifer Alsever, "What Is Crowdsourcing?"

3 Revising, editing, and proofreading

To revise is to *re-see*, and the comments you receive from reviewers — instructors, peers, and writing center tutors — will help you re-see your draft through readers' eyes. Asking readers simple questions such as "Do you understand my main idea?" and "Is my draft organized?" will help you shape your draft in progress. Writing multiple drafts allows you to write in stages, seek feedback, and strengthen your paper through revising and editing.

3a Use peer review: Revise with comments.

Peer review gives you the benefit of real readers who offer their suggestions and answer your questions. The following guidelines will help you learn from your reviewers' comments and revise successfully.

Be active. Help reviewers understand your purpose for writing and provide background about why you chose your topic and what you hope to accomplish in your draft. Tell reviewers your specific questions and concerns so that they can focus their feedback.

Listen with an open mind. After you've worked hard on a draft, you might be surprised to hear reviewers tell you it still needs more development. Don't take criticism personally. Consider why a reader is confused, and figure out how to clarify your point.

Weigh feedback carefully. Your reviewers will offer more suggestions than you can use, so be strategic. Sort through all the comments you receive, with your original goals in mind, and focus on global concerns first.

Keep a revision and editing log.   To help you learn about your strengths and challenges as a writer, make a list of the global and sentence-level concerns that keep coming up in your reviewers' comments.

3b Use peer review: Give constructive comments.

Peer review provides an opportunity for you to read the work of your classmates and for all of you to learn from one another. It isn't your job to rewrite, correct, or proofread the work of your peers. It is your job, as a peer reviewer, to offer thoughtful, encouraging comments.

An excerpt from an online peer review session (see p. 30) shows a peer reviewer offering constructive comments that lead the writer to a stronger idea about how to connect to her audience.

3c Approach global revision in cycles.

Revision is more effective when you approach it in cycles, rather than attempting to change everything all at once. You may, for example, take one pass through your draft to make sure you are addressing the expectations of a particular audience, and then a second pass to make sure the draft is focused on one central idea or argument. Yet a third pass or cycle may be dedicated to thinking through the logic or the evidence. As you revise, use the following checklist to help you focus on global issues.

3d Revise and edit sentences.

When you *revise* sentences, you focus on clarity and effectiveness; when you *edit*, you check for correctness. Read each sentence slowly to determine if it uses correct grammar and punctuation and if it communicates your meaning clearly and specifically.

Write helpful peer review comments

1 **View yourself as a coach, not a judge.** Think of yourself as asking questions and proposing possibilities, not dictating solutions. Help your peer identify the strengths of a draft and build on those strengths. Try phrasing comments this way: "Have you thought about . . . ?" or "How can you help a reader understand this point?"

2 **Pay attention to global issues first.** Focus on the big picture—purpose, thesis, organization, and content—before sentence structure, word choice, and grammar. Help your peer see whether their essay is logically organized and fulfills its overall purpose (to make a claim, to inform, to propose a solution, or something else).

3 **Restate the writer's main idea.** As a reader, you can help the writer see whether he or she is expressing points clearly. Can you follow the writer's train of thought? Restate the writer's thesis to check your understanding.

4 **Be specific.** Point to specific places in a draft to show your peer how, why, and where a draft is effective or confusing. Instead of saying "I like your introduction," say exactly what you like: "You use a surprising statistic in your introduction, and it really hooks me as a reader."

Excerpt from an online peer review session

Juan (peer reviewer): Rachel, your essay makes a great point that credit card companies often hook students on a cycle of spending. But it sounds as if you're blaming students for their spending habits and credit card companies for their deceptive actions. Is this what you want to say?

Peer reviewer restates writer's main point and asks a question to help her clarify her ideas.

Rachel (writer): No, I want to keep the focus on the credit card companies. I didn't realize I was blaming students. What could I change?

Writer takes comment seriously and asks reviewer for specific suggestion.

Juan: In paragraphs three and four, you group all students together as if all students have the same bad spending habits. If students are your audience, you'll be insulting them. What reader is motivated to read something that's alienating? What is your purpose for writing this draft?

Peer reviewer points to specific places in the draft and asks questions to help writer focus on audience and purpose.

Rachel: Well . . . It's true that students don't always have good spending habits, but I don't want to blame students. My purpose is to call students to action about the dangers of credit card debt. Any suggestions for narrowing the focus?

Writer is actively engaged with peer reviewer's comments and doesn't take criticism personally.

Juan: Most students know about the dangers of credit card debt, but they might not know about specific deceptive practices companies use to lure them. Maybe ask yourself what would surprise your audience about these practices.

Peer reviewer responds as a reader and acts as a coach to suggest possible solutions.

Rachel: Juan, that's a good idea. I'll try it.

Writer thanks reviewer for his help and leaves session with a specific revision strategy.

|

POST COMMENT

Checklist for global revision

Purpose and audience

- Does the draft address a question, a problem, or an issue that readers care about?
- Is the draft appropriate for its audience? Does it address the audience's knowledge of and attitudes toward the subject?

Focus

- Is the thesis clear? Is it prominently placed?
- Does the thesis answer a reader's "So what?" question?
- If the draft has no thesis, do you have a good reason for omitting one?

Organization and paragraphing

- Is each paragraph unified around a main point?
- Does each paragraph support and develop the thesis with evidence?
- Have you stated the main point of the paragraph in a topic sentence?
- Have you presented ideas in a logical order?

Content

- Is the supporting material relevant and persuasive?
- Which ideas need further development? Have you left your readers with any unanswered questions?
- Do major ideas receive enough attention?
- Where might you delete redundant or irrelevant material?

Point of view

- Is the dominant point of view—first person (*I* or *we*), second person (*you*), or third person (*he, she, it, one,* or *they*)—appropriate for your purpose and audience? (See 13a.)

Improve your writing with an editing log

An important aspect of becoming a college writer is learning how to identify the grammar, punctuation, and spelling errors that you make frequently. You can use an editing log to keep a list of your common errors, anticipate error patterns, and learn the rules needed to correct the errors.

 When your instructor or tutor returns a draft, review any errors he or she has identified.

 Note which errors you commonly make. For example, have you seen "run-on sentence" or "need a transition" in other drafts?

Identify the advice in the handbook that will help you correct the errors.

 Make an entry in your editing log to identify each error. A suggested format appears below.

SAMPLE EDITING LOG PAGE

Original Sentence

Athletes who use any type of biotechnology give themselves an unfair

advantage they should be banned from competition.

Edited Sentence

Athletes who use any type of biotechnology give themselves an unfair
, and
advantage they should be banned from competition.
^

Rule or Pattern Applied

To edit a run-on sentence, use a comma and a coordinating conjunction (*and, but, or*).

Handbook section 21a

3e Format and proofread the final version of your writing.

Before you submit your writing, make sure your formatting is correct and follows appropriate guidelines. Use the format recommended by your instructor or for your academic discipline. For an example of formatting in MLA style, see 51b. For an example that shows APA formatting, see 53b.

As a final step, be sure to proofread your writing. Proofreading is a special kind of reading: a slow and methodical search for misspellings, typographical mistakes, and omitted words or word endings. Try one or more of the following tips.

PROOFREADING TIPS

- Remove distractions and allow yourself ten to fifteen minutes of pure concentration—without your cell phone.

- Proofread out loud, articulating each word as it is actually written.

- Proofread your sentences in reverse order.

- Proofread hard-copy pages; mistakes can be difficult to catch on screen.

- Don't rely too heavily on spell checkers and grammar checkers. Before automatically accepting their changes, consider the accuracy and appropriateness of the suggestions.

- Ask a volunteer (a friend, roommate, or co-worker) to proofread after you. A second reader may catch something you didn't.

3f Reflect on your writing.

Reflection—the process of stepping back periodically to examine your decisions, preferences, strengths, and challenges as a writer—helps you recognize your progress as a writer. Thinking about who you are as a writer, and what you've learned about writing, makes it possible for you to transfer your learning from one writing assignment to the next. When you complete a piece of writing, reflect on questions such as the following:

- What have you learned about yourself as a writer?
- What parts of the writing process are easy for you? What parts are challenging?
- What do you want to do differently the next time you write?
- Can you identify two or three decisions you made that were successful?
- Can you identify two or three pieces of feedback that helped you revise? What did the feedback teach you?
- What lessons have you learned about writing? How will these lessons help you with your next writing assignment?

PART 2

Academic Reading and Writing

4 Reading critically; writing analytically

One of the best ways to become a strong college writer is to become a critical reader. When you read critically, you read with an open, curious mind, trying to understand both what is said and why. And when you write analytically, you respond to a text and its author with thoughtful observations and insights. The more you take from your reading, the more you have to give as a writer.

4a Read actively.

Reading, like writing, is an active process that happens in steps. Most texts, such as the ones assigned in college, don't yield their meaning with one quick reading. Rather, they require you to read and reread to understand the main ideas and the evidence used to support the ideas.

The following guidelines will help you read actively—previewing, annotating, and conversing with a text you read, whether it is a traditional text composed of words or a multimodal text composed of any combination of words, static images, moving images, and sound.

Guidelines for active reading

Preview the text.

The following questions can be useful as you look through a text before reading or viewing it.

- Who is the author? What are the author's credentials?
- What is the author's purpose: To inform? To persuade? To call to action?
- Who is the expected audience?

- When was the text written or created? Where was it published or posted?
- What kind of text is it: A book? A scholarly article? An ad? A public service video? An online news report?

Annotate the text.

The following questions can help you write more useful notes about the text as you read or view it and can help you understand the author's message.

- What surprises, puzzles, or intrigues you about the text?
- What question does the text attempt to answer or what problem does it attempt to solve?
- What is the author's thesis, or main idea?
- What type of evidence does the author provide to support the thesis? How persuasive is this evidence?
- If the text includes sound or images, what purpose do they serve? If color is important, what can you say about the author's choices?

Converse with the text.

The following questions can prepare you to write analytically about a text after you've read and thought about it for a while.

- What are the strengths and limitations of the text? If it is a multimodal text, has the author chosen the best combination of modes for the message?
- Has the author drawn conclusions that you want to question? Do you have a different interpretation of the evidence?
- Does the text raise questions that it does not answer?
- Does the author consider opposing points of view? Does the author seem to treat sources fairly?

Ask the "So what?" question.

To put an author's thesis to the "So what?" test, use phrases like the following: *The author overlooks this important point: . . .* and *The author's argument is convincing because. . . .*

- Why does the author's thesis need to be argued, explained, or explored? What's at stake?
- What has the author overlooked or failed to consider in presenting the message? What's missing?
- Could a reasonable person draw different conclusions?

The following example shows how one student, Emilia Sanchez, practiced active reading by annotating an article from *CQ Researcher*, a newsletter about social and political issues.

ANNOTATED ARTICLE

Big Box Stores Are (Bad) for Main Street

BETSY TAYLOR

Title states Taylor's position.

There is plenty of reason to be concerned about the proliferation of Wal-Marts and other so-called "big box" stores. The question, however, is not whether or not these types of stores create jobs (although several studies claim they produce a net job loss in local communities) or whether they ultimately save consumers money. The real concern about having a 25-acre slab of concrete with a 100,000 square foot box of stuff land on a town is whether it's good for a community's soul.

Assumes readers are concerned.

Main point of article. But what does she mean by "community's soul"?

The worst thing about "big boxes" is that they have a tendency to produce Ross Perot's famous "big sucking sound" — sucking the life out of cities and small towns across the country. On the other hand, small businesses are great for a community. They offer more personal service; they won't threaten to pack up and leave town if they don't get tax breaks, free roads and other blandishments; and small-business owners are much more responsive to a customer's needs. (Ever try to complain about bad service or poor quality products to the president of Home Depot?)

Lumps all big boxes together.

"Either/or" argument — Main Street is good, big boxes are bad.

Assumes all small businesses are attentive.

Yet, if big boxes are so bad, why are they so successful? One glaring reason is that we've become a nation of hyper-consumers, and the big-box boys know this. Downtown shopping districts comprised of small businesses take some of the efficiency out of over-consumption. There's all that hassle of having to travel from store to store, and having to pull out your credit card so many times. Occasionally, we even find ourselves chatting with the shopkeeper, wandering into a coffee shop to visit with a friend or otherwise wasting precious time that could be spent on acquiring more stuff.

But let's face it—bustling, thriving city centers are fun. They breathe life into a community. They allow cities and towns to stand out from each other. They provide an atmosphere for people to interact with each other that just cannot be found at Target, or Wal-Mart or Home Depot.

Is it anti-American to be against having a retail giant set up shop in one's community? Some people would say so. On the other hand, if you board up Main Street, what's left of America?

True?

Word choice makes author seem sentimental.

Shopping at Target to save money — is that bad?

Author's argument seems one-sided and makes assumptions about consumers.

Ends with emotional appeal. Seems too simplistic!

Read like a writer

Reading like a writer helps you identify the techniques writers use so that you can use them, too. To read like a writer is to pay attention to *how* a text is written and *how* it creates an effect on you.

1 **Review any notes you've made on the text.** What passages did you find effective? What words did you underline? If you think the text is powerful or well written, commit yourself to figuring out *why* and *how* the text works.

2 **Ask *what*, *why*, and *how* questions about the techniques writers use.** *What* introductory techniques, for instance, do writers use to hook readers? *Why* and *how* are these techniques effective? *How* do they keep readers reading? As a reader, identify the specific techniques you appreciate so that they become part of your repertoire as a writer.

3 **Observe how writers use specific writing techniques you want to learn.** For instance, if you're interested in learning how writers vary their sentence structure, pay attention to these techniques when you read.

4 **Use your experiences as a reader to plan the effect you want to create for your readers.** Make deliberate choices to create this effect.

Guidelines for writing a summary

- In the first sentence, mention the title of the text, the name of the author, and the author's thesis.
- Maintain a neutral tone; be objective.
- As you present the author's ideas, use the third-person point of view and the present tense: *Taylor argues. . . .* (If you are writing in APA style, see 49c.)
- Keep your focus on the text. Don't state the author's ideas as if they were your own.
- Put all or most of your summary in your own words; if you borrow a phrase or a sentence from the text, put it in quotation marks and give the page number in parentheses.
- Limit yourself to presenting the text's key points, not every detail.

4b Summarize to deepen your understanding.

When you read critically, you ask "What is this text about?" to understand a text's main ideas and key points. When you summarize, you test your understanding of a text by putting the main ideas in your own words—concisely, objectively, and accurately.

4c Analyze to demonstrate your critical reading.

Whereas a summary most often answers the question of *what* a text says, an analysis looks at *how* a text conveys its main idea. Start your analysis with questions you have about the text. What puzzles you or doesn't make sense about the text? Is there a contradiction in the text or a misguided assumption? Do you have questions about the author's thesis or use of evidence? Your analytical questions will lead you to formulate a thesis and will establish the reason your audience needs to read your essay.

Balancing summary with analysis

Summary and analysis need each other in an analytical essay; you can't have one without the other. Your readers may or may not be familiar with the text you are analyzing, so you should summarize the text briefly to orient readers and to help them understand the basis of your analysis. The following strategies will help you balance summary with analysis.

- Remember that readers are interested in your ideas about the text.
- Pose *why* and *how* questions that lead to an interpretation of the text rather than to a summary.
- Formulate a strong position (thesis) to answer your questions about the text.
- Make sure your summary sentences serve a purpose and provide a context for analysis.

Drafting an analytical thesis statement

An effective thesis statement for analytical writing responds to a question about a text or tries to resolve a problem in the text. Remember that your thesis isn't the same as the text's thesis or main idea. Your thesis presents your judgment of the text's argument.

If Emilia Sanchez had started her analysis of "Big Box Stores Are Bad for Main Street" (pp. 38–39) with the following thesis statement, she merely would have repeated the main idea of the article.

INEFFECTIVE ANALYTICAL THESIS STATEMENT

Big-box stores such as Wal-Mart and Home Depot promote consumerism by offering endless goods at low prices, but they do nothing to promote community.

Instead, Sanchez wrote the following thesis statement, which offers *her judgment* of the assumptions that form the basis of Taylor's argument.

EFFECTIVE ANALYTICAL THESIS STATEMENT

By ignoring the complex economic relationship between large chain stores and their communities, Taylor incorrectly assumes that simply getting rid of big-box stores would have a positive effect on America's communities.

Draft an analytical thesis statement

Analysis begins with asking questions about a text. Answering these questions will help you form a judgment about the text. Let the following steps guide you as you develop an analytical thesis statement.

 Review your notes to remind yourself of the author's main idea, supporting evidence, and, if possible, his or her purpose (reason for writing) and audience (intended reader).

 Ask *what, why,* **or** *how* **questions** such as the following: What has the author overlooked or failed to consider? Why might a reasonable person draw a conclusion different from the author's? How does the text complicate or clarify something you've been thinking about or reading about?

 Write your thesis as an answer to the questions you have posed or the resolution of a problem you have identified in the text. Remember that your thesis isn't the same as the text's thesis. Your thesis presents your judgment of the text's thesis.

 Test your thesis. Is your position clear? Is your position debatable? The answer to both questions should be yes.

Revise your thesis. Why does your position matter? Put your working thesis to the "So what?" test (see p. 8). Consider adding a *because* clause to your thesis (see p. 7).

4d Sample student writing: Analysis of an article

Following is Emilia Sanchez's analysis of the article by Betsy Taylor (see p. 38). Sanchez used MLA (Modern Language Association) style to format her paper and cite the source.

Sanchez 1

Emilia Sanchez

Professor Goodwin

English 10

20 October 2017

Rethinking Big-Box Stores

Opening briefly summarizes the article's purpose and thesis.

In her essay "Big Box Stores Are Bad for Main Street," Betsy Taylor focuses not on the economic effects of large chain stores but on the effects these stores have on the "soul" of America. She argues that stores like Home Depot, Target, and Wal-Mart are bad for America because they draw people out of downtown shopping districts and cause them to focus on consumption. In contrast, she believes that small businesses are good for America because they provide personal attention, encourage community interaction, and make each city and town unique. But Taylor's argument is unconvincing because it is based on sentimentality — on idealized images of a quaint Main Street — rather than on the roles that businesses play in consumers' lives and communities. By ignoring the complex economic relationship between large chain stores and their communities, Taylor incorrectly assumes that simply getting rid of big-box stores would have a positive effect on America's communities.

Sanchez begins to analyze Taylor's argument.

Thesis expresses Sanchez's judgment of Taylor's article.

Taylor's use of colorful language reveals that she has a sentimental view of American society and does not understand economic realities. In her first paragraph, Taylor refers to a big-box store as a "25-acre slab of concrete with a 100,000 square foot box of stuff " that "land[s] on a town," evoking images of a powerful monster crushing the American way

Signal phrase introduces quotations from the source.

Marginal annotations indicate MLA-style formatting and effective writing.

of life (1011). But she oversimplifies a complex issue. Taylor does not consider that many downtown business districts failed long before chain stores moved in, when factories and mills closed and workers lost their jobs. In cities with struggling economies, big-box stores can actually provide much-needed jobs. Similarly, while Taylor blames big-box stores for harming local economies by asking for tax breaks, free roads, and other perks, she doesn't acknowledge that these stores also enter into economic partnerships with the surrounding communities by offering financial benefits to schools and hospitals.

> Sanchez uses an MLA in-text citation.

> Sanchez identifies and challenges Taylor's assumptions.

Taylor's assumption that shopping in small businesses is always better for the customer also seems driven by nostalgia for an old-fashioned Main Street rather than by the facts. While she may be right that many small businesses offer personal service and are responsive to customer complaints, she does not consider that many customers appreciate the service at big-box stores. Just as customer service is better at some small businesses than at others, it is impossible to generalize about service at all big-box stores. For example, customers depend on the lenient return policies and the wide variety of products at stores like Target and Home Depot.

> Clear topic sentence announces a shift to a new topic.

> Sanchez refutes Taylor's claim.

Taylor blames big-box stores for encouraging American "hyper-consumerism," but she oversimplifies by equating big-box stores with bad values and small businesses with good values. Like her other points, this claim ignores the economic and social realities of American society today. Big-box stores do not force Americans to buy more. By offering lower prices in a convenient setting, however, they allow consumers to save time and purchase goods they might not be able to afford from small businesses. The existence of more small businesses would not change what most Americans can afford, nor would it reduce their desire to buy affordable merchandise.

Sanchez 3

Sanchez treats
the author fairly.

Taylor may be right that some big-box stores have a negative
impact on communities and that small businesses offer certain

Conclusion
returns to the
thesis and
shows the wider
significance
of Sanchez's
analysis.

advantages. But she ignores the economic conditions that support big-
box stores as well as the fact that Main Street was in decline before the
big-box store arrived. Getting rid of big-box stores will not bring back a
simpler America populated by thriving, unique Main Streets; in reality,
Main Street will not survive if consumers cannot afford to shop there.

Sanchez 4

Work Cited

Work cited page
is in MLA style.

Taylor, Betsy. "Big Box Stores Are Bad for Main Street." *CQ Researcher,*
vol. 9, no. 44, 1999, p. 1011.

How to write an analytical essay

An **analysis** of a text allows you to examine the parts of a text to understand *what* it means and *how* it makes its meaning. Your goal is to offer your judgment of the text and to persuade readers to see it through your analytical perspective. Sample analytical essays begin on pages 44 and 51.

Key features

- **A careful and critical reading** of a text reveals what the text says, how it works, and what it means. In an analytical essay, you pay attention to the details of the text, especially its thesis, evidence, and—in the case of a multimodal text—its visual or audio presentation.

- **A thesis that offers a clear judgment** of a text anchors your analysis. Your thesis might be the answer to a question you have posed about a text or the resolution of a problem you have identified in the text.

- **Support for the thesis** comes from evidence in the text. You summarize, paraphrase, and quote passages that support the claims you make about the text.

- **A balance of summary and analysis** helps readers who are not familiar with the text you are analyzing. Summary answers the question of *what* a text says; analysis looks at *how* a text makes its point.

Thinking ahead: Presenting and publishing

You may have the opportunity to present or publish your analysis in the form of a multimodal text such as a slide show. Consider how adding images or sound might strengthen your analysis or help you to better reach your audience.

Writing your analytical essay

Explore

Generate ideas for your analysis by responding to questions such as the following:

- What is the text about?
- What do you find most interesting, surprising, or puzzling about this text?
- What is the author's thesis or central idea? Put the author's thesis to the "So what?" test.
- What do your annotations of the text reveal about your response to it?

Draft

- Draft a working thesis to focus your analysis. Remember that your thesis is not the same as the author's thesis or message. Your thesis presents *your* judgment of the text.
- Draft a plan to organize your paragraphs. Your introductory paragraph will briefly summarize the text and offer your thesis. Your body paragraphs will support your thesis with evidence from the text. Your conclusion will pull together the major points and show the significance of your analysis.
- Identify specific words, phrases, sentences, or design features as evidence to support your thesis.

Revise

Ask your reviewers to give you specific comments. You can use the following questions to guide their feedback.

- Is the introduction effective and engaging?
- Is summary balanced with analysis?
- Does the thesis offer a clear judgment of the text?
- What objections might other writers pose to your analysis?
- Is the analysis well organized? Are there clear topic sentences and transitions?
- Have you provided sufficient evidence? Have you analyzed the evidence?
- Have you cited words, phrases, or sentences that are summarized or quoted?

4e Read and write about multimodal texts.

In many of your college classes, you'll have the opportunity to read and write about multimodal texts, such as advertisements, videos, or websites. Multimodal texts combine two or more of the following modes: words, static images, moving images, and sound. Like a print text, a multimodal text can be read carefully to understand *what* it says and *how* it communicates its purpose and reaches its audience.

Use the guidelines for active reading on pages 36–37 to help you preview, annotate, and converse with a multimodal text.

Annotate a multimodal text to understand the message and ask questions

The first step is to become familiar enough with the text that you can state its central idea and key points simply and objectively. Taking notes on the text will help you do that. One student, Ren Yoshida, annotated an advertisement for fairly traded coffee. He made an effort to understand the message of the ad and questioned some of the language used by the composer. You can see the ad and his annotations on the next page.

Analyze a multimodal text to demonstrate your critical reading

When you analyze a multimodal text, you say to readers "Here's my reading of this text. This is what the text means and why it matters." Analysis begins with asking *why* and *how* questions about a multimodal text to help you form a judgment about it. When Ren Yoshida analyzed the Equal Exchange advertisement, he asked questions about the ad's design details and its emotional and logical appeals, and he focused his thesis by questioning a single detail in the ad. On the following pages is the Equal Exchange advertisement with Yoshida's notes, followed by his analysis of the ad.

When you choose Equal Exchange fairly traded coffee, tea or chocolate, you join a network that empowers farmers in Latin America, Africa, and Asia to:

- Stay on their land
- Care for the environment
- Farm organically
- Support their family
- Plan for the future

www.equalexchange.coop

Photo: Jesus Choqueheranca de Quevero,
Coffee farmer & CEPICAFE Cooperative member, Peru

Annotated advertisement

What is being exchanged?

Why is "fairly traded" so hard to read?

"Empowering" — why in an elegant font? Who is empowering farmers?

"Farmers" in all capital letters — shows strength?

Straightforward design and not much text.

Outstretched hands. Is she giving a gift? Inviting partnership?

Hands: heart-shaped, foregrounded.

Raw coffee beans are red: earthy, natural, warm.

Positive verbs: consumers choose, join, empower; farmers stay, care, farm, support, plan.

How do consumers know their money helps farmers stay on their land?

Yoshida 1

Ren Yoshida

Professor Marcotte

English 101

4 November 2015

Sometimes a Cup of Coffee Is Just a Cup of Coffee

A farmer, her hardworking hands full of coffee beans, reaches out from an Equal Exchange advertisement ("Empowering"). The hands, in the shape of a heart, offer to consumers the fruit of the farmer's labor. The ad's message is straightforward: in choosing Equal Exchange, consumers become global citizens, partnering with farmers to help save the planet. Suddenly, a cup of coffee is more than just a morning ritual; a cup of coffee is a moral choice that empowers both consumers and farmers. This simple exchange appeals to a consumer's desire to be a good person—to protect the environment and do the right thing. Yet the ad is more complicated than it first seems, and its design raises some logical questions about such an exchange. Although the ad works successfully on an emotional level, it is less successful on a logical level because of its promise for an equal exchange between consumers and farmers.

The focus of the ad is a farmer, Jesus Choqueheranca de Quevero, and, more specifically, her outstretched, cupped hands. Her hands are full of red, raw coffee, her life's work. The ad successfully appeals to consumers' emotions, assuming they will find the farmer's welcoming face and hands, caked with dirt, more appealing than startling statistics about the state of the environment or the number of farmers who lose their land each year. It seems almost rude not to accept the farmer's generous offering since we know her name and, as the ad implies, have the choice to "empower" her. In fact, how can a consumer resist helping the farmer "[c]are for the environment" and "[p]lan for the future," when it is a simple matter of choosing the right coffee? The ad sends the message that our future is a global future in which producers and consumers are bound together.

The source is cited in the text. No page number is available for the online source.

Yoshida summarizes the content of the ad.

Thesis expresses Yoshida's analysis of the ad.

Details show how the ad appeals to consumers' emotions.

Yoshida interprets details such as the farmer's hands.

Marginal annotations indicate MLA-style formatting and effective writing.

Yoshida 2

First impressions play a major role in the success of an advertisement. Consumers are pulled toward a product, or pushed away, by an ad's initial visual and emotional appeal. Here, the intended audience is busy people, so the ad tries to catch viewers' attention and make a strong impression immediately. Yet with a second or third viewing, consumers might start to ask some logical questions about Equal Exchange before buying their morning coffee. Although the farmer extends her heart-shaped hands to consumers, they are not actually buying a cup of coffee or the raw coffee directly from her. In reality, consumers are buying from Equal Exchange, even if the ad substitutes the more positive word *choose* for *buy*. Furthermore, consumers aren't actually empowering the farmer; they are joining "a network that empowers farmers." The idea of a network makes a simple transaction more complicated. How do consumers know their money helps farmers "[s]tay on their land" and "[p]lan for the future" as the ad promises? They don't.

The ad's design elements raise questions about the use of the key terms *equal exchange* and *empowering farmers*. The Equal Exchange logo suggests symmetry and equality, with two red arrows facing each other, but the words of the logo appear almost like an eye exam poster, with each line decreasing in font size and clarity. The words *fairly traded* are tiny. Below the logo, the words *empowering farmers* are presented in contradictory fonts. *Empowering* is written in a flowing, cursive font, almost the opposite of what might be considered empowering, whereas *farmers* is written in a plain, sturdy font. The ad's varying fonts communicate differently and make it hard to know exactly what is being exchanged and who is becoming empowered.

What is being exchanged? The logic of the ad suggests that consumers will improve the future by choosing Equal Exchange. The first exchange is economic: consumers give one thing—dollars—and receive

Yoshida begins to challenge the logic of the ad.

Words from the ad serve as evidence.

Clear topic sentence announces a shift.

Summary of the ad's key features serves Yoshida's analysis.

Yoshida 3

something in return—a cup of coffee—and the farmer stays on her land. The second exchange is more complicated because it involves a moral exchange. The ad suggests that if consumers don't choose "fairly traded" products, farmers will be forced off their land and the environment destroyed. This exchange, when put into motion by consumers choosing to purchase products not "fairly traded," has negative consequences for both consumers and farmers. The message of the ad is that the actual exchange taking place is not economic but moral; after all, nothing is being bought, only chosen. Yet the logic of this exchange quickly falls apart. Consumers aren't empowered to become global citizens simply by choosing Equal Exchange, and farmers aren't empowered to plan for the future by consumers' choices. And even if all this empowerment magically happened, there is nothing equal about such an exchange.

> Yoshida shows why his thesis matters.

    Advertisements are themselves about empowerment—encouraging viewers to believe they can become someone or do something by identifying, emotionally or logically, with a product. In the Equal Exchange ad, consumers are emotionally persuaded to identify with a farmer whose face is not easily forgotten and whose heart-shaped hands hold a collective future. On a logical level, though, the ad raises questions because empowerment, although a good concept to choose, is not easily or equally exchanged. Sometimes a cup of coffee is just a cup of coffee.

> Conclusion includes a detail from the introduction.

> Conclusion returns to Yoshida's thesis.

Yoshida 4

Work Cited

"Empowering Farmers." Equal Exchange, equalexchange.coop/.
Advertisement. Accessed 14 Oct. 2015.

> Yoshida gives date of access for an undated source.

5 Reading arguments

Many of your college assignments will ask you to read arguments about debatable issues. The questions being debated might be matters of public policy (*Should corporations be allowed to advertise on public school property?*) or they might be scholarly issues (*What role do genes play in determining behavior?*). On such questions, reasonable people may disagree. You'll find the critical reading strategies introduced in section 4 to be useful as you enter debates and ask questions about an argument's logic, evidence, and use of appeals.

5a Read with an open mind and a critical eye.

As you read arguments and enter into academic or public policy debates, keep an open mind about opposing viewpoints. Be curious about and open to the wide range of positions in the arguments you are reading. Examine an author's assumptions (ideas the author accepts as true), assess the evidence, and weigh the conclusions. Reading with an open mind means

- **Reading carefully.** Read to understand an author's argument and point of view. Ask questions: What is the author's thesis? What evidence does the author use to support the thesis?

- **Reading skeptically.** Read to test the strengths and weaknesses of an author's argument. Ask questions: Are any of the author's assumptions or conclusions problematic? Is the author's evidence persuasive and sufficient? How does the author handle opposing views?

- **Reading evaluatively.** Read to judge the usefulness and significance of an author's argument. Put the argument to the "So what?" test: Why does the thesis matter? Why does it need to be argued?

Recognizing logical fallacies

When you evaluate an argument, look closely at the reasoning behind it. Some arguments use unreasonable argumentative tactics known as logical fallacies.

Hasty generalization is a conclusion based on insufficient or unrepresentative evidence.

> *In a single year, scores on standardized tests in California's public schools rose by ten points. Therefore, more children than ever are succeeding in America's public school systems.*

Stereotypes are hasty generalizations about a group.

> *All politicians are corrupt.*
>
> *Children are always curious.*

False analogy is a comparison that points out a similarity between two things that are unrelated.

> *If we can send a spacecraft to Mars, we should be able to find a cure for the common cold.*

Post hoc fallacy assumes that because one event follows another, the first is the cause of the second.

> *Since Governor Cho took office, unemployment of minorities in the state has decreased by 7 percent. Governor Cho should be applauded for reducing unemployment among minorities.*

Either/or fallacy oversimplifies an argument by suggesting that there are only two alternatives when in fact there are more.

> *Our current war against drugs has not worked. Either we should legalize drugs or we should turn the drug war over to our armed forces and let them fight it.*

5b Evaluate ethical, logical, and emotional appeals.

Ancient Greek rhetoricians distinguished among three kinds of appeals used to influence readers: ethical, logical, and emotional. As you evaluate arguments, identify these appeals and question their effectiveness. Are they appropriate for the audience and the argument? Are they balanced and legitimate or lopsided and misleading?

Evaluating ethical, logical, and emotional appeals as a reader

Ethical appeals (*ethos*)

Ethical arguments call upon a writer's character, knowledge, and authority. Ask questions such as the following when you evaluate the ethical appeal of an argument.

- Is the writer informed and trustworthy? How does the writer establish authority and credibility?
- Is the writer fair-minded and unbiased? How does the writer establish reasonableness and good judgment?
- Does the writer use sources knowledgeably and responsibly?
- How does the writer describe the views of others and deal with opposing views?

Logical appeals (*logos*)

Reasonable arguments appeal to readers' sense of logic, rely on evidence, and use inductive and deductive reasoning. Ask questions such as the following to evaluate the logical appeal of an argument.

- Is the evidence accurate, sufficient, representative, and relevant?
- Is the reasoning sound?
- Does the argument contain any logical fallacies or unwarranted assumptions?
- Are there any missing or mistaken premises?

Emotional appeals (*pathos*)

Emotional arguments appeal to readers' beliefs and values. Ask questions such as the following to evaluate the emotional appeal of an argument.

- What values or beliefs does the writer address, either directly or indirectly?
- Are the emotional appeals legitimate and fair?
- Does the writer oversimplify or dramatize an issue?
- Do the emotional arguments highlight or shift attention away from the evidence?

DON'T BUY THIS JACKET

THIS SEASON, SHARE SOME VALUES
Learn more about our Common Threads Initiative,
and take the pledge to reduce consumption

TAKE THE PLEDGE

Advertising makes use of ethical, logical, and emotional appeals to persuade consumers to buy a product or embrace a brand. This ad makes an ethical appeal with its copy that invites customers to rethink their purchasing practices.

EXERCISE 5–1 In the following paragraph, identify the type of appeal used in each sentence for which a choice is given: *ethos* (ethical appeal), *logos* (logical appeal), or *pathos* (emotional appeal).

Elderspeak, the use of pet names such as "dear" and "sweetie" directed toward older adults, is generally intended as an endearment. However, the use of such language suggests a view of seniors as childlike or cognitively impaired. It should be no surprise, then, that older adults find these pet names condescending and demeaning (*ethos / logos / pathos*). Unfortunately, the effects of elderspeak go far beyond insulting older adults. Health care professionals have found that residents in nursing facilities, even those with dementia, respond to patronizing language by becoming uncooperative, aggressive, or depressed. In a 2009 study published in the *American Journal of Alzheimer's Disease and Other Dementias*, Ruth Herman and Kristine L. Williams reported that older adults responded to elderspeak by resisting care, yelling, or crying ("Elderspeak's Influence") (*ethos / logos / pathos*). Surprisingly, despite widely published research on the negative effects of elderspeak, the worst offenders are health care workers, the very people we trust to treat our elderly family members with respect and dignity—and the very people who are old enough to know better (*ethos / logos / pathos*).

5c Evaluate the evidence behind an argument.

Writers draw on facts, statistics, examples, expert opinion, and appeals to support their arguments. As you read arguments, look closely at the evidence behind the argument. Ask questions:

- Is the evidence **accurate** and **unbiased**?
- Is the evidence **sufficient**?
- Is the evidence **representative**?
- Is the evidence **relevant**?

The chart on the next page offers an example of how to evaluate evidence in the arguments you read. See also section 46 for more on identifying false and misleading sources.

5d Evaluate how fairly a writer handles opposing views.

The way in which a writer deals with opposing views is telling. Some writers address the arguments of the opposition fairly, conceding points when necessary and countering others, all in a civil spirit. Other writers will do almost anything to win an argument: either ignoring opposing views altogether or misrepresenting such views and attacking their proponents.

Writers build credibility — *ethos* — by addressing opposing arguments fairly. As you read arguments, evaluate how writers deal with views that don't line up with their own. Trustworthy writers deal with opposing arguments by

- respectfully acknowledging counterpositions
- incorporating elements of the opposition into their arguments
- using precise language to describe opposing views
- quoting opposing views accurately and fairly
- not misrepresenting a source by taking it out of context
- finding common ground among differing positions

Questioning the evidence behind the argument

Argument

The majority of students on our campus would volunteer at least five hours a week in a community organization if the school provided a placement service for volunteers.

Evidence

In a recent survey of students on our campus, 723 of 1,215 participants said they would volunteer at least five hours a week in a community organization if the school provided a placement service for volunteers.

1. **Is the evidence accurate and unbiased?** The evidence is accurate and trustworthy if the author has conducted the survey fairly and objectively without bias. In weighing the accuracy of survey evidence, ask questions about an author's purpose for conducting the survey and methods used to collect data.

2. **Is the evidence sufficient?** That depends. On a small campus (say, 3,000 students), the pool of students surveyed would be sufficient for research, but on a large campus (say, 30,000), 1,215 students are only 4 percent of the population. If those 4 percent were known to be truly representative of the other 96 percent, however, even such a small sample would be sufficient.

3. **Is the evidence representative?** The evidence is representative if those responding to the survey reflect the entire student population with respect to the characteristics of age, gender, race, field of study, number of extracurricular commitments, etc. If most of those surveyed are majoring in a field such as social work, the researchers should question the survey's conclusion.

4. **Is the evidence relevant?** Yes. The survey results are directly linked to the conclusion. A survey about the number of hours students work for pay, by contrast, would not be relevant because it would not be about *choosing to volunteer.*

Checklist for reading and evaluating arguments

- What is the writer's thesis, or central claim?
- Are there any gaps in reasoning?
- On what assumptions does the argument rest? Are any of the assumptions unstated?
- What appeals—ethical, logical, or emotional—does the writer make? Are these appeals effective?
- What evidence does the writer use? Could there be alternative interpretations of the evidence?
- How does the writer handle opposing views?
- If you are not persuaded by the writer's argument, what counterarguments would you make to the writer?

6 Writing arguments

▶ Writing guide: How to write an argument essay, 74
▶ Sample argument essay, 69

As you write for various college courses, you'll be asked to take a stance in academic debates, propose solutions to problems, and persuade readers to accept your arguments. Writing an argument gives you the opportunity to take a position on a debatable issue. You say to your readers, "Here is my position in the debate, here is the evidence that supports the position, and here is my response to other positions on the issue." Just as you evaluate arguments with openness, you'll want to construct arguments with the same openness—acknowledging disagreements and presenting your arguments fully and fairly to your audience.

6a View your audience as a panel of jurors.

As you build your argument, think about how you will appeal to your audience. It is useful to envision your audience as skeptical readers who, like a panel of jurors, will make up their minds after listening to all sides of the argument. To construct a convincing argument, you need to establish your credibility (*ethos*) and appeal to your readers' sense of logic and reason (*logos*) as well as to their values and beliefs (*pathos*).

Let the following chart guide your use of ethical, logical, and emotional appeals to reach your audience.

Using ethical, logical, and emotional appeals as a writer

Ethical appeals (*ethos*)

To accept your argument, a reader must see you as trustworthy, fair, and reasonable. When you acknowledge alternative positions, you build common ground with readers; by showing that you are knowledgeable, you also gain their trust. And when you use sources responsibly and respectfully, you inspire readers' confidence in your judgment.

Logical appeals (*logos*)

To persuade readers, you need to appeal to their sense of logic and reason. When you provide sufficient evidence, you offer readers logical support for your argument. In addition, when you clarify the assumptions (ideas that you accept as true or certain) that underlie your arguments, you appeal to readers' desire for reason.

Emotional appeals (*pathos*)

To establish common ground with readers, you need to appeal to their beliefs and values as well as to their minds. When you offer vivid examples and illustrations, surprising statistics, or compelling visuals, you engage readers and deepen their interest in your argument. When you balance emotional appeals with logical appeals, you highlight the human dimension of an issue to show readers why they should care about your argument.

For Multilingual Writers

Some cultures value writers who argue with force; other cultures value writers who argue subtly or indirectly. Academic audiences in the United States will expect your writing to be assertive and confident—neither aggressive nor passive. You can create an assertive tone by acknowledging different positions and supporting your ideas with specific evidence.

TOO AGGRESSIVE	Of course only registered organ donors should be eligible for organ transplants. It's selfish and shortsighted to think otherwise.
TOO PASSIVE	I might be wrong, but I think that maybe people should have to register as organ donors if they want to be considered for a transplant.
ASSERTIVE TONE	If only registered organ donors are eligible for transplants, more people will register as donors.

6b In your introduction, establish credibility and state your position.

When you are constructing an argument, make sure your introduction includes a thesis statement that sets out your position on the issue you have chosen to debate and that gives some sense of your reasoning. In the sentences leading up to the thesis, establish your credibility (*ethos*) with readers by showing that you are knowledgeable and fair-minded. If possible, build common ground (*pathos*) with readers who may not at first agree with your views, and show them why they should consider your thesis.

In the following introduction, student writer Kevin Smith presents himself as someone worth listening to. Because Smith introduces both sides of the debate, readers are likely to approach his essay with an open mind.

Smith shows familiarity with the legal issues surrounding school prayer.

Although the Supreme Court has ruled against prayer in public schools on First Amendment grounds, many people still feel that prayer should be allowed. Such people value prayer as a practice central to their faith and believe that prayer is a way for schools to reinforce moral principles. They also compellingly point out a paradox in the First Amendment itself: at what point does the separation of church and state restrict the freedom of those who wish to practice their religion? What proponents of school prayer fail to realize, however, is that the Supreme Court's decision, although it was made on legal grounds, makes sense on religious grounds as well. Prayer is too important to be trusted to our public schools.

Smith is fair-minded, presenting the views of both sides.

Thesis builds common ground.

—Kevin Smith, student

6c Back up your thesis with persuasive lines of argument.

Arguments of any complexity contain lines of argument that, when taken together, might reasonably persuade readers that the thesis has merit. You can think of lines of argument as your *reasons*. Below, for example, are the main lines of argument that student writer Sam Jacobs used in his paper about the shift from print to online news (see pages 69–73).

CENTRAL CLAIM

Thesis: The shift from print to online news provides unprecedented opportunities for readers to become more engaged with the news, to hold journalists accountable, and to participate as producers, not simply as consumers.

SUPPORTING CLAIMS

- Print news has traditionally had a one-sided relationship with its readers, delivering information for passive consumption.
- Online news invites readers to participate in a collaborative process — to question and even contribute to the content.

- Links within news stories provide transparency, allowing readers to move easily from the main story to original sources, related articles, or background materials.
- Technology has made it possible for readers to become news producers—posting text, audio, images, and video of news events.
- Citizen journalists can provide valuable information, sometimes more quickly than traditional journalists can.

6d Support your thesis with specific evidence.

You will support your thesis with evidence: facts and statistics, examples and illustrations, visuals (charts, slides, photos), expert opinion, and so on.

Using facts and statistics

Most arguments are supported to some extent by facts and statistics. A fact is something that is known with certainty because it has been objectively verified: carbon has an atomic weight of 12; John F. Kennedy was assassinated on November 22, 1963. Statistics are collections of numerical facts: alcohol impairment is a factor in nearly 31 percent of traffic fatalities; more than four in ten businesses in the United States are owned by women.

Writers often use statistics in selective ways to bolster their own positions. If you suspect that a writer's handling of statistics is not fair, track down the original sources for those statistics or read authors with opposing views, who may give you a fuller understanding of the numbers.

Using examples

Examples rarely prove a point by themselves, but when used in combination with other forms of evidence, they add detail to an argument and bring it to life. Because examples are often concrete and sometimes vivid, they can reach readers in ways that statistics and abstract ideas cannot.

Draft a thesis statement for an argument

1 **Identify the various positions in the debate you're writing about.** At the heart of a good argument are debate and disagreement. An argumentative thesis takes a clear position on a debatable issue and is supported by evidence. Identify the points in the debate on which there is disagreement. Consider your own questions and thoughts about the topic.

2 **Review any notes you have taken** to clarify your own thoughts about the debate.

3 **Pose a question that needs to be asked and doesn't have an easy yes/no answer.** Write this question either in your draft or in your notes to guide your thinking. An open-ended question will make a stronger thesis. If your question can be answered with a factual yes or no, add *why* or *how* to the question to add an argumentative edge.

4 **Write your thesis as an answer to your question.** Include the topic, your position, and language that previews the organization of your argument or shows why you are making the argument.

5 **Test your thesis.** A good way to test a thesis while drafting and revising is to imagine a counterargument to your argument. If you can't think of an opposing point of view, rethink your thesis or ask a classmate or writing center tutor to respond to your argument.

6 **Revise your thesis.** Why does your position matter? Put your working thesis to the "So what?" test. Consider adding a *because* clause to your thesis to show readers the significance of your position.

Using visuals

Visuals can support your argument by providing vivid and detailed evidence and by capturing your readers' attention. Bar or line graphs, for instance, can describe and organize complex statistical data; photographs can convey abstract ideas; a map can illustrate geography. As you consider using visual evidence, ask whether the evidence will appeal to readers logically, ethically, or emotionally.

The following graph could appeal to *logos* (home ownership rates have risen steadily since the 1950s) or to *pathos* (the American dream is coming true for more and more Americans).

THE PURSUIT OF PROPERTY
Home ownership rates in the United States

Citing expert opinion

Although they are no substitute for careful reasoning of your own, the views of an expert can contribute to the force of your argument. To help readers recognize the expert, provide credentials showing why your source is worth listening to, perhaps listing the person's position or title alongside his or her name. For example, to help make the case that print journalism has a one-sided relationship with its readers, student writer Sam Jacobs cites an expert, Dan Gillmor, and provides his credentials.

> With the rise of the Internet, however, this model has been criticized by journalists such as Dan Gillmor, founder of the Center for Citizen Media, who argues that traditional print journalism treats "news as a lecture," whereas online news is "more of a conversation" (xxiv).

> ### Anticipating and countering objections
>
> To anticipate possible objections to your argument, consider the following questions.
>
> - Could a reasonable person draw a different conclusion from your facts or examples?
> - Might a reader question any of your assumptions or offer an alternative explanation?
> - Is there any evidence that might weaken your position?
>
> The following questions may help you respond to potential objections.
>
> - Can you concede the point to the opposition but challenge the point's importance or usefulness?
> - Can you explain why readers should consider a new perspective or question a piece of evidence?
> - Should you explain how your position responds to contradictory evidence?
> - Can you suggest a different interpretation of the evidence?
>
> Use sentence openers to signal to readers that you're about to present an objection.
>
> Critics of this view argue that _____.
>
> Some readers might point out that _____.
>
> Researchers challenge these claims by _____.

6e Anticipate objections; counter opposing arguments.

It might seem at first that drawing attention to an opposing point of view or contradictory evidence would weaken your argument. But by anticipating and countering objections to your argument, you show your *ethos* as a reasonable and well-informed writer who has a thorough understanding of the significance of the issue.

There is no best place in an essay to deal with opposing views. Often it is useful to summarize the opposing position early in your essay. After stating your thesis but before developing your own arguments, you might include a paragraph that takes up the most important counterargument. Or you can anticipate objections paragraph by paragraph as you build your case. Wherever you decide to address opposing arguments, you will enhance your credibility if you explain the arguments of others accurately and fairly.

6f Build common ground.

As you counter opposing arguments, try to find one or two assumptions you might share with readers who do not initially agree with your views. If you can show that you share their concerns, your readers will be more likely to accept that your argument is valid. For example, to convince parents that school uniforms will have a positive effect on academic achievement, a school board would want to create common ground with parents by emphasizing shared values regarding learning. Having established these values in common, the board might convince parents that school uniforms will reduce distractions, save money, and focus students' attention on learning rather than on clothes.

6g Sample student writing: Argument

In the following paper, student writer Sam Jacobs argues that the shift from print to online news benefits readers by providing them with new opportunities to produce news and to think more critically as consumers of news. Notice how he appeals to his readers by presenting opposing views fairly before providing his own arguments.

When Jacobs quotes, summarizes, or paraphrases information from a source, he cites the source with an in-text citation formatted in MLA style. Citations in the paper refer readers to the list of works cited at the end of the paper. (For more details about citing sources, see section 48.)

Sam Jacobs

Professor Alperini

English 101

11 October 2016

From Lecture to Conversation: Redefining What's "Fit to Print"

"All the news that's fit to print," the motto of *The New York Times* since 1896, plays with the word *fit*, asserting that a news story must be newsworthy and must not exceed the limits of the printed page. The increase in online news consumption, however, challenges both meanings of the word *fit*, allowing producers and consumers alike to rethink who decides which topics are worth covering and how extensive that coverage should be. Any cultural shift usually means that something is lost, but in this case there are clear gains. The shift from print to online news provides unprecedented opportunities for readers to become more engaged with the news, to hold journalists accountable, and to participate as producers, not simply as consumers.

Guided by journalism's code of ethics — accuracy, objectivity, and fairness — print news reporters have gathered and delivered stories according to what editors decide is fit for their readers. Except for op-ed pages and letters to the editor, print news has traditionally had a one-sided relationship with its readers. The print news media's reputation for objective reporting has been held up as "a stop sign" for readers, sending a clear message that no further inquiry is necessary (Weinberger). With the rise of the Internet, however, this model has been criticized by journalists such as Dan Gillmor, founder of the Center for Citizen Media, who argues that traditional print journalism treats "news as a lecture," whereas online news is "more of a conversation" (xxiv). Print news arrives on the doorstep every morning as a fully formed lecture, a product created without participation from its readership. By contrast, online news invites readers to participate in a collaborative process — to question and even help produce the content.

In his opening sentences, Jacobs provides background for his thesis.

Thesis states the main point.

Jacobs does not need a citation for common knowledge.

Source is cited in MLA style.

Marginal annotations indicate MLA-style formatting and effective writing.

Jacobs 2

Transition moves
from Jacobs's
main argument
to specific
examples.

One of the most important advantages online news offers over print news is the presence of built-in hyperlinks, which carry readers from one electronic document to another. If readers are curious about the definition of a term, the roots of a story, or other perspectives on a topic, links provide a path. Links help readers become more critical consumers of information by engaging them in a totally new way. For instance, the link embedded in the story "Credit-Shy: Younger Generation Is More Likely to Stick to a Cash-Only Policy" (Sapin) allows readers to find out more about the financial trends of young adults and provides statistics that confirm the article's accuracy (see fig. 1). Other links in the article widen the conversation. These kinds of links give readers the opportunity to conduct their own evaluation of the evidence and verify the journalist's claims.

Jacobs clarifies
key terms
(transparency
and
accountability).

Links provide a kind of transparency impossible in print because they allow readers to see through online news to the "sources, disagreements, and the personal assumptions and values" that may have influenced a news story (Weinberger). The International Center for Media and the Public Agenda underscores the importance of news organizations letting "consumers in on the often tightly held little secrets of journalism." To do so, they suggest, will lead to accountability, and "accountability leads to credibility" ("Openness"). These tools alone don't guarantee that news producers will be responsible and trustworthy, but they encourage an open and transparent environment that benefits news consumers.

Jacobs develops
the thesis.

Not only has technology allowed readers to become more critical news consumers, but it also has helped some to become news producers. The Web gives ordinary people the power to report on the day's events. Anyone with an Internet connection can publish on blogs and Web sites, engage in online discussion forums, and contribute video and audio recordings. Citizen journalists with laptops, cell phones, and digital camcorders have become news producers alongside large news organizations.

Jacobs 3

Fig. 1. Links embedded in online news articles allow readers to move from the main story to original sources, related articles, or background materials. The link in this online article (Sapin) points to a statistical report by the Pew Research Center, the original source of the author's data on young adults' spending practices.

Not everyone embraces the spread of unregulated news reporting online. Critics point out that citizen journalists are not necessarily trained to be fair or ethical, for example, nor are they subject to editorial oversight. Acknowledging that citizen reporting is more immediate and experimental, critics also question its accuracy and accountability: "While it has its place . . . it really isn't journalism at all,

Opposing views are presented fairly.

and it opens up information flow to the strong probability of fraud and
abuse. . . . Information without journalistic standards is called gossip,"
writes David Hazinski in *The Atlanta Journal-Constitution* (23A). In his
book *Losing the News,* media specialist Alex S. Jones argues that what
passes for news today is in fact "pseudo news" and is "far less reliable"
than traditional print news (27). Even a supporter like Gillmor is willing
to agree that citizen journalists are "nonexperts," but he argues that
they are "using technology to make a profound contribution, and a real
difference" (140).

Citizen reporting made a difference in the wake of Hurricane
Katrina in 2005. Armed with cell phones and laptops, regular citizens
relayed critical news updates in a rapidly developing crisis, often before
traditional journalists were even on the scene. In 2006, the enormous
contributions of citizen journalists were recognized when the New
Orleans *Times-Picayune* received the Pulitzer Prize in public service for
its online coverage—largely citizen-generated—of Hurricane Katrina.
In recognizing the paper's "meritorious public service," the Pulitzer
Prize board credited the newspaper's blog for "heroic, multi-faceted
coverage of [the storm] and its aftermath" ("2006"). Writing for the
Online Journalism Review, Mark Glaser emphasizes the role that blog
updates played in saving storm victims' lives. Further, he calls *The Times-
Picayune's* partnership with citizen journalists a "watershed for online
journalism."

The Internet has enabled consumers to participate in a new way
in reading, questioning, interpreting, and reporting the news. Decisions
about appropriate content and coverage are no longer exclusively in the
hands of news editors. Ordinary citizens now have a meaningful voice
in the conversation—a hand in deciding what's "fit to print." Some
skeptics worry about the apparent free-for-all and loss of tradition. But
the expanding definition of news provides opportunities for consumers
to be more engaged with events in their communities, their nations, and
the world.

Jacobs counters opposing arguments.

A vivid example helps Jacobs make his point.

Jacobs uses specific evidence for support.

Conclusion echoes the thesis without merely repeating it.

Jacobs 5

Works Cited

Gillmor, Dan. *We the Media: Grassroots Journalism by the People, for the People.* O'Reilly Media, 2006.

Glaser, Mark. "NOLA.com Blogs and Forums Help Save Lives after Katrina." *OJR: The Online Journalism Review,* Knight Digital Media Center, 13 Sept. 2005, www.ojr.org/050913glaser/.

Hazinski, David. "Unfettered 'Citizen Journalism' Too Risky." *The Atlanta Journal-Constitution,* 13 Dec. 2007, p. 23A. General OneFile. go. galegroup.com/ps/.

Jones, Alex S. *Losing the News: The Future of the News That Feeds Democracy.* Oxford UP, 2009.

"Openness and Accountability: A Study of Transparency in Global Media Outlets." *ICMPA: International Center for Media and the Public Agenda,* 2006, www.icmpa.umd.edu/pages/studies/transparency/main.html/.

Sapin, Rachel. "Credit-Shy: Younger Generation Is More Likely to Stick to a Cash-Only Policy." *The Denver Post,* 26 Aug. 2013, www.denverpost.com/ci_23929523/credit-shy-younger-generation-stick-cash-only-policy/.

"The 2006 Pulitzer Prize Winners: Public Service." *The Pulitzer Prizes.* Columbia U, www.pulitzer.org/prize-winners-by-year/2006/. Accessed 2 Oct. 2016.

Weinberger, David. "Transparency Is the New Objectivity." *Joho the Blog,* 19 July 2009, www.hyperorg.com/blogger/2009/07/19/transparency-is-the-new-objectivity/.

Works cited page uses MLA style.

List is alphabetized by authors' last names (or by title when a work has no author).

Access date is used for a web source that has no update date.

How to write an argument essay

When you compose an **argument**, you propose a reasonable solution to a debatable issue. You state your position, provide evidence to support it, and respond to other positions on the issue. A sample argument essay begins on page 69.

Key features

- **A thesis, stated as a clear position on a debatable issue,** frames an argument essay. The issue is debatable because reasonable people disagree about it.

- **An examination of the issue's context** indicates why the issue is important, why readers should care about it, or how your position fits into the debates surrounding the topic.

- **Sufficient, representative, and relevant evidence** supports the argument's claims. Evidence needs to be specific and persuasive; quoted, summarized, or paraphrased fairly and accurately; and cited correctly.

- **Opposing positions are summarized and countered.** By anticipating and countering objections to your position, you establish common ground with readers and show yourself to be a reasonable and well-informed writer.

Thinking ahead: Presenting or publishing

You may have some flexibility in how you present or publish your argument. If you submit your argument as an audio or video essay, make sure you understand the genre's conventions and think through how your voice or a combination of sounds and images can help you establish your *ethos*. If you are taking a position on a local issue, consider publishing your argument in the form of a newspaper op-ed or letter to the editor. The benefit? A real-world audience.

Writing your argument

Explore

Generate ideas by responding to questions such as the following.

- What is the debate around your issue? What sources will help you learn more about your issue?
- What position will you take? Why does your position need to be argued?
- What evidence supports your position? What evidence makes you question your position?
- What types of appeals—*ethos, logos, pathos*—might you use to persuade readers? How will you build common ground with your readers?

Draft

Try to figure out the best way to structure your argument. A typical approach might include the following steps: capture readers' attention; state your thesis; give background information; support your major claims with specific evidence; recognize and respond to opposing points of view; and end by reinforcing your thesis and reminding readers why it matters.

As you draft, think about the best order for your claims. You could organize by strength, building up to your strongest argument (instead of starting with your strongest), or by concerns your audience might have.

Revise

Ask your reviewers for specific feedback. Here are some questions to guide their comments.

- Is the thesis clear? Is the issue debatable?
- Is the evidence persuasive? Is more needed?
- Is your argument organized logically?
- Are there any flaws in your reasoning or assumptions that weaken the argument?
- Have you presented yourself as a knowledgeable, trustworthy writer?
- Does the conclusion pull together your entire argument? How might the conclusion be made more effective?

7 Writing in the disciplines

College courses introduce you to the thinking of scholars in many disciplines, such as the humanities (literature, music, art), the social sciences (psychology, anthropology, sociology), and the sciences (biology, physics, chemistry). In a criminal justice course, for example, you may be asked to write a policy memo or a legal brief; in a nursing course, you may be asked to write a treatment plan or a case study. To write in these courses is to think like a criminologist or a nurse and to engage in the debates of the discipline.

7a Recognize the questions that writers in a discipline ask.

Disciplines are characterized by the kinds of questions their scholars and practitioners attempt to answer. For example, social scientists, who analyze human behavior, might ask about the factors that cause people to act in certain ways. Historians, who seek an understanding of the past, often ask about the causes and effects of events and about connections between current and past events.

Whenever you write for a college course, try to determine the kinds of questions scholars in the field might ask about a topic. You can find clues in assigned readings, lecture topics, discussion groups, and the writing assignment itself.

7b Understand the kinds of evidence that writers in a discipline use.

Regardless of the discipline in which you are writing, you must support any claims with evidence—facts, data, examples, and expert opinion.

The kinds of evidence used in different disciplines may overlap. Students of geography, media studies, and political science, for example, might use census data to explore different topics. The evidence that one discipline values, however, might not be sufficient to support an interpretation or a conclusion in another field. You might use interviews in an anthropology paper, for example, but such evidence would be irrelevant in a biology lab report. The following box lists the kind of evidence used in various disciplines.

What counts as evidence in various disciplines?

Humanities: literature, art, film, music, philosophy

- Passages of text, lines of a poem, or passages of a musical composition
- Details from an image, film, or other work of art
- Critical essays that analyze original works

Humanities: history

- Primary sources such as photos, letters, maps, and government documents
- Scholarly books and articles that interpret evidence

Social sciences: psychology, sociology, political science, anthropology

- Data from original experiments
- Results of field research such as interviews or surveys
- Statistics from government agencies
- Scholarly books and articles that interpret findings from other researchers' studies
- Primary sources such as maps, artifacts, or government documents

Sciences and health fields: biology, chemistry, physics, nursing

- Data from original experiments
- Notes from lab or clinical work
- Models, diagrams, or animations
- Scholarly articles that report findings from experiments

Questions to ask about literature

All good writing about literature attempts to answer a question about the text—for example, how does street language function in Gwendolyn Brooks's "We Real Cool"? The goal of a literature analysis is to answer such questions with a meaningful and persuasive interpretation. Focus your reading by asking questions about the text. Keep in mind that readers are interested in your ideas about a work; pose questions that lead to your interpretation or a judgment of the work rather than to a summary. The following list can help you get started.

Questions about technique

PLOT What conflicts drive the plot? Are they internal (within a character) or external (between characters or between a character and a force)? How are conflicts resolved? Why do events happen in a particular order?

SETTING Does the setting (time and place) create an atmosphere, give insight into a character, suggest symbolic meaning, or hint at the theme?

CHARACTER What seems to motivate the central characters? Do any characters change significantly? If so, what have they learned from their experiences? Do contrasts between characters highlight important themes?

POINT OF VIEW Does the point of view—the perspective from which the story is narrated or the poem is spoken—influence our understanding of events? Does the narration reveal the character traits of the speaker, or does the speaker merely observe others?

THEME Does the work have an overall theme (a central insight about people or a truth about life, for example)? If so, how do details in the work serve to illuminate this theme?

LANGUAGE Does language—formal or informal, standard or dialect, ordinary or poetic—reveal the character of speakers? How do metaphors, similes, and sensory images contribute to the work? How do recurring images enrich the work and hint at its meaning?

Questions about social context

HISTORICAL CONTEXT What does the work reveal about—or how was it shaped by—the time and place in which it was written? Does the work appear to promote or undermine a philosophy that was popular in its time, such as social Darwinism in the late nineteenth century or feminism in the mid-twentieth century?

QUESTIONS TO ASK ABOUT LITERATURE (*cont.*)

CLASS How does social class shape or influence characters' choices and actions? How does class affect the way characters view—or are viewed by—others?

RACE AND CULTURE Are any characters portrayed as being caught between cultures: between a traditional and an emerging culture, for example? Are any characters engaged in a conflict with society because of their race or ethnic background? Does the work celebrate a specific culture and its traditions?

GENDER Are any characters' choices limited because of gender? What are the power relationships between the sexes, and do these change during the course of the work? Do any characters resist the gender roles assigned to them? Do other characters choose to conform to those roles?

ARCHETYPES (OR UNIVERSAL TYPES) Does a character, an image, or a plot fit a pattern—a type—that has been repeated in stories throughout history and across cultures? (For example, nearly every culture has stories about heroes, quests, redemption, and revenge.) How is an archetypal character, image, or plot line similar to or different from others like it?

7c Become familiar with a discipline's preferred genres.

As you write in various disciplines, pay attention to the genre, or type of writing, assigned. Each genre is a category of writing meant for a specific purpose and audience, with its own set of agreed-upon expectations and conventions for style, structure, and format. When you are asked to write a business memo for a management course, a lab report for a biology class, or a case study for an education class, you are being asked to adopt a discipline's method for communicating among its members. When you are assigned a type of document you are unfamiliar with, seek samples from your instructor or your school's writing center.

7d Become familiar with a discipline's language conventions.

Every discipline has a specialized vocabulary. As you read the articles and books in a field, you'll notice that certain words and phrases come up repeatedly. Sociologists, for example, use terms such as *independent variables* and *dyads* to describe social phenomena; computer scientists might refer to *algorithm design* and *loop invariants* to describe programming methods. Practitioners in health fields such as nursing use terms like *treatment plan* and *systemic assessment* to describe patient care. Use discipline-specific terms only when you are certain that you and your readers fully understand their meaning.

7e Use a discipline's preferred citation style.

In any discipline, you must give credit to those whose ideas or words you have borrowed. It is your responsibility to avoid plagiarism by citing sources honestly and accurately.

While all disciplines emphasize careful documentation, each follows a particular system of citation that its members have agreed on. Writers in the humanities usually use the system established by the Modern Language Association (MLA). Scholars in some social sciences, such as psychology and anthropology, follow the style guidelines of the American Psychological Association (APA). Scholars in history and other humanities typically follow *The Chicago Manual of Style*.

PART 3

Clear Sentences

8 Prefer active verbs.

Choose an active verb whenever possible. Active verbs express meaning more vigorously than forms of the verb *be* or verbs in the passive voice. Forms of *be* (*be, am, is, are, was, were, being, been*) lack vigor because they convey no action. Passive verbs lack strength because their subjects receive the action instead of doing it.

BE VERB	A surge of power *was* responsible for the destruction of the pumps.
PASSIVE	The pumps *were destroyed* by a surge of power.
ACTIVE	A surge of power *destroyed* the pumps.

8a Choose the active voice or the passive voice depending on your writing situation.

In the active voice, the subject does the action; in the passive voice, the subject receives the action. Although both voices are grammatically correct, the active voice is usually more effective because it is clearer and more direct.

ACTIVE	Hernando *caught* the fly ball.
PASSIVE	The fly ball *was caught* by Hernando.

In passive sentences, the actor (in this case, *Hernando*) frequently does not appear: *The fly ball was caught.*

Most of the time, you will want to emphasize the actor, so you should use the active voice. To replace a passive verb with an active one, make the actor the subject of the sentence.

> The settlers stripped the land of timber before realizing
> ~~The land was stripped of timber before the settlers realized~~
> ^
> the consequences of their actions.

The revision emphasizes the actors (*settlers*) by naming them in the subject.

The decision to use the active or the passive voice will be influenced by your purpose but also by your audience's expectations. In much scientific writing, for example, the passive voice properly emphasizes an experiment or a process, not a person: *Just before harvest, the tobacco plants are sprayed with a chemical to prevent the growth of suckers.*

8b Replace *be* verbs that result in dull or wordy sentences.

Not every *be* verb needs replacing. The forms of *be* (*be, am, is, are, was, were, being, been*) work well when you want to link a subject to a noun that clearly renames it or to an adjective that describes it: *Orchard House was the home of Louisa May Alcott. The harvest will be bountiful this year.*

If using a *be* verb makes a sentence needlessly wordy, consider replacing it. Often a phrase following the verb contains a noun or an adjective (such as *violation, resistant*) that suggests a more vigorous, active verb (*violate, resist*).

▶ Burying nuclear waste in Antarctica would ~~be in violation of~~ an international treaty.
  violate

▶ When Rosa Parks ~~was resistant to~~ giving up her seat on the bus, she became a civil rights hero.
  resisted

EXERCISE 8–1   Revise any weak, unemphatic sentences by replacing passive verbs or *be* verbs with active alternatives. If a sentence is emphatic, do not change it. Possible revisions appear in the back of the book.

~~The campfire was doused by the ranger before we were given~~
The ranger doused the campfire before giving us
a ticket for unauthorized use of a campsite.

a. The Saxons were defeated by the Prussians in 1745.
b. The entire operation is managed by Ahmed, the producer.

c. The sea kayaks were expertly paddled by the tour guides.

d. At the crack of rocket and mortar blasts, I jumped from the top bunk and landed on my buddy below, who was crawling on the floor looking for his boots.

e. The protestors' shouts were heard by the congresswoman as she walked up the Capitol steps.

9 Balance parallel ideas.

If two or more ideas are parallel, they should be expressed in parallel grammatical form. Single words should be balanced with single words, phrases with phrases, clauses with clauses.

A kiss can be a comma, a question mark, or an exclamation point.
—Mistinguett

This novel is not to be tossed lightly aside, but to be hurled with great force.
—Dorothy Parker

9a Balance parallel ideas in a series.

Balance all items in a series by presenting them in parallel grammatical form.

▶ Children who study music also learn confidence,
creativity.
discipline, and ~~they are creative.~~
^

The revision presents all the items in the series as nouns: _confidence,_ _discipline,_ and _creativity._

▶ Racing to get to work on time, Sam drove down the middle of the
road, ran one red light, ^{ignored} and two stop signs.
  ^

The revision adds a verb to make the three items parallel: *drove, ran*, and
ignored.

9b Balance parallel ideas presented as pairs.

When pairing ideas, underscore their connection by expressing them in
similar grammatical form. Paired ideas are usually connected with coordinating conjunctions, with correlative conjunctions, or with *than* or *as*.

Parallel ideas linked with coordinating conjunctions

Coordinating conjunctions (*and, but, or, nor, for, so*, and *yet*) link ideas of
equal importance. When those ideas are closely parallel in content, they
should be expressed in parallel grammatical form.

▶ Many states are reducing property taxes for home owners
and ^{extending} ~~extend~~ tax credits to renters.
  ^

The revision balances the verb *reducing* with the verb *extending*.

Parallel ideas linked with correlative conjunctions

Correlative conjunctions come in pairs: *either ... or, neither ... nor, not only ...
but also, both ... and, whether ... or.* Make sure that the grammatical structure following the second half of the pair is the same as that following the
first half.

▶ Thomas Edison was not only a prolific inventor but also ~~was~~ a

successful entrepreneur.

The words *a prolific inventor* follow *not only*, so *a successful entrepreneur*
should follow *but also*. Repeating *was* creates an unbalanced effect.

▶ The clerk told me either to change my flight or ^to^ take the train.

To change my flight, which follows *either*, should be balanced with *to take the train*, which follows *or*.

Comparisons linked with than or as

In comparisons linked with *than* or *as*, the elements being compared should be expressed in parallel grammatical structure.

▶ It is easier to speak in abstractions than ~~grounding~~ ^to ground^ one's thoughts in reality.

To speak is balanced with *to ground*.

EXERCISE 9–1   Edit the following sentences to correct faulty parallelism. Possible revisions appear in the back of the book.

Rowena began her workday by pouring a cup of coffee and ~~checked~~ ^checking^ her email.

a. Police dogs are used for finding lost children, tracking criminals, and the detection of bombs and illegal drugs.

b. Hannah told her rock-climbing partner that she bought a new harness and of her desire to climb Otter Cliffs.

c. It is more difficult to sustain an exercise program than starting one.

d. During basic training, I was not only told what to do but also what to think.

e. Jan wanted to drive either to wine country or Sausalito.

10 Add needed words.

Sometimes writers leave out words intentionally without affecting meaning. But often the result is a confusing or an ungrammatical sentence. Readers need to see at a glance how the parts of a sentence are connected.

10a Add words needed to complete compound structures.

In compound structures, words are often omitted for economy: *Tom is a man who means what he says and [who] says what he means.* Such omissions are acceptable as long as the omitted words are common to both parts of the compound structure.

If omitting a word from a sentence would make the sentence ungrammatical because the word is not common to both parts of the compound structure, the word must be left in.

> Mayor Davis never has and never will accept a bribe.
>   ^accepted

Has . . . accept is not grammatically correct.

10b Add the word *that* where needed for clarity.

Add the word *that* if there is any danger of misreading without it.

> In his famous obedience experiments, psychologist Stanley Milgram
> discovered ordinary people were willing to inflict physical pain on
>   ^that
> strangers.

Milgram didn't discover people; he discovered that people were willing to inflict pain on strangers.

10c Add words needed to make comparisons logical and complete.

Comparisons should be made between items that are alike. To compare unlike items is illogical and distracting.

▶ The forests of North America are much more extensive
     those of
than Europe.
  ^

Forests must be compared with forests, not with all of Europe.

                                             singer's.
▶ Beyoncé's music videos are better than any other ~~singer.~~
                                             ^

Beyoncé's music videos cannot logically be compared with a singer. The revision uses the possessive form *singer's*, with the word videos being implied.

          as
▶ The city of Lowell is as old, if not older than, the neighboring city of
                        ^

Lawrence.

The construction *as old* is not complete without a second *as: as old as . . . the neighboring city of Lawrence.*

Comparisons should be complete so that readers will understand what is being compared.

INCOMPLETE	Depression is more common in adolescent girls.
COMPLETE	Depression is more common in adolescent girls than in adolescent boys.

Also, comparisons should leave no ambiguity for readers. If a sentence lends itself to more than one interpretation, revise the sentence to state clearly which interpretation you intend. In the following ambiguous sentence, two interpretations are possible.

AMBIGUOUS	Ken helped me more than my roommate.
CLEAR	Ken helped me more than *he helped* my roommate.
CLEAR	Ken helped me more than my roommate *did*.

EXERCISE 10–1 Add to the following sentences any words needed for grammatical or logical completeness. Possible revisions appear in the back of the book.

> that
> **The officer feared the prisoner would escape.**
>   ^

a. Oranges are a better source of vitamin C.

b. The women entering the military academy can expect haircuts as short as the male cadets.

c. Looking out the family room window, Sarah saw her favorite tree, which she had climbed as a child, was gone.

d. The graphic designers are interested and knowledgeable about producing posters for the balloon race.

e. My town's high school is much larger than the neighboring town.

11 Untangle mixed constructions.

A mixed construction contains sentence parts that do not sensibly fit together. The mismatch may be a matter of grammar or of logic.

11a Untangle the grammatical structure.

You should not begin a sentence with one grammatical plan and switch without warning to another. Often you must rethink the purpose of the sentence and revise.

>   Most
> ▶ ~~For most~~ drivers who have a blood alcohol content of .05 percent
>   ^
>   increase their risk of causing an accident.

In the original sentence, the prepositional phrase beginning with *For* is incorrectly made the subject of the verb *increase*. This revision makes *drivers* the subject.

For Multilingual Writers

English does not allow double subjects, nor does it allow an object or an adverb to be repeated in an adjective clause. English also does not allow a noun and a pronoun to be repeated in a sentence if they have the same grammatical function. See 29c.

▶ For most drivers who have a blood alcohol content of .05 percent , the risk of causing an accident is doubled. ~~increase their risk of causing an accident.~~
     ^

Here, the writer begins with the prepositional phrase and finishes the sentence with a proper subject and verb (*risk . . . is doubled*).

▶ Although the United States is a wealthy nation, ~~but~~ more than

20 percent of our children live in poverty.

The coordinating conjunction *but* cannot link a subordinate clause (*Although the United States . . .*) with an independent clause (*more than 20 percent of our children live in poverty*).

11b Straighten out the logical connections.

A sentence's subject and verb should make sense together.

                          Tiffany
▶ The court decided that ~~Tiffany's welfare~~ would be safer living with
                           ^
her grandparents.

Tiffany, not her welfare, would be safer.

                                   benefits for the
▶ Under the revised plan, the elderly/ ~~who now receive benefits,~~ will be
                                   ^
abolished.

The benefits, not the elderly, will be abolished.

11c Avoid *is when, is where,* and *reason . . . is because* constructions.

In formal English, readers sometimes object to *is when, is where,* and *reason . . . is because* constructions on grammatical or logical grounds.

▶ Anorexia nervosa is ~~where people~~ think they are too fat and diet to
  ^{a disorder suffered by people who}
  ∧
  the point of starvation.

> *Where* refers to places. Anorexia nervosa is a disorder, not a place.

▶ The ~~reason the~~ experiment failed ~~is~~ because conditions in the lab
  were not sterile.

> The writer might have changed *because* to *that* (*The reason the experiment failed is that conditions in the lab were not sterile*), but the preceding revision is more concise.

EXERCISE 11–1   Edit the following sentences to untangle mixed constructions. Possible revisions appear in the back of the book.

Taking
~~By taking~~ the oath of allegiance made Ling a US citizen.
∧

a. Using surgical gloves is a precaution now worn by dentists to prevent contact with patients' blood and saliva.

b. A physician, the career my brother is pursuing, requires at least ten years of challenging work.

c. The reason the pharaohs had bad teeth was because tiny particles of sand found their way into Egyptian bread.

d. Recurring bouts of flu among team members set a record for number of games forfeited.

e. In this box contains the key to your future.

12 Repair misplaced and dangling modifiers.

Modifiers should point clearly to the words they modify. As a rule, related words should be kept together.

12a Put limiting modifiers in front of the words they modify.

Limiting modifiers such as *only, even, almost, nearly,* and *just* should appear in front of a verb only if they modify the verb. If they limit the meaning of some other word in the sentence, they should be placed in front of that word.

> Research shows that students ~~only~~ learn new vocabulary
> only
> words when they are encouraged to read.
> ^
>
> *Only* limits the meaning of the *when* clause.

> just
> If you ~~just~~ interview chemistry majors, your picture of the student
> ^
> response to the new policies will be incomplete.
>
> The adverb *just* limits the meaning of *chemistry majors,* not *interview.*

When the limiting modifier *not* is misplaced, the sentence usually suggests a meaning the writer did not intend.

> not
> In the United States in 1860, all black southerners were ~~not~~ slaves.
> ^
>
> The original sentence means that no black southerners were slaves. The revision makes the writer's real meaning clear.

12b Place phrases and clauses so that readers can see at a glance what they modify.

Although phrases and clauses can appear at some distance from the words they modify, make sure your meaning is clear.

MISPLACED   The soccer player returned to the clinic where he had undergone emergency surgery in 2018 in a limousine sent by Adidas.

REVISED   Traveling in a limousine sent by Adidas, the soccer player returned to the clinic where he had undergone emergency surgery in 2018.

The revision corrects the false impression that the soccer player underwent emergency surgery in a limousine.

▶ *On the walls*
~~There~~ are many pictures of comedians who have performed at
 ^
Gavin's. ~~on the walls.~~
 ^

The comedians weren't performing on the walls; the pictures were on the walls.

12c Avoid split infinitives when they are awkward.

An infinitive consists of *to* plus the base form of a verb: *to think, to breathe.* When a modifier appears between *to* and the verb, the infinitive is said to be "split": *to completely understand.*

If a split infinitive is awkward, move the modifier to another position in the sentence.

▶ Cardiologists encourage their patients to ~~more carefully~~ watch their
                          more carefully.
cholesterol levels/
           ^

Attempts to avoid split infinitives can result in equally awkward sentences. When alternative phrasing sounds unnatural, most experts allow—and even encourage—splitting the infinitive.

| AWKWARD | We decided actually to enforce the law. |
| BETTER | We decided to actually enforce the law. |

EXERCISE 12–1   Edit the following sentences to correct misplaced or awkwardly placed modifiers. Possible revisions appear in the back of the book.

in a telephone survey
Answering questions can be annoying, in a telephone survey.
                      ^   ^

a. The manager asked her employees to if they had time submit their reports today.
b. Many students graduate with debt from college totaling more than fifty thousand dollars.
c. It is a myth that humans only use 10 percent of their brains.
d. Daria found the old nightgown she used to wear to sleep in the closet.
e. All geese do not fly beyond Narragansett for the winter.

12d Repair dangling modifiers.

A dangling modifier fails to refer logically to any word in the sentence. Dangling modifiers are easy to repair, but they can be hard to recognize, especially in your own writing.

Dangling modifiers are usually introductory word groups (such as verbal phrases) that suggest but do not name an actor. When a sentence opens with such a modifier, readers expect the subject of the next clause to name the actor. If it doesn't, the modifier dangles.

Upon entering the doctor's office, a skeleton caught my attention.

Deciding to join the navy, the recruiter enthusiastically pumped Joe's hand.

These dangling modifiers falsely suggest that the recruiter decided to join the navy and that the skeleton entered the doctor's office.

To repair a dangling modifier, you can revise the sentence in one of two ways:

- Name the actor in the subject of the sentence.
- Name the actor in the modifier.

Depending on your sentence, one of these revision strategies may be more appropriate than the other.

ACTOR NAMED IN SUBJECT

                      I noticed
▶ Upon entering the doctor's office, a skeleton. ~~caught my attention.~~
                                  ^   ^

ACTOR NAMED IN MODIFIER

   When Joe decided
▶ ~~Deciding~~ to join the navy, the recruiter enthusiastically
    ^   *his*
   pumped ~~Joe's~~ hand.
          ^

You cannot repair a dangling modifier simply by moving it: *A skeleton caught my attention upon entering the doctor's office.* The sentence still suggests that the skeleton entered the office.

EXERCISE 12–2   Edit the following sentences to correct dangling modifiers. Most sentences can be revised in more than one way. Possible revisions appear in the back of the book.

                           a student must complete
To acquire a degree in almost any field, two science courses. ~~must be~~
                                 ^   ^

~~completed.~~

a. To complete an online purchase with a credit card, the expiration date and the security code must be entered.

b. Though only sixteen, UCLA accepted Martha's application.

c. Settled in the cockpit, the pounding of the engine was muffled only slightly by my helmet.

d. After studying polymer chemistry, computer games seemed less complex to Phuong.

e. When a young man, my mother enrolled me in tap dance classes.

13 Eliminate distracting shifts.

This section can help you avoid unnecessary shifts that might distract or confuse your readers: shifts in point of view, in verb tense, in mood or voice, or from indirect to direct questions or quotations.

13a Make the point of view consistent in person and number.

The point of view of a piece of writing is the perspective from which it is written: first person (*I* or *we*), second person (*you*), or third person (*he, she, it, one,* or *they*).

The *I* (or *we*) point of view, which emphasizes the writer, is a good choice for informal writing based on personal experience. The *you* point of view, which emphasizes the reader, works well for giving advice or explaining how to do something. The third-person point of view, which emphasizes the subject, is appropriate in most formal academic and professional writing.

Once you settle on an appropriate point of view, stick with it. Shifting points of view within a piece of writing confuses readers.

> Our class practiced rescuing a victim trapped in a wrecked car.
>
> We learned to dismantle the car with the essential tools. ~~You~~ were
>   We ^
> graded on ~~your~~ speed and ~~your~~ skill in freeing the victim.
>   our ^   our ^
>
> The writer should have stayed with the *we* point of view. *You* is inappropriate because the writer is not addressing readers directly. *You* should not be used in a vague sense meaning "anyone." (See 24d.)

EXERCISE 13-1 Edit the following paragraph to eliminate distracting shifts in point of view (person and number). Create two versions. First, imagine that this is an introductory paragraph designed to engage the reader with a personal story; write it in the first person (using *I* and *we*). Can you think of other contexts in which the first-person point of view would be the best choice? Then write the paragraph in the third person (using *people* and *they*). In what contexts would this version be the best choice?

When online dating first became available, many people thought that it would simplify romance. We believed that you could type in a list of criteria—sense of humor, college education, green eyes, good job—and a database would select the perfect mate. Thousands of people signed up for services and filled out their profiles, confident that true love was only a few mouse clicks away. As it turns out, however, virtual dating is no easier than traditional dating. I still have to contact the people I find, exchange emails and phone calls, and meet him in the real world. Although a database might produce a list of possibilities and screen out obviously undesirable people, you can't predict chemistry. More often than not, people who seem perfect online just don't click in person. Electronic services do help a single person expand their pool of potential dates, but it's no substitute for the hard work of romance.

13b Maintain consistent verb tenses.

Consistent verb tenses clearly establish the time of the actions being described. When a passage begins in one tense and then shifts without warning and for no reason to another, readers are distracted and confused.

▶ Our candidate lost in the debate. Just as we gave up hope,
       soared
she ~~soars~~ ahead in the polls.
      ^

The writer thought that the present tense (*soars*) would convey excitement. But having begun in the past tense (*lost, gave up*), the writer should follow through in the past tense.

14 Emphasize key ideas.

Within each sentence, emphasize your point by expressing it in the subject and verb of an independent clause, the words that receive the most attention from readers.

14a Coordinate equal ideas; subordinate minor ideas.

When combining two or more ideas in one sentence, you have two choices: coordination or subordination. Choose coordination to indicate that the ideas are equal or nearly equal in importance. Choose subordination to indicate that one idea is less important than another.

Coordination

Coordination draws attention equally to two or more ideas. To coordinate single words or phrases, join them with a coordinating conjunction or with a pair of correlative conjunctions: *bananas **and** strawberries*; ***not only** a lackluster plot **but also** inferior acting* (see 40g).

To coordinate independent clauses—word groups that express a complete thought and that can stand alone as a sentence—join them with a comma and a coordinating conjunction or with a semicolon and a word such as *therefore*. (See the following chart.)

> **For Multilingual Writers**
>
> Conjunctions (words such as *and* and *but*) and conjunctive adverbs (words such as *therefore* or *meanwhile*) can help you express relationships between ideas when you write in English.

> **Using coordination to combine sentences of equal importance**
>
> 1. Consider using a comma and a coordinating conjunction. (See 30a.)
>
> | and | but | or | nor |
> |-----|-----|----|-----|
> | for | so | yet | |
>
> ▶ In Orthodox Jewish funeral ceremonies, the shroud is a simple
> linen vestment/. ~~The~~ *and the* coffin is plain wood.
> ^
>
> 2. Consider using a semicolon followed by a conjunctive adverb or a transitional phrase. (See 32b.)
>
> | also | however | next |
> |------|---------|------|
> | as a result | in addition | now |
> | besides | in fact | of course |
> | consequently | in other words | otherwise |
> | finally | in the first place | still |
> | for example | meanwhile | then |
> | for instance | moreover | therefore |
> | furthermore | nevertheless | thus |
>
> ▶ Alicia scored well on the SAT/; *in addition, she* ~~She also~~ had excellent grades and a
> ^
> record of community service.
>
> 3. Consider using a semicolon alone. (See 32a.)
>
> ▶ In youth we learn/; *in* ~~In~~ age we understand.
> ^

Subordination

To give unequal emphasis to two or more ideas, express the major idea in an independent clause and place any minor ideas in subordinate clauses or phrases. (For specific subordination strategies, see the following chart.)

> ## Using subordination to combine sentences of unequal importance
>
> 1. Consider putting the less important idea in a subordinate clause beginning with one of the following words. (See 42e.)
>
> | | | | |
> |---|---|---|---|
> | after | before | that | which |
> | although | even though | unless | while |
> | as | if | until | who |
> | as if | since | when | whom |
> | because | so that | where | whose |
>
>   When
> ▶ Elizabeth Cady Stanton proposed a convention to discuss the status of
>   ^
>   women in America/, Lucretia Mott agreed.
>   ^
>
> 2. Consider putting the less important idea in an appositive phrase. (See 42c.)
>
> ▶ Karate, ~~is~~ a discipline based on the philosophy of nonviolence/,
>   ^   ^
>   ~~It~~ teaches the art of self-defense.
>
> 3. Consider putting the less important idea in a participial phrase. (See 42b.)
>
>   E
> ▶ ~~American essayist Cheryl Peck was~~ encouraged by friends to write
>   ^
>   American essayist Cheryl Peck
>   about her life/, ~~She~~ began combining humor and irony in her essays
>   ^
>   about being overweight.

Let your intended meaning determine which idea you emphasize. Thinking about your purpose and your audience will often help you decide which ideas deserve emphasis.

14b Combine choppy sentences.

Short sentences demand a reader's attention, so you should use them primarily for emphasis. Too many short sentences, one after the other, make for a choppy style.

If an idea is not important enough to deserve its own sentence, try combining it with a sentence close by. Put any minor ideas in subordinate structures such as phrases or subordinate clauses. (See 42.)

▶ The Parks Department keeps the use of insecticides to a minimum/
  because the
  ~~The~~ city is concerned about the environment.
  ^

The writer wanted to emphasize that the Parks Department minimizes its use of chemicals, so she put the reason in a subordinate clause beginning with *because*.

▶ The Chesapeake and Ohio Canal, ~~is~~ a 184-mile waterway
  ^
  constructed in the 1800s/, ~~It~~ was a major source of transportation
  ^
  for goods during the Civil War.

A minor idea is now expressed in an appositive phrase (*a 184-mile waterway constructed in the 1800s*).

For Multilingual Writers

Unlike some other languages, English does not allow repetition of objects or adverbs in adjective clauses.

▶ The apartment that we rented ~~it~~ needed repairs.

The pronoun *it* cannot repeat the relative pronoun *that*.

EXERCISE 14–1   Combine the following sentences by subordinating minor ideas or by coordinating ideas of equal importance. You must decide which ideas are minor because the sentences are given out of context. Possible revisions appear in the back of the book.

Agnes, ~~was~~ a girl I worked with/, ~~She~~ was a hyperactive child.
     ^   ^
a. The X-Men comic books and Japanese woodcuts of kabuki dancers were part of Marlena's research project on popular culture. They covered the tabletop and the chairs.

b. Our waitress was costumed in a kimono. She had painted her face white. She had arranged her hair in a beehive.

c. Students can apply for a spot in the leadership program. The program teaches thinking and communication skills.

d. Shore houses were flooded. Beaches were washed away. Brant's Light-house was swallowed by the sea.

e. Laura Thackray was an engineer at Volvo. She addressed women's safety needs. She designed a pregnant crash-test dummy.

14c Avoid ineffective or excessive coordination.

Coordinate structures are appropriate only when you intend to draw readers' attention equally to two or more ideas: *Professor Liu praises loudly, and she criticizes softly.* If one idea is more important than another — or if a coordinating conjunction does not clearly signal the relationship between the ideas — you should subordinate the less important idea.

INEFFECTIVE COORDINATION	Closets were taxed as rooms, and most colonists stored their clothes in chests or clothespresses.
IMPROVED WITH SUBORDINATION	Because closets were taxed as rooms, most colonists stored their clothes in chests or clothespresses.

The revision subordinates the less important idea (*closets were taxed as rooms*). Notice that the subordinating conjunction *Because* signals the relation between the ideas more clearly than the coordinating conjunction *and*.

Because it is so easy to string ideas together with *and*, writers often rely too heavily on coordination in their rough drafts. The cure for excessive coordination is simple: look for opportunities to tuck minor ideas into subordinate clauses or phrases.

▶ After four hours,
    ~~Four hours went by, and~~ a rescue truck finally arrived, but by that
    ^
    time we had been evacuated in a helicopter.

Having three independent clauses was excessive. The least important idea has become a prepositional phrase.

EXERCISE 14–2 The following sentences show coordinated ideas (ideas joined with a coordinating conjunction or a semicolon). Restructure the sentences by subordinating minor ideas. You must decide which ideas are minor because the sentences are given out of context. Possible revisions appear in the back of the book.

> *where they*
> The rowers returned to shore, ~~and~~ had a party on the beach
> *to celebrate* ∧
> ~~and celebrated~~ the start of the season.
> ∧

a. These particles are known as "stealth liposomes," and they can hide in the body for a long time without detection.

b. Irena is a competitive gymnast and majors in biochemistry; her goal is to apply her athletic experience and her science degree to a career in sports medicine.

c. Students, textile workers, and labor unions have loudly protested sweat-shop abuses, so apparel makers have been forced to examine their labor practices.

d. IRC (Internet relay chat) was developed in a European university; it was created as a way for a group of graduate students to talk about projects from their dorm rooms.

e. The cafeteria's new menu has an international flavor, and it includes every-thing from enchiladas and pizza to pad thai and sauerbraten.

14d Do not subordinate major ideas.

If a sentence buries its major idea in a subordinate construction, readers may not give the idea enough attention. Make sure to express your major idea in an independent clause and to subordinate any minor ideas.

> *defeated Thomas E. Dewey,*
> ► Harry S. Truman, who was the unexpected winner of the 1948
> ∧
> presidential election/. ~~defeated Thomas E. Dewey.~~
> ∧

The writer wanted to focus on Truman's unexpected victory, but the original sentence buried this information in an adjective clause. The revision puts the more important idea in an independent clause and tucks the less important idea into an adjective clause (*who defeated Thomas E. Dewey*).

As
▶ I was driving home from my new job, heading down Ranchitos
  ^
  Road, ~~when~~ my car suddenly overheated.

> The writer wanted to emphasize that the car overheated, not the fact of
> driving home. The revision expresses the major idea in an independent clause
> and places the less important idea in an adverb clause (*As I was driving home
> from my new job*).

15 Provide some variety.

When a rough draft is filled with too many sentences that begin the same
way or have the same structure, try injecting some variety—as long as
you can do so without sacrificing clarity or ease of reading.

15a Vary your sentence openings.

Most sentences in English begin with the subject, move to the verb, and
continue to the object, with modifiers tucked in along the way or put at
the end. For the most part, such sentences are fine. Put too many of them
in a row, however, and they become monotonous.

Words, phrases, or clauses modifying the verb can often be inserted
ahead of the subject.

Eventually a
▶ A few drops of sap ~~eventually~~ began to trickle into the aluminum
  ^
  bucket.

> Like most adverbs, *eventually* does not need to appear close to the verb it
> modifies (*began*).

Just as the sun was coming up, a
▶ A pair of black ducks flew over the pond. ~~just as the sun was coming up.~~
  ^   ^
> The adverb clause, which modifies the verb *flew*, is as clear at the beginning
> of the sentence as it is at the end.

Adjectives and participial phrases can frequently be moved to the beginning of a sentence without loss of clarity.

> *Dejected and withdrawn,*
> ▶ Edward/~~dejected and withdrawn,~~ nearly gave up his search for
>   ^
>   a job.

NOTE: When beginning a sentence with an adjective or a participial phrase, make sure that the subject of the sentence names the person or thing described in the introductory phrase. If it doesn't, the phrase will dangle. (See 12d.)

15b Use a variety of sentence structures.

A writer should not rely too heavily on simple sentences and compound sentences. The effect tends to be both monotonous and choppy. (See 14b and 14c.) Too many complex or compound-complex sentences, however, can be equally monotonous. Try to achieve a mix of sentence types to strengthen your writing.

SIMPLE	Lowering the bedroom temperature often leads to better sleep.
COMPOUND	Several factors affect sleep quality, but research has shown that simply lowering the bedroom temperature often leads to better sleep.
COMPLEX	When other factors are taken out of the equation, simply lowering the bedroom temperature has been shown to lead to better sleep.
COMPOUND-COMPLEX	Some people turn to sleep aids for a better night's sleep, but often, because core body temperature is a factor in restful sleep, just lowering the bedroom temperature can be equally effective.

For a fuller discussion of sentence types, see 43.

15c Try inverting sentences occasionally.

A sentence is inverted if it does not follow the normal subject-verb-object pattern. Many inversions sound artificial and should be avoided except in the most formal contexts. If an inversion sounds natural, though, it can provide a welcome touch of variety.

▶ Set at the top two corners of the stage were huge ~~Huge~~ lavender hearts outlined in bright white lights. ~~were set at the top two corners of the stage.~~

In the revision, the subject, *hearts*, appears after the verb, *were set*. Notice that the two parts of the verb are also inverted—and separated from each other (*Set . . . were*)—without any awkwardness or loss of meaning.

PART 4

Word Choice

16 Tighten wordy sentences.

Long sentences are not necessarily wordy, nor are short sentences always concise. A sentence is wordy if it can be tightened without loss of meaning.

16a Eliminate redundancies.

Redundancies such as *cooperate together*, *yellow in color*, or *basic essentials* are a common source of wordiness. There is no need to say the same thing twice.

▶ Daniel ~~is now employed~~ at a private rehabilitation center ~~working~~
_{works}

as a registered physical therapist.

Modifiers are redundant when their meanings are suggested by other words in the sentence.

▶ Sylvia ~~very quickly~~ scribbled her name, address, and phone number

on a greasy napkin.

The word *scribbled* already suggests that Sylvia wrote *very quickly*.

16b Cut empty or inflated phrases.

An empty word or phrase can be cut with little or no loss of meaning. Common examples are word groups that weaken the writer's authority by apologizing or hedging: *in my opinion*, *I think that*, *it seems that*, and so on.

▶ ~~In my opinion,~~ Our current economic policy is misguided.

Readers understand that they are hearing the writer's opinion.

Inflated phrases can be reduced to a word or two without loss of meaning.

▶ We are unable to provide funding ~~at this point in time.~~ ^now.^

INFLATED	CONCISE
along the lines of	like
as a matter of fact	in fact
at the present time	now, currently
due to the fact that	because
for the purpose of	for
in order to	to
in spite of the fact that	although, though
in the event that	if

16c Simplify the structure.

Simplifying sentences and using stronger verbs can make writing more direct. Look for opportunities to strengthen the verb.

▶ The financial analyst claimed that because of volatile market conditions she could not ~~make an~~ estimate ~~of~~ the company's future profits.

The verb *estimate* is more vigorous and concise than *make an estimate of.*

The colorless verbs *is, are, was,* and *were* frequently generate excess words.

▶ Investigators ~~were involved in studying~~ ^studied^ the effect of classical music on unborn babies.

The revision is more direct and concise. The action (*studying*), originally appearing in a subordinate structure, has become a strong verb, *studied.*

16d Reduce clauses to phrases, phrases to single words.

Word groups functioning as modifiers can often be made more compact. Look for any opportunities to reduce clauses to phrases or phrases to single words.

▶ We took a side trip to Monticello, ~~which was~~ the home of Thomas Jefferson.

EXERCISE 16-1   Edit the following sentences to reduce wordiness. Possible revisions appear in the back of the book.

The Wilsons moved into the house ~~in spite of the fact that~~ *even though* the back door was only ten yards from the train tracks.

a.   Martin Luther King Jr. was a man who set a high standard for future leaders to meet.
b.   Alice has been deeply in love with cooking since she was little and could first peek over the edge of a big kitchen tabletop.
c.   In my opinion, Bloom's race for the governorship is a futile exercise.
d.   It is pretty important in being a successful graphic designer to have technical knowledge and at the same time an eye for color and balance.
e.   Your task will be to set up digital mail communications capabilities for all employees in the company.

17 Choose appropriate language.

Language is appropriate when it suits your subject, engages your audience, and blends naturally with your own voice.

17a Choose an appropriate level of formality.

In deciding on a level of formality, consider both your subject and your audience. Does the subject demand a formal treatment, or is a relaxed tone more suitable? Will readers be put off if you assume too close a relationship with them, or might you alienate them by seeming too distant?

For most college and professional writing, some degree of formality is appropriate. In a job application letter, for example, it is a mistake to sound breezy and informal.

> **TOO INFORMAL**　　I'd like to get that sales job you've got on the website.
>
> **MORE FORMAL**　　I would like to apply for the position of sales manager advertised on LinkedIn.

Informal writing is appropriate for social media posts, personal email and text messages, and business correspondence between close associates. Like spoken conversation, informal writing allows contractions (*don't*, *I'll*) and colloquial words (*kids*, *kinda*). Vocabulary and sentence structure are rarely complex.

In choosing a level of formality, above all be consistent. When a writer's voice shifts from one level of formality to another, readers receive mixed messages.

> ▶ Residents are ~~entreating~~ the property manager for ~~recurring~~ trash
>   　　　　　　asking　　　　　　　　　　　　　　　　　　　　regular
>   pick-up. So far their efforts have ~~floundered~~.
>   　　　　　　　　　　　　　　failed
>
> Words such as *entreating*, *recurring*, and *floundered* are inappropriate for the subject matter.

17b Avoid jargon, except in specialized writing situations.

Jargon is specialized language used among members of a trade, discipline, or professional group. Use jargon only when readers will be familiar with it and when plain English will not do as well.

| JARGON | We outsourced the work to an outfit in Ohio because we didn't have the bandwidth to tackle it in-house. |
| REVISED | We hired a company in Ohio because we had too few employees to do the work. |

Sentences with jargon are hard to read and are often wordy.

▶ The CEO should ~~dialogue~~ *talk* with investors about ~~partnering~~ *working* with clients to ~~purchase~~ *buy* land in ~~economically deprived zones~~ *poor neighborhoods*.

17c Avoid most euphemisms and doublespeak.

Euphemisms — nice-sounding words or phrases substituted for words thought to sound harsh or ugly — are sometimes appropriate. We may use euphemisms out of concern for someone's feelings. Telling parents, for example, that their daughter is "unmotivated" is more sensitive than saying she's lazy. Tact or politeness, then, can occasionally justify euphemisms, but use them sparingly.

Most euphemisms are needlessly evasive or even deceitful.

EUPHEMISM	PLAIN ENGLISH
preowned automobile	used car
revenue enhancers	taxes
chemical dependency	drug addiction
correctional facility	prison

The term *doublespeak* applies to any deliberately evasive or deceptive language, including euphemisms. Doublespeak is especially common in politics and business. A military retreat is described as *tactical redeployment*; *enhanced interrogation* is a euphemism for "torture"; and *downsizing* really means "firing employees."

17d In most contexts, avoid slang.

Slang is an informal and sometimes private vocabulary that expresses the solidarity of a group such as teenagers, rap musicians, or sports fans.

It is subject to more rapid change than Standard English. For example, the slang teenagers use to express approval changes every few years; *cool, groovy, neat, awesome, sick,* and *dope* have replaced one another within the last several decades.

Although slang has a certain vitality, it is an informal code that not everyone understands. Avoid using it in academic writing, unless you have a specific purpose for doing so.

▶ When the server crashed unexpectedly, three hours of unsaved data. *we lost*
  ~~went down the tubes.~~

17e Avoid sexist language.

Sexist language is language that stereotypes or demeans women or men. Using nonsexist language is a matter of courtesy—of respect for and sensitivity to the feelings of others.

Recognizing sexist language

Some sexist language is easy to recognize because it reflects genuine contempt for women: referring to a woman as a "chick," for example, or calling a lawyer a "lady lawyer."

Other forms of sexist language are less blatant. The following practices reflect stereotypical thinking: referring to members of one profession as exclusively male or exclusively female (teachers as women or engineers as men, for instance) or using different conventions when naming or identifying women and men.

STEREOTYPICAL LANGUAGE

After a nursing student graduates, *she* must face a difficult state board examination. [Not all nursing students are women.]

Running for city council are Boris Stotsky, an attorney, and *Mrs.* Cynthia Jones, a professor of English and *mother of three*. [The title *Mrs.* and the phrase *mother of three* are irrelevant.]

Sometimes sexist language arises from the practice of using the pronouns *he*, *him*, and *his* to refer generically to persons of either sex.

GENERIC PRONOUNS

A journalist is motivated by *his* deadline.

A good interior designer treats *her* clients' ideas respectfully.

Both sentences are sexist—for excluding one sex entirely and for making assumptions about the members of a particular profession.

Similarly, terms including *man* and *men* were once used to refer generically to persons of either sex. Current usage demands gender-neutral terms for references to both men and women.

INAPPROPRIATE	APPROPRIATE
chairman	chairperson, moderator, chair, head
congressman	representative, legislator
fireman	firefighter
to man	to operate, to staff
mankind	people, humans
manpower	personnel, staff
policeman	police officer

Revising sexist language

When revising sexist language, some writers substitute *he or she* and *his or her*. This strategy is wordy and can become awkward when repeated throughout an essay. Also, some readers may think *he or she* and *his or her* exclude transgender individuals. Other writers alternate female pronouns (*she*, *her*, *hers*) with male pronouns, a strategy that can confuse readers. A more effective revision strategy is to use plural nouns and pronouns or to rewrite the sentence to avoid problems with sexist or noninclusive language. Yet another strategy might be to use the plural pronouns *they* and *them*, gender-neutral options, to refer to all nouns, including singular nouns: *A journalist is motivated by their deadline.* (You may want to check with your instructor for any preferences.)

SEXIST

A journalist is motivated by *his* deadline.

A good interior designer treats *her* clients' ideas respectfully.

BETTER: USING THE PLURAL

Journalists are motivated by *their* deadlines.

Good interior designers treat *their* clients' ideas respectfully.

BETTER: REVISING THE SENTENCE

A journalist is motivated by *a* deadline.

A good interior designer treats clients' ideas respectfully.

For more examples of these revision strategies, see 23.

EXERCISE 17-1 Edit the following sentences to eliminate sexist language and sexist assumptions. Possible revisions appear in the back of the book.

> *Scholarship athletes* *their*
> A scholarship athlete must be as concerned about ~~his~~ academic
>
> *they are* *their*
> performance as ~~he is~~ about ~~his~~ athletic performance.

a. Mrs. Geralyn Farmer, who is the mayor's wife, is the chief surgeon at University Hospital. Dr. Paul Green is her assistant.

b. Every applicant wants to know how much he will earn.

c. An elementary school teacher should understand the concept of nurturing if she intends to be effective.

d. An obstetrician needs to be available to his patients at all hours.

e. If man does not stop polluting his environment, mankind will perish.

18 Find the exact words.

Two reference works will help you find words to express your meaning exactly: a good dictionary, such as *The American Heritage Dictionary* or *Merriam-Webster* online, and a collection of synonyms and antonyms, such as *Roget's International Thesaurus*.

NOTE: Do not turn to a thesaurus in search of impressive words. Look instead for precise words that express your meaning exactly.

18a Select words with appropriate connotations.

In addition to their strict dictionary meanings (or *denotations*), words have *connotations*, emotional colorings that affect how readers respond to them. The word *steel* denotes "commercial iron that contains carbon," but it also calls up images associated with steel. These associations give the word its connotations—cold, hard, smooth, unbending.

If the connotation of a word does not seem appropriate for your purpose, your audience, or your subject matter, you should change the word. When a more appropriate synonym does not come quickly to mind, consult a dictionary or a thesaurus.

> When American soldiers returned home after World War II, many
> women ~~abandoned~~ left their jobs in favor of marriage.
>
> The word *abandoned* is too negative for the context.

18b Prefer specific, concrete nouns.

Unlike general nouns, which refer to broad classes of things, specific nouns point to particular items. *Film*, for example, names a general class, *fantasy film* names a narrower class, and *The Fellowship of the Ring* is more specific still. Other examples are *team, football team, Denver Broncos; music, symphony, Beethoven's Ninth*.

Unlike abstract nouns, which refer to qualities and ideas (*justice*, *beauty*, *dignity*), concrete nouns point to immediate, often sensory experiences and to physical objects (*steeple*, *asphalt*, *lilac*, *stone*).

Specific, concrete nouns express meaning more vividly than general or abstract ones. Although general and abstract language is sometimes necessary to convey your meaning, use specific, concrete words whenever possible.

▶ The senator spoke about the challenges of the future:
pollution, dwindling resources, and terrorism.
~~the environment and world peace.~~
^

Nouns such as *thing*, *area*, *aspect*, *factor*, and *individual* are especially dull and imprecise.

▶ Toni Morrison's *Beloved* is about slavery, ~~among other things.~~
motherhood, and memory.
^

18c Use standard idioms.

Idioms are speech forms that follow no easily specified rules. The English say "Bernice went *to hospital*," an idiom strange to American ears, which are accustomed to hearing *the* in front of *hospital*. Native speakers of a language seldom have problems with idioms, but prepositions (such as *with*, *to*, *at*, and *of*) occasionally cause trouble, especially when they follow certain verbs and adjectives. When in doubt, consult a dictionary.

UNIDIOMATIC	IDIOMATIC
angry at (a person)	angry with (a person)
preferable than	preferable to
superior than	superior to
think on	think of, about
try and	try to

For Multilingual Writers

Because idioms follow no particular rules, it's best to learn them individually. You may find it helpful to keep a list of idioms that you frequently encounter in conversation and in reading.

18d Do not rely heavily on clichés.

The pioneer who first announced that he had "slept like a log" no doubt amused his companions with a fresh, unlikely comparison. Today, however, that comparison is a cliché, a saying that can no longer add emphasis or surprise.

To see just how dully predictable clichés are, put your hand over the right-hand column in the following list and then finish the phrases on the left.

cool as a	cucumber
beat around	the bush
busy as a	bee, beaver
crystal	clear
light as a	feather
avoid clichés like the	plague

The solution for clichés is simple: delete them or rewrite them.

▶ When I received a full scholarship from my second-choice school, I
  felt pressured to settle for second best.
  ~~found myself between a rock and a hard place.~~
  ^

18e Use figures of speech with care.

A figure of speech is an expression that uses words imaginatively (rather than literally) to make abstract ideas concrete. Most often, figures of speech compare two seemingly unlike things to reveal surprising similarities.

In a *simile*, the writer makes the comparison explicitly, typically by using *like* or *as*: *By the time cotton had to be picked, Grandfather's neck was as red as the clay he plowed.* In a *metaphor*, the *like* or *as* is omitted, and the comparison is implied. For example, in the Old Testament Song of Solomon, a young woman compares the man she loves to a fruit tree: *With great delight I sat in his shadow, and his fruit was sweet to my taste.*

Although figures of speech are useful devices, writers can misuse them if they don't think about the images they evoke. The result is sometimes a *mixed metaphor*, the combination of two or more images that don't make sense together.

▶ Our manager decided to put all controversial issues ~~in a holding~~

~~pattern~~ on a back burner until after the annual meeting.

Here the writer is mixing airplanes and stoves. Simply deleting one of the images corrects the problem.

EXERCISE 18–1 Edit the following sentences to replace worn-out expressions and to clarify mixed figures of speech. Possible revisions appear in the back of the book.

the color drained from his face.
When he heard about the accident, ~~he turned white as a sheet.~~
                                                        ^

a. John stormed into the room like a bull in a china shop.
b. Some people insist that they'll always have your back, even when they haven't before.
c. The Cubs easily beat the Mets, who were in over their heads early in the game today at Wrigley Field.
d. We ironed out the sticky spots in our relationship.
e. My mother accused me of beating around the bush when in fact I was just talking off the top of my head.

19 Use the right words. (Glossary of usage)

This glossary includes words commonly confused, words commonly misused, and words that are nonstandard. It also lists words that may be appropriate in informal speech but that are inappropriate in formal writing.

accept, except *Accept* is a verb meaning "to receive." *Except* is usually a preposition meaning "excluding." *I will accept all the packages except that one.* *Except* is also a verb meaning "to exclude." *Please except that item from the list.*

advice, advise *Advice* is a noun, *advise* a verb. *We advise you to follow John's advice.*

affect, effect *Affect* is usually a verb meaning "to influence." *Effect* is usually a noun meaning "result." *The drug did not affect the disease, and it had adverse side effects. Effect* can also be a verb meaning "to bring about." *Only the president can effect such a dramatic change.*

agree to, agree with *Agree to* means "to give consent to." *Agree with* means "to be in accord with" or "to come to an understanding with." *He agrees with me about the need for change, but he won't agree to my plan.*

all ready, already *All ready* means "completely prepared." *Already* means "previously." *Susan was all ready for the concert, but her friends had already left.*

all together, altogether *All together* means "everyone or everything in one place." *Altogether* means "entirely." *We were not altogether certain that we could bring the family all together for the reunion.*

allusion, illusion An *allusion* is an indirect reference. An *illusion* is a misconception or false impression. *Did you catch my allusion to Shakespeare? Mirrors give the room an illusion of depth.*

a lot *A lot* is two words. Do not write *alot*. *Sam lost a lot of weight.* See also *lots, lots of.*

amount, number Use *amount* with quantities that cannot be counted; use *number* with those that can. *This recipe calls for a large amount of sugar. We have a large number of toads in our garden.*

anymore Use the adverb *anymore* in a negative context to mean "any longer" or "now." *The factory isn't producing shoes anymore.* Using *anymore* in a positive context is colloquial; in formal writing, use *now* instead. *We order all our food online now* (not *anymore*).

anyone, any one *Anyone*, an indefinite pronoun, means "any person at all." *Any one*, the pronoun *one* preceded by the adjective *any*, refers to a particular person or thing in a group. *Anyone from the winning team may choose any one of the games on display.*

anyplace *Anyplace* is colloquial. In formal writing, use *anywhere*.

as Do not use *as* to mean "because" if there is any chance of ambiguity. *We canceled the picnic because* (not *as*) *it began raining. As* here could mean either "because" or "when."

awhile, a while *Awhile* is an adverb; it can modify a verb, but it cannot be the object of a preposition such as *for.* The two-word form *a while* is a noun preceded by an article and therefore can be the object of a preposition. *Stay awhile. Stay for a while.*

being as, being that *Being as* and *being that* are nonstandard expressions. Write *because* instead. *Because* (not *Being as*) *I slept late, I had to skip breakfast.*

beside, besides *Beside* is a preposition meaning "at the side of" or "next to." *Annie sleeps with a flashlight beside her bed. Besides* is a preposition meaning "except" or "in addition to." *No one besides Terrie can have that ice cream. Besides* is also an adverb meaning "in addition." *I'm not hungry; besides, I don't like ice cream.*

between, among Ordinarily, use *among* with three or more entities, *between* with two. *The prize was divided among several contestants. You have a choice between carrots and beans.*

bring, take Use *bring* when an object is being transported toward you, *take* when it is being moved away. *Please bring me a glass of water. Please take these forms to Mr. Scott.*

can, may *Can* is traditionally reserved for ability, *may* for permission. *Can you speak French? May I help you?*

capital, capitol *Capital* refers to a city, *capitol* to a building where law-makers meet. *The residents of the state capital protested plans to close the streets surrounding the capitol. Capital* can also refer to wealth or resources.

cite, site *Cite* means "to quote as an authority or example." *Site* is usually a noun meaning "a particular place." *He cited the zoning law in his argument against the proposed site of the gas station.* Locations on the Internet are usually referred to as *sites. The library's website improves every week.*

compare to, compare with *Compare to* means "to represent as similar." *She compared him to a wild stallion. Compare with* means "to examine similarities and differences." *The study compared the language ability of apes with that of dolphins.*

complement, compliment *Complement* is a verb meaning "to go with or complete" or a noun meaning "something that completes." As a verb, *compliment* means "to flatter"; as a noun, it means "flattering remark." *Her skill at rushing the net complements his skill at volleying. Martha's flower arrangements receive many compliments.*

conscience, conscious *Conscience* is a noun meaning "moral principles." *Conscious* is an adjective meaning "aware or alert." *Let your conscience be your guide. Were you conscious of his love for you?*

continual, continuous *Continual* means "repeated regularly and frequently." *She grew weary of the continual telephone calls. Continuous* means "extended or prolonged without interruption." *The broken siren made a continuous wail.*

could of *Could of* is nonstandard for *could have*. *We could have* (not *could of*) *taken the train.*

council, counsel A *council* is a deliberative body, and a *councilor* is a member of such a body. *Counsel* usually means "advice" and can also mean "lawyer"; a *counselor* is one who gives advice or guidance. *The councilors met to draft the council's position paper. The pastor offered wise counsel to the troubled teenager.*

data *Data* is a plural noun technically meaning "facts or propositions." But *data* is increasingly being accepted as a singular noun. *The new data suggest* (or *suggests*) *that our theory is correct.* (The singular *datum* is rarely used.)

different from, different than Ordinarily, write *different from. Your sense of style is different from Jim's.* However, *different than* is acceptable to avoid an awkward construction. *Please let me know if your plans are different than* (to avoid *from what*) *they were six weeks ago.*

disinterested, uninterested *Disinterested* means "impartial, objective"; *uninterested* means "not interested." *We sought the advice of a disinterested counselor to help us solve our problem. Mark was uninterested in anyone's opinion but his own.*

e.g. In formal writing, replace the Latin abbreviation *e.g.* with its English equivalent: *for example* or *for instance.*

emigrate from, immigrate to *Emigrate* means "to leave one country or region to settle in another." *In 1903, my great-grandfather emigrated from Russia to escape the religious pogroms. Immigrate* means "to enter another country and reside there." *More than fifty thousand Bosnians immigrated to the United States in the 1990s.*

etc. Avoid ending a list with *etc.* It is more emphatic to end with an example, and in most contexts readers will understand that the list is not exhaustive. When you don't wish to end with an example, *and so on* is more graceful than *etc.*

everyone, every one *Everyone* is an indefinite pronoun. *Every one*, the pronoun *one* preceded by the adjective *every*, means "each individual or thing in a particular group." *Every one* is usually followed by *of. Everyone wanted to go. Every one of the missing books was found.*

explicit, implicit *Explicit* means "expressed directly" or "clearly defined"; *implicit* means "implied, unstated." *I gave him explicit instructions not to go swimming. My mother's silence indicated her implicit approval.*

farther, further *Farther* usually describes distances. *Further* usually suggests quantity or degree. *Chicago is farther from Miami than I thought. I would be grateful for further suggestions.*

fewer, less Use *fewer* for items that can be counted; use *less* for items that cannot be counted. *Fewer people are living in the city. Please put less sugar in my tea.*

firstly *Firstly* sounds pretentious, and it leads to the ungainly series *firstly, secondly, thirdly*, and so on. Write *first, second, third* instead.

good, well *Good* is an adjective, *well* an adverb. (See 27a, 27b, and 27c.) *He hasn't felt good about his game since he sprained his wrist last season. She performed well on the uneven parallel bars.*

hanged, hung *Hanged* is the past-tense and past-participle form of the verb *hang* meaning "to execute." *The prisoner was hanged at dawn. Hung* is the past-tense and past-participle form of the verb *hang* meaning "to fasten or suspend." *The stockings were hung by the chimney with care.*

hopefully *Hopefully* means "in a hopeful manner." *We looked hopefully to the future.* Some usage experts object to the use of *hopefully* as a sentence adverb, apparently on grounds of clarity. To be safe, avoid using *hopefully* in sentences such as the following: *Hopefully, your son will recover soon.* Instead, indicate who is doing the hoping: *I hope that your son will recover soon.*

however In the past, some writers objected to using *however* at the beginning of a sentence, but current experts allow placing the word according to the intended meaning and emphasis. All of the following sentences are correct. *Pam decided, however, to attend the lecture. However, Pam decided to attend the lecture.* (She had been considering other activities.) *Pam, however, decided to attend the lecture.* (Unlike someone else, Pam chose to attend the lecture.)

i.e. In formal writing, use "in other words" or "that is" rather than the Latin abbreviation *i.e.* to introduce a clarifying statement. *Exposure to borax usually causes only mild skin irritation; in other words* (not *i.e.*), *it's not especially toxic.*

if, whether Use *if* to express a condition and *whether* to express alternatives. *If you go on a trip, whether to Nebraska or Italy, remember to bring identification.*

imply, infer *Imply* means "to suggest or state indirectly"; *infer* means "to draw a conclusion." *John implied that he knew all about databases, but the interviewer inferred that John was inexperienced.*

in, into *In* indicates location or condition; *into* indicates movement or a change in condition. *They found the lost letters in a box after moving into the house.*

irregardless *Irregardless* is nonstandard. Use *regardless*.

kind of, sort of Avoid using *kind of* or *sort of* to mean "somewhat." *The movie was somewhat* (not *sort of*) *boring*. Do not put *a* after either phrase. *That kind of* (not *kind of a*) *salesclerk annoys me.*

lead, led *Lead* is a metallic element; it is a noun. *Led* is the past tense of the verb *lead*. *He led me to the treasure.*

lie, lay *Lie* is an intransitive verb meaning "to recline or rest on a surface." Its forms are *lie, lay, lain*. *Lay* is a transitive verb meaning "to put or place." Its forms are *lay, laid, laid*. *I'm going to lay my phone on the picnic table and lie in the hammock.*

like, as *Like* is a preposition, not a subordinating conjunction. It can be followed only by a noun or a noun phrase. *As* is a subordinating conjunction that introduces a subordinate clause. In casual speech, you may say *She looks like she hasn't slept*. But in formal writing, use *as*. *She looks as if she hasn't slept.*

loose, lose *Loose* is an adjective meaning "not securely fastened." *Lose* is a verb meaning "to misplace" or "to not win." *Did you lose your only loose pair of work pants?*

lots, lots of *Lots* and *lots of* are informal substitutes for *many*, *much*, or *a lot*. Avoid using them in formal writing.

maybe, may be *Maybe* is an adverb meaning "possibly." *Maybe the sun will shine tomorrow*. *May be* is a verb phrase. *Tomorrow may be brighter.*

of Use the verb *have*, not the preposition *of*, after the verbs *could, should, would, may, might*, and *must*. *They must have* (not *must of*) *left early.*

off of *Off* is sufficient. Omit *of*. *The ball rolled off* (not *off of*) *the table.*

passed, past *Passed* is the past tense of the verb *pass*. *Ann passed me another slice of cake*. *Past* usually means "belonging to a former time" or "beyond a time or place." *Our past president spoke until past midnight. The hotel is just past the next intersection.*

precede, proceed *Precede* means "to come before." *Proceed* means "to go forward." *As we proceeded up the mountain path, we noticed fresh tracks in the mud, evidence that a group of hikers had preceded us.*

principal, principle *Principal* is a noun meaning "the head of a school or an organization" or "a sum of money." It is also an adjective meaning "most important." *Principle* is a noun meaning "a basic truth or law." *The principal expelled her for three principal reasons. We believe in the principle of equal justice for all.*

quote, quotation *Quote* is a verb; *quotation* is a noun. Avoid using *quote* as a shortened form of *quotation. Her quotations* (not *quotes*) *from current movies intrigued us.*

raise, rise *Raise* is a transitive verb meaning "to move or cause to move upward." It takes a direct object. *I raised the shades. Rise* is an intransitive verb meaning "to go up." *Heat rises.*

reason why The expression *reason why* is redundant. *The reason* (not *The reason why*) *Jones lost the election is clear.*

respectfully, respectively *Respectfully* means "showing or marked by respect." *Respectively* means "each in the order given." *He respectfully submitted his opinion to the judge. John, Tom, and Larry were a butcher, a baker, and a lawyer, respectively.*

set, sit *Set* is a transitive verb meaning "to put" or "to place." Its past tense is *set. She set the dough in a warm corner of the kitchen. Sit* is an intransitive verb meaning "to be seated." Its past tense is *sat. The cat sat in the doorway.*

should of *Should of* is nonstandard for *should have. They should have* (not *should of*) *been home an hour ago.*

since Do not use *since* to mean "because" if there is any chance of ambiguity. *Because* (not *Since*) *we won the game, we have been celebrating with a pitcher of root beer. Since* here could mean "because" or "from the time that."

sometime, some time, sometimes *Sometime* is an adverb meaning "at an indefinite time." *Some time* is the adjective *some* modifying the noun *time* and means "a period of time." *Sometimes* is an adverb meaning "at times, now and then." *I'll see you all sometime soon. I haven't lived there for some time. Sometimes I see him at work.*

suppose to *Suppose to* is nonstandard for *supposed to. I was supposed to* (not *suppose to*) *be there by noon.*

sure and Write *sure to. We were all taught to be sure to* (not *sure and*) *look both ways before crossing a street.*

than, then *Than* is a conjunction used in comparisons; *then* is an adverb denoting time. *That pizza is more than I can eat. Tom laughed, and then we recognized him.*

there, their, they're *There* is an adverb specifying place; it is also an expletive (placeholder). Adverb: *Sylvia is sitting there patiently.* Expletive: *There are two plums left. Their* is a possessive pronoun: *Fred and Jane finally washed their car. They're* is a contraction of *they are: They're later than usual today.*

to, too, two *To* is a preposition; *too* is an adverb; *two* is a number. *Too many of your shots slice to the left, but the last two were just right.*

toward, towards *Toward* and *towards* are generally interchangeable, although *toward* is preferred in American English.

try and *Try and* is nonstandard for *try to. The teacher asked us all to try to* (not *try and*) *write a haiku.*

wait for, wait on *Wait for* means "to be in readiness for" or "to await." *Wait on* means "to serve." *We're waiting for* (not *waiting on*) *Ruth to take us to the museum.*

weather, whether The noun *weather* refers to the state of the atmosphere. *Whether* is a conjunction referring to a choice between alternatives. *We wondered whether the weather would clear.*

while Avoid using *while* to mean "although" or "whereas" if there is any chance of ambiguity. *Although* (not *While*) *Gloria lost money in the slot machine, Tom won it at roulette.* Here *While* could mean either "although" or "at the same time that."

who, which, that Do not use *which* to refer to persons. Use *who* instead. *That*, though generally used to refer to things, may be used to refer to a group or class of people. *The player who* (not *that* or *which*) *made the basket at the buzzer was named MVP. The team that scores the most points in this game will win the tournament.*

who, whom *Who* is used for subjects and subject complements; *whom* is used for objects. (See 26.)

who's, whose *Who's* is a contraction of *who is; whose* is a possessive pronoun. *Who's ready for more popcorn? Whose coat is this?* (See 33c and 33e.)

would of *Would of* is nonstandard for *would have. She would have* (not *would of*) *had a chance to play if she had arrived on time.*

your, you're *Your* is a possessive pronoun; *you're* is a contraction of *you are. Is that your new bike? You're in the finals.*

PART 5

Grammatical Sentences

20 Repair sentence fragments.

A sentence fragment is a word group that pretends to be a sentence. Sentence fragments are easy to recognize when they appear out of context, like these:

> When the cat leaped onto the table.

> Running for the bus.

When fragments appear next to related sentences, however, they are harder to spot.

> We had just sat down to dinner. When the cat leaped onto the table.

> I tripped and twisted my ankle. Running for the bus.

To be a sentence, a word group must consist of at least one full independent clause. An independent clause includes a subject and a verb, and it either stands alone or could stand alone.

For Multilingual Writers

Unlike some other languages, English requires a subject and a verb in every sentence (except in commands, where the subject *you* is understood but not present: *Sit down*).

> Students usually very busy at the end of the semester.
>
> ^ are

You can repair most fragments in one of two ways:

- Pull the fragment into a nearby sentence.

- Rewrite the fragment as a complete sentence.

> We had just sat down to dinner/ ~~When~~ the cat leaped onto the table.
> ^ when

> I tripped and sprained my ankle. ~~Running for the bus.~~
> ^ Running for the bus,

20a Attach fragmented subordinate clauses or turn them into sentences.

A subordinate clause is patterned like a sentence, with both a subject and a verb, but it begins with a word that marks it as subordinate. The following words commonly introduce subordinate clauses: *after, although, because, before, if, so that, though, unless, until, when, where, which,* and *who.*

Most fragmented clauses can be pulled into a sentence nearby.

▶ Americans have come to fear the West Nile virus/ ~~Because~~ it is

                                                because

   transmitted by the common mosquito.

If a fragmented clause cannot be attached to a nearby sentence, try rewriting it. The simplest way to turn a fragmented clause into a sentence is to delete the opening word or words that mark it as subordinate.

▶ Uncontrolled development is taking a toll on the environment.
   Across
   ~~So that across~~ the globe, fragile ecosystems are collapsing.

20b Attach fragmented phrases or turn them into sentences.

Like subordinate clauses, phrases function within sentences as adjectives, as adverbs, or as nouns. They cannot stand alone. Fragmented phrases are often prepositional or verbal phrases; sometimes they are appositives, words or word groups that rename nouns or pronouns. (See 42a, 42b, and 42c.)

Often a fragmented phrase may simply be pulled into a nearby sentence.

                                  examining
▶ The archaeologists worked slowly/ ~~Examining~~ and labeling every

   pottery shard they uncovered.

The word group beginning with *Examining* is a verbal phrase.

▶ The patient displayed symptoms of ALS/. A neurodegenerative disease.
(a)

A neurodegenerative disease is an appositive renaming the noun *ALS*.
(For punctuation of appositives, see 30e.)

If a fragmented phrase cannot be pulled into a nearby sentence effectively, turn the phrase into a sentence. You may need to add a subject, a verb, or both.

▶ In the training session, Jamie explained how to access our new
database. ~~Also~~ how to submit expense reports and request vendor
She also taught us
payments.

The revision turns the fragmented phrase into a sentence by adding a subject and a verb.

20c Attach other fragmented word groups or turn them into sentences.

Other word groups that are commonly fragmented include parts of compound predicates, lists, and examples introduced by *for example, in addition*, or similar expressions.

▶ The woodpecker finch of the Galápagos Islands carefully selects a
twig of a certain size and shape/~~And~~ then uses this tool to pry out
and
grubs from trees.

The subject is *finch*, and the compound predicate is *selects . . . and . . . uses.*
(For punctuation of compound predicates, see 31a.)

▶ It has been said that there are only three indigenous American art
forms/: ~~Musical~~ comedy, jazz, and soap opera.
musical

To correct a fragmented list, often you can attach it to a nearby sentence with a colon or a dash. When terms such as *especially, namely, like*, and *such as* introduce fragmented lists, the fragments can usually be attached to the preceding sentence.

▶ In the twentieth century, the South produced some great American
    such
  writers/, ~~Such~~ as Flannery O'Connor, William Faulkner, Alice
           ^
  Walker, Tennessee Williams, and Thomas Wolfe.

Although you may begin a sentence with some of the following words or phrases, make sure that what follows has a subject and a verb.

also	for example	mainly
and	for instance	or
but	in addition	that is

Often the easiest solution is to turn the fragment into a sentence.

▶ In his memoir, Primo Levi describes the horrors of living in a
                              he worked
  concentration camp. For example, ~~working~~ without food and
  suffered   ^
  ~~suffering~~ emotional abuse.
  ^

EXERCISE 20–1 Repair each fragment by attaching it to a nearby sentence or by rewriting it as a complete sentence. If a word group is correct, write "correct" after it. Possible revisions appear in the back of the book.

                                                            a
One Greek island that should not be missed is Mykonos/, ~~A~~ vacation
                                                      ^
spot for Europeans and a playground for the rich.

a. Listening to the CD her sister had sent, Mia was overcome with a mix of emotions. Happiness, homesickness, and nostalgia.

b. Cortés and his soldiers were astonished when they looked down from the mountains and saw Tenochtitlán. The magnificent capital of the Aztecs.

c. Although my spoken Spanish is not very good. I can read the language with ease.

d. There are several reasons for not eating meat. One reason being that dangerous chemicals are used throughout the various stages of meat production.

e. To learn how to sculpt beauty from everyday life. This is my intention in studying art and archaeology.

21 Revise run-on sentences.

Run-on sentences are independent clauses that have not been joined correctly. An independent clause is a word group that can stand alone as a sentence. (See 43a.) When two independent clauses appear in one sentence, they must be joined in one of these ways:

- with a comma and a coordinating conjunction (*and, but, or, nor, for, so, yet*)
- with a semicolon (or occasionally with a colon or a dash)

There are two types of run-on sentences. When a writer puts no mark of punctuation and no coordinating conjunction between independent clauses, the result is called a *fused sentence*.

FUSED ┌───── INDEPENDENT CLAUSE ─────┐┌── INDEPENDENT CLAUSE ──┐ Air pollution poses risks to all humans it can be deadly for asthma sufferers.

A far more common type of run-on sentence is the *comma splice* — two or more independent clauses joined with a comma but without a coordinating conjunction. In some comma splices, the comma appears alone.

COMMA SPLICE Air pollution poses risks to all humans, it can be deadly for asthma sufferers.

In other comma splices, the comma is accompanied by a joining word that is *not* a coordinating conjunction.

COMMA SPLICE Air pollution poses risks to all humans, however, it can be deadly for asthma sufferers.

However is a transitional expression, not a coordinating conjunction, and it cannot be used with only a comma to join two independent clauses (see 21b).

To revise a run-on sentence, you have four choices.

1. Use a comma and a coordinating conjunction (*and*, *but*, *or*, *nor*, *for*, *so*, *yet*). See 21a.
2. Use a semicolon (or, if appropriate, a colon or a dash). A semicolon may be used alone; it can also be accompanied by a transitional expression. See 21b.
3. Make the clauses into separate sentences. See 21c.
4. Restructure the sentence, perhaps by subordinating a clause. See 21d.

As you revise, decide which of these revision techniques will work best for a particular sentence.

21a Consider separating the clauses with a comma and a coordinating conjunction.

There are seven coordinating conjunctions in English: *and*, *but*, *or*, *nor*, *for*, *so*, and *yet*. When a coordinating conjunction joins independent clauses, it is usually preceded by a comma. (See 30a.)

▶ Air pollution poses risks to all humans, _∧ it can be deadly for people
    ^{but}
    with asthma.

21b Consider separating the clauses with a semicolon, a colon, or a dash.

When the independent clauses are closely related and their relation is clear without a coordinating conjunction, inserting a semicolon is one method of revision. (See 32a.)

▶ Tragedy depicts the individual confronted with the fact of death/;

    comedy depicts the adaptability of human nature.

A semicolon is required between independent clauses that have been linked with a transitional expression such as *however*, *therefore*, *moreover*, *in fact*, or *for example*. For a longer list, see 32b.

▶ In her film adaptation, the director changed key details of the plot/; in fact, she added new scenes that do not appear in the novel.

A colon or a dash may be more appropriate if the first independent clause introduces the second or if the second clause summarizes or explains the first. (See 32e and 36a.) In formal writing, the colon is usually preferred to the dash.

Inserting a colon is an appropriate method of revision if the first independent clause introduces a quoted sentence.

▶ Nobel Peace Prize winner Al Gore had this to say about climate change/:"The truth is that our circumstances are not only new; they are completely different than they have ever been in all of human history."

21c Consider making the clauses into separate sentences.

▶ Why should we spend money on space exploration/?
We
~~we~~ have enough underfunded programs here on Earth.

A question and a statement should be separate sentences.

21d Consider restructuring the sentence, perhaps by subordinating one of the clauses.

If one of the independent clauses is less important than the other, turn the less important clause into a subordinate clause or phrase. (For more about subordination, see 14, especially the chart on p. 100.)

▶ One of the most famous advertising slogans is Wheaties cereal's
which
"Breakfast of Champions," ~~it~~ associated the cereal with famous athletes.

▶ Mary McLeod Bethune, ~~was~~ the seventeenth child of former slaves,

                ^

~~she~~ founded the National Council of Negro Women in 1935.

Minor ideas in these sentences are now expressed in a subordinate clause or phrase.

EXERCISE 21–1   Revise the following run-on sentences using the method of revision suggested in brackets. Possible revisions appear in the back of the book.

    Because
Orville had been obsessed with his weight as a teenager, he rarely ate
  ^
anything sweet. [*Restructure the sentence.*]

a. The city had one public swimming pool, it stayed packed with children all summer long. [*Restructure the sentence.*]

b. The building is being renovated, therefore at times we have no heat, water, or electricity. [*Use a comma and a coordinating conjunction.*]

c. The view was not what the travel agent had described, where were the rolling hills and the shimmering rivers? [*Make two sentences.*]

d. Walker's coming-of-age novel is set against a gloomy scientific backdrop, the Earth's rotation has begun to slow down. [*Use a semicolon.*]

e. City officials had good reason to fear a major earthquake, most of the business district was built on landfill. [*Use a colon.*]

22   Make subjects and verbs agree.

In the present tense, verbs agree with their subjects in number (singular or plural) and in person (first, second, third): *I sing, you sing, she sings, we sing, they sing.* Even if your ear recognizes the standard subject-verb combinations in 22a, you will no doubt encounter tricky situations such as those described in 22b–22j.

22a Learn to recognize standard subject-verb combinations.

The present-tense ending -s (or -es) is used on a verb if its subject is third-person singular (*he*, *she*, *it*, and singular nouns); otherwise the verb takes no ending. Consider, for example, the present-tense forms of the verb *give*.

	SINGULAR	PLURAL
FIRST PERSON	I give	we give
SECOND PERSON	you give	you give
THIRD PERSON	he/she/it gives	they give
	Yolanda gives	parents give

The verb *be* varies from this pattern; it has special forms in *both* the present and the past tense.

PRESENT-TENSE FORMS OF *BE*		PAST-TENSE FORMS OF *BE*	
I am	we are	I was	we were
you are	you are	you were	you were
he/she/it is	they are	he/she/it was	they were

22b Make the verb agree with its subject, not with a word that comes between.

Word groups often come between the subject and the verb. Such word groups, usually modifying the subject, may contain a noun that at first appears to be the subject. By mentally stripping away such modifiers, you can isolate the noun that is in fact the subject.

▶ High levels of air pollution causes damage to the respiratory tract.

The subject is *levels*, not *pollution*.

▶ The slaughter of pandas for their pelts ~~have~~ ^{has} caused the panda

  population to decline drastically.

  The subject is *slaughter*, not *pandas* or *pelts*.

NOTE: Phrases beginning with expressions such as *as well as, in addition to, accompanied by, together with,* and *along with* do not make a singular subject plural: *The governor as well as his press secretary was on the plane.* To emphasize that two people were on the plane, the writer could use *and* instead: *The governor and his press secretary were on the plane.*

22c Treat most subjects joined with *and* as plural.

A subject with two or more parts is said to be compound. If the parts are connected with *and*, the subject is nearly always plural.

▶ Bleach and ammonia create**s** a toxic gas when mixed.

EXCEPTIONS: When the parts of the subject form a single unit or when they refer to the same person or thing, treat the subject as singular: *Fish and chips is always on the menu.* When a compound subject is preceded by *each* or *every*, treat it as singular: *Each tree, shrub, and vine needs to be sprayed.*

22d With subjects joined with *or* or *nor* (or with *either . . . or* or *neither . . . nor*), make the verb agree with the part of the subject nearer to the verb.

▶ If an infant or a child ~~have~~ ^{has} a high fever, call a doctor.

▶ Neither the chief financial officer nor the marketing managers ~~was~~ ^{were}

  able to convince the client to reconsider.

  The verb must be matched with the part of the subject closer to it: *child has* in the first sentence, *managers were* in the second.

NOTE: If one part of the subject is singular and the other is plural, put the plural part last to avoid awkwardness.

22e Treat most indefinite pronouns as singular.

Indefinite pronouns are pronouns that do not refer to specific persons or things. The following commonly used indefinite pronouns are singular.

anybody	each	everyone	nobody	somebody
anyone	either	everything	no one	someone
anything	everybody	neither	nothing	something

Many of these words appear to have plural meanings, and they are often treated as plural in casual speech. In formal written English, however, they are nearly always treated as singular.

> has
> ▶ Each of the essays ~~have~~ been graded.
>   ^

> was
> ▶ Nobody who participated in the clinical trials ~~were~~ given a placebo.
>   ^

> The subjects of these sentences are *Each* and *Nobody*. These indefinite pronouns are third-person singular, so the verbs must be *has* and *was*.

A few indefinite pronouns (*all, any, none, some*) may be singular or plural depending on the noun or pronoun they refer to: *Some of our luggage was lost. Some of the rocks were slippery. None of his advice makes sense. None of the eggs were broken.*

22f Treat collective nouns as singular unless the meaning is clearly plural.

Collective nouns such as *jury, committee, audience, crowd, troop, family,* and *couple* name a class or a group. In American English, collective nouns are nearly always treated as singular, to emphasize the group as a unit.

> meets
> ▶ The board of trustees ~~meet~~ in Denver twice a year.
>   ^

Occasionally, to draw attention to the individual members of the group, a collective noun may be treated as plural: *The class are debating among themselves.* Many writers prefer to add a clearly plural noun such as *members: The class members are debating among themselves.*

NOTE: In general, when a fraction or unit of measurement is used with a singular noun, treat it as singular; when it is used with a plural noun, treat it as plural: *Three-fourths* of the pie *has* been eaten. *One-fourth* of the drivers *were* texting.

22g Make the verb agree with its subject even when the subject follows the verb.

Verbs ordinarily follow subjects. When this normal order is reversed, it is easy to become confused. Sentences beginning with *there is* or *there are* (or *there was* or *there were*) are inverted; the subject follows the verb.

▶ There ~~is~~ surprisingly few honeybees left in southern China.
      ^are

The subject, *honeybees*, is plural, so the verb must be *are*.

Occasionally you may decide to invert a sentence for variety or effect. When you do so, check to make sure that your subject and verb agree.

▶ Of particular concern ~~is~~ penicillin and tetracycline, antibiotics used
      ^are

to make animals more resistant to disease.

The subject, *penicillin and tetracycline*, is plural, so the verb must be *are*.

22h Make the verb agree with its subject, not with a subject complement.

One basic sentence pattern in English consists of a subject, a linking verb, and a subject complement: *Jack is a lawyer.* Because the subject complement (*lawyer*) names or describes the subject (*Jack*), it is sometimes mistaken for the subject.

▶ A major force in today's economy ~~are~~ children — as consumers,
                                      ^is

decision makers, and trend spotters.

Force is the subject, not *children*. If the corrected version seems too awkward, make *children* the subject: *Children are a major force in today's economy — as consumers, decision makers, and trend spotters.*

22i With *who, which,* and *that,* use verbs that agree with their antecedents.

Like most pronouns, the relative pronouns *who, which,* and *that* have antecedents, nouns or pronouns to which they refer. A relative pronoun used as the subject of a subordinate clause takes a verb that agrees with its antecedent.

ANT PN   V
Take a *course that prepares* you for classroom management.

Constructions such as *one of the students who* [or *one of the things that*] cause problems for writers. Do not assume that the antecedent must be *one.* Instead, consider the logic of the sentence.

▶ Our ability to use language is one of the things that sets us apart

from animals.

The antecedent of *that* is *things,* not *one.* Several things set us apart from animals.

When the word *only* comes before *one,* you are safe in assuming that *one* is the antecedent of the relative pronoun.

▶ Veronica was the only one of the first-year Spanish students who
was
~~were~~ fluent enough to apply for the exchange program.
^
The antecedent of *who* is *one,* not *students.* Only one student was fluent enough.

22j Treat titles of works, company names, and words mentioned as words as singular.

describes
▶ *Lost Cities* ~~describe~~ the discoveries of fifty ancient civilizations.
^
specializes
▶ Delmonico Brothers ~~specialize~~ in organic produce and additive-free
^
meats.

is
▶ *Controlled substances* ~~are~~ a euphemism for illegal drugs.
^

EXERCISE 22–1 Edit the following sentences to eliminate problems with subject-verb agreement. If a sentence is correct, write "correct" after it. Answers appear in the back of the book.

> *were*
> Jack's first days in the military ~~was~~ grueling.
> ^

a. One of the main reasons for elephant poaching are the profits received from selling the ivory tusks.

b. Not until my interview with Dr. Hwang were other possibilities opened to me.

c. A number of students in the seminar was aware of the importance of joining the discussion.

d. Batik cloth from Bali, blue and white ceramics from Delft, and a bocce ball from Turin has made Angelie's room the talk of the dorm.

e. The board of directors, ignoring the wishes of the neighborhood, has voted to allow further development.

23 Make pronouns and antecedents agree.

A pronoun is a word that substitutes for a noun. Many pronouns have antecedents, nouns or pronouns to which they refer. A pronoun and its antecedent agree when they are both singular or both plural. (See 23a for advice on using plural *they* with singular nouns and pronouns in some cases.)

SINGULAR   *Dr. Ava Berto* finished *her* rounds.

PLURAL   The hospital *interns* finished *their* rounds.

For Multilingual Writers

The pronouns *he, his, she, her, it,* and *its* must agree in gender (masculine, feminine, or neuter) with their antecedents, not with the words they modify.

Steve visited *his* [not *her*] sister in Seattle.

23a Take care with indefinite pronouns (*anybody, everyone*) and generic nouns.

Writers are frequently tempted to use plural pronouns to refer to two kinds of singular antecedents: indefinite pronouns and generic nouns.

Indefinite pronouns

Indefinite pronouns refer to nonspecific persons or things.

anybody	each	everyone	nobody	somebody
anyone	either	everything	no one	someone
anything	everybody	neither	nothing	something

Traditionally, indefinite pronouns have been treated as singular in formal English. However, using a singular pronoun usually results in a sentence that is sexist, and the traditional alternative (*he or she*) is now often considered noninclusive.

SEXIST   Everyone performs at his own fitness level.

NONINCLUSIVE   Everyone performs at his or her own fitness level.

Since using *he/his* or *she/her* to refer generically to any person is considered sexist and using *he or she* or *his or her* is wordy and doesn't include people who prefer not to refer to themselves as *he* or *she*, it is becoming increasingly acceptable in many contexts to use the plural pronoun *they* to refer to an indefinite pronoun. You may want to check with your instructor for any preferences.

The following are usually your best options for revision.

1. Make the antecedent plural.

2. Rewrite the sentence so that no problem of agreement exists.

3. Use the plural pronoun *they* to refer to the singular antecedent.

▶ If ~~a singer~~ singers wants to audition, ~~he or she~~ they should sign up.

▶ Anyone who If ~~a singer~~ wants to audition, ~~he or she~~ should sign up.

▶ If ~~a singer~~ anyone wants to audition, ~~he or she~~ they should sign up.

NOTE: When using pronouns to refer to people, choose the pronouns that the individuals themselves would use. Doing so communicates your respect and audience awareness. Some transgender and gender-fluid individuals refer to themselves by new pronouns (*ze/hir*, for example), but if you are unfamiliar with such preferences, *they* and *them* are acceptable gender-neutral options.

Generic nouns

A generic noun represents a typical member of a group, such as a *typical student*, or any member of a group, such as *any lawyer*. Although generic nouns may seem to have plural meanings, they have traditionally been considered singular. However, you should avoid using *he* to refer to generic nouns, as in *A runner must train if he wants to excel.* As with indefinite pronouns, the singular use of *they* is becoming increasingly acceptable with generic nouns.

When a plural pronoun refers to a generic noun, you will usually have the same three options as for indefinite pronouns.

▶ ~~A medical student~~ must study hard if ~~he wants~~ to succeed.
  (Medical students / they want)

▶ A medical student must study hard ~~if he wants~~ to succeed.

23b Treat collective nouns as singular unless the meaning is clearly plural.

Collective nouns such as *jury, committee, audience, crowd, class, troop, family, team,* and *couple* name a group. Ordinarily the group functions as a unit, so the noun should be treated as singular; if the members of the group function as individuals, however, the noun should be treated as plural. (See also 22f.)

AS A UNIT The *committee* granted *its* permission to build.

AS INDIVIDUALS The *committee* put *their* signatures on the document.

When treating a collective noun as plural, many writers prefer to add a clearly plural antecedent such as *members* to the sentence: *The members of the committee put their signatures on the document.*

> After only an hour of deliberation, the jury returned ~~their~~ verdict.
> (inserted above: *its*)

There is no reason to draw attention to the individual members of the jury, so *jury* should be treated as singular.

23c Take care with compound antecedents.

President Obama and Chinese President Xi held a meeting at which *they* formally signed the 2016 Paris Climate Agreement.

With compound antecedents joined with *or* or *nor* (or with *either . . . or* or *neither . . . nor*), make the pronoun agree with the nearer antecedent.

Either *Bruce* or *Sebastian* should receive first prize for *his* poem.

Neither the *mouse* nor the *rats* could find *their* way through the maze.

NOTE: If one of the antecedents is singular and the other plural, as in the second example, put the plural antecedent last to avoid awkwardness.

EXCEPTION: If one antecedent is male and the other female, do not follow the traditional rule. The sentence *Either Bruce or Elizabeth should receive first prize for her short story* makes no sense. The best solution is to recast the sentence: *The prize for best short story should go to either Bruce or Elizabeth.*

EXERCISE 23-1 Edit the following sentences to eliminate problems with pronoun-antecedent agreement. Most of the sentences can be revised in more than one way, so experiment before choosing a solution. If a sentence is correct, write "correct" after it. Possible revisions appear in the back of the book.

Recruiters
~~The recruiter~~ may tell the truth, but there is much that they choose not to tell.

a. Every presidential candidate must appeal to a wide variety of ethnic and social groups if he wants to win the election.

b. If someone wants to ride David's motorcycle, he/she has to wear a helmet.

c. The trainer motioned for everyone to move his or her arms in wide, slow circles.

d. The parade committee was unanimous in its decision to allow all groups and organizations to join the festivities.

e. The applicant should be bilingual if she wants to qualify for this position.

24 Make pronoun references clear.

In the sentence *When Andrew got home, he took a nap*, the noun *Andrew* is the antecedent of the pronoun *he*. A pronoun should refer clearly to its antecedent.

24a Avoid ambiguous pronoun reference.

Ambiguous pronoun reference occurs when a pronoun could refer to two possible antecedents.

> ~~When Gloria set the pitcher~~ The pitcher broke when Gloria set it on the glass-topped table~~,~~. ~~it broke.~~

> Tom told James, "You have ~~that he had~~ won the lottery."

What broke — the pitcher or the table? Who won the lottery—Tom or James? The revisions eliminate the ambiguity.

24b Generally, avoid making broad references with *this, that, which,* and *it.*

For clarity, the pronouns *this, that, which,* and *it* should ordinarily refer to specific antecedents rather than to whole ideas or sentences. When a pronoun's reference is needlessly broad, either replace the pronoun with a noun or supply an antecedent to which the pronoun clearly refers.

▶ TV advertising has created new demand for prescription drugs.

the ads
Patients respond to ~~this~~ by requesting drugs they might not need.
∧

The writer substituted the noun *ads* for the pronoun *this,* which referred broadly to the idea expressed in the preceding sentence.

▶ Romeo and Juliet were both too young to have acquired much

a fact
wisdom, ~~and~~ that accounts for their rash actions.
∧

The writer added an antecedent (*fact*) that the pronoun *that* clearly refers to.

24c Do not use a pronoun to refer to an implied antecedent.

A pronoun should refer to a specific antecedent, not to a word that is implied but not present in the sentence.

the braids
▶ After braiding Ann's hair, Sue decorated ~~them~~ with ribbons.
∧

The pronoun *them* referred to Ann's braids (implied by the term *braiding*), but the word *braids* did not appear in the sentence.

24d Avoid the indefinite use of *they* and *it.*

The pronoun *they* should refer to a specific antecedent. Do not use the pronoun *they* to refer to persons who have not been specifically mentioned.

the school board
▶ In June, ~~they~~ voted to charge a fee for students to participate in
∧

sports and music programs.

The word *it* should not be used indefinitely in constructions such as *It is said on television . . .* or *In the article, it says that. . . .*

> The
> ▶ ~~In the~~ encyclopedia ~~it~~ states that male moths can smell female
> ^
> moths from several miles away.

24e To refer to persons, use *who, whom,* or *whose,* not *which* or *that.*

In most contexts, use *who, whom,* or *whose* to refer to persons, and use *which* or *that* to refer to animals or things.

> ▶ During the two-day festival El Día de los Muertos (Day of the
>   who
> Dead), Mexican families celebrate loved ones ~~that~~ have died.
>   ^

EXERCISE 24–1 Edit the following sentences to correct errors in pronoun reference. In some cases, you will need to decide on an antecedent that the pronoun might logically refer to. Possible revisions appear in the back of the book.

> Although Apple makes the most widely recognized tablet device,
>   The competition
> other companies have gained a share of the market. ~~This~~ has kept
>   ^
> prices from skyrocketing.

a. They say that engineering students should have hands-on experience with dismantling and reassembling machines.

b. She had decorated her living room with posters from chamber music festivals. This led her date to believe that she was interested in classical music. Actually she preferred rock.

c. The high school principal congratulated the seniors that were graduating later that day.

d. Marianne told Jenny that she was worried about her mother's illness.

e. Though Lewis cried for several minutes after scraping his knee, eventually it subsided.

25 Choose between pronouns such as *I* and *me*.

The personal pronouns in the following chart change what is known as *case form* according to their grammatical function in a sentence. Pronouns functioning as subjects or subject complements appear in the *subjective* case; those functioning as objects appear in the *objective* case; and those showing ownership appear in the *possessive* case.

	SUBJECTIVE CASE	OBJECTIVE CASE	POSSESSIVE CASE
SINGULAR	I	me	my
	you	you	your
	he/she/it	him/her/it	his/her/its
PLURAL	we	us	our
	you	you	your
	they	them	their

Pronouns in the subjective and objective cases are frequently confused. Most of the rules in this section specify when to use one or the other of these cases (*I* or *me*, *he* or *him*, and so on). Section 25g explains a special use of pronouns and nouns in the possessive case.

25a Use the subjective case (*I, you, he, she, it, we, they*) for subjects and subject complements.

When personal pronouns are used as subjects, ordinarily your ear will tell you the correct pronoun. Problems sometimes arise, however, with compound word groups containing a pronoun, so it is not always safe to trust your ear.

▶ Joel ran away because his stepfather and ~~him~~ he had argued.

His stepfather and he is the subject of the verb *had argued*.
If we strip away the words *his stepfather and*, the correct pronoun becomes clear: *he had argued* (not *him had argued*).

When a pronoun is used as a subject complement (a word following a linking verb), your ear may mislead you, since the incorrect form is frequently heard in casual speech.

▶ During the trial, the defendant repeatedly denied that the kidnapper
                he.
  was ~~him.~~
       ^

If *kidnapper was he* seems awkward, rewrite the sentence: *During the trial,* the defendant *repeatedly denied that he was the kidnapper.*

25b Use the objective case (*me, you, him, her, it, us, them*) for all objects.

When a personal pronoun is used as a direct object, an indirect object, or the object of a preposition, ordinarily your ear will lead you to the correct pronoun. When an object is compound, however, you may occasionally become confused.

▶ Janice was indignant when she realized that the salesclerk was
                            her.
  insulting her mother and ~~she.~~
                    ^

Strip away the words *her mother and* to hear the correct pronoun: *was insulting her* (not *was insulting she*).

▶   me
  The most traumatic experience for her father and ~~I~~ occurred long
                                  ^
  after her operation.

Strip away the words *her father and* to test for the correct pronoun: *for me* (not *for I*).

▶   me
  Nidra gave my cousin and ~~myself~~ some good tips on traveling in
                    ^
  New Delhi.

In this situation, the reflexive pronoun *myself* is nonstandard. *My cousin and me* is the indirect object of the verb *gave*.

25c Put an appositive and the word to which it refers in the same case.

Appositives are noun phrases that rename nouns or pronouns. A pronoun used as an appositive has the same function (usually subject or object) as the word or words it renames.

▶ The managers, Dr. Bell and ~~me,~~ could not agree on a plan.
    I,
    ^

The appositive *Dr. Bell and I* renames the subject, *managers*.
Test: *I could not agree* (not *me could not agree*).

▶ The reporter found only two witnesses, the bicyclist and ~~I.~~
                                                              me.
                                                               ^

The appositive *the bicyclist and me* renames the direct object, *witnesses*.
Test: *found me* (not *found I*).

25d Following *than* or *as*, choose the pronoun that expresses your intended meaning.

When a comparison begins with *than* or *as*, your choice of a pronoun will depend on your intended meaning. To test for the correct pronoun, mentally complete the sentence.

▶ We respected no other candidate as much as ~~she.~~
                                              her.
                                               ^

Test: *as much as [we respected] her.*

25e For *we* or *us* before a noun, choose the pronoun that would be appropriate if the noun were omitted.

▶ ~~Us~~ tenants would rather fight than move.
  We
   ^

Test: *We would rather fight* (not *Us would rather fight*).

25f Use the objective case for subjects and objects of infinitives.

An infinitive is the word *to* followed by the base form of a verb. (See 42b.) Both subjects and objects of infinitives take the objective case.

▶ Sue asked John and ~~I~~ *me* to drive the mayor and ~~she~~ *her* to the airport.

John and me is the subject of the infinitive *to drive; mayor and her* is the direct object of the infinitive.

25g Use the possessive case to modify a gerund.

A pronoun that modifies a gerund or a gerund phrase should be in the possessive case (*my, our, your, his, her, its, their*). A gerund is a verb form ending in *-ing* that functions as a noun.

▶ The chances of ~~you~~ *your* being hit by lightning are about two million to one.

Your modifies the gerund phrase *being hit by lightning.*

Nouns as well as pronouns may modify gerunds. To form the possessive case of a noun, use an apostrophe and an *-s* (*victim's*) or just an apostrophe (*victims'*). (See 33a.)

▶ The old order in France paid a high price for the ~~aristocracy~~ *aristocracy's* exploiting the lower classes.

The possessive noun *aristocracy's* modifies the gerund phrase *exploiting the lower classes.*

Gerund phrases should not be confused with participial phrases, which function as adjectives, not as nouns: *We saw him driving a yellow convertible.* Here *driving a yellow convertible* is a participial phrase modifying the pronoun *him.* (See 42b.)

The choice between the objective case and the possessive case depends on the meaning you intend; sometimes the distinction is subtle.

We watched *them* dancing.

We watched *their* dancing.

In the first sentence, the emphasis is on the people; we watched *them*, and they happened to be dancing. In the second sentence, the emphasis is on the dancing; we watched the *dancing*—a noun form modified by the possessive *their*.

NOTE: Do not use the possessive if it creates an awkward effect. Try to reword the sentence instead.

AWKWARD	The president agreed to the applications' being reviewed by a faculty committee.
REVISED	The president agreed that the applications could be reviewed by a faculty committee.
REVISED	The president agreed that a faculty committee could review the applications.

EXERCISE 25–1 Edit the following sentences to eliminate errors in pronoun case. If a sentence is correct, write "correct" after it. Answers appear in the back of the book.

he.
Grandfather cuts down trees for neighbors much younger than ~~him.~~
^

a. Rick applied for the job even though he heard that other candidates were more experienced than he.
b. The volleyball team could not believe that the coach was she.
c. She appreciated him telling the truth in such a difficult situation.
d. The director has asked you and I to draft a proposal for a new recycling plan.
e. Five close friends and myself rented an SUV, packed it with food, and drove two hundred miles to Mardi Gras.

26 Choose between *who* and *whom*.

The choice between *who* and *whom* (or *whoever* and *whomever*) occurs primarily in subordinate clauses and in questions. *Who* and *whoever*, subjective-case pronouns, are used for subjects and subject complements. *Whom* and *whomever*, objective-case pronouns, are used for objects.

26a Use *who* and *whom* correctly in subordinate clauses.

When *who* and *whom* (or *whoever* and *whomever*) introduce subordinate clauses, their case is determined by their function *within the clause they introduce*.

In the following two examples, the pronouns *who* and *whoever* function as the subjects of the clauses they introduce.

▶ First prize goes to the runner ~~whom~~ who earns the most points.

> The subordinate clause is *who earns the most points*. The verb of the clause is *earns*, and its subject is *who*.

▶ Maya Angelou's *I Know Why the Caged Bird Sings* should be read by ~~whomever~~ whoever is interested in the effects of racial prejudice on children.

> The object of the preposition *by* is the entire subordinate clause *whoever is interested in the effects of racial prejudice on children*. The verb of the clause is *is*, and the subject of the verb is *whoever*.

26b Use *who* and *whom* correctly in questions.

When deciding whether to use *who* or *whom* in a question, check for the word's function within the question.

> Who
> ► ~~Whom~~ was responsible for creating that computer virus?
>   ^
> *Who* is the subject of the verb *was.*

> Whom
> ► ~~Who~~ did the Democratic Party nominate in 1952?
>   ^
> *Whom* is the direct object of the verb *did nominate.* This becomes clear if you
> restructure the question: *The Democratic Party did nominate whom in 1952?*

EXERCISE 26–1 Edit the following sentences to eliminate errors in the use of *who* and *whom* (or *whoever* and *whomever*). If a sentence is correct, write "correct" after it. Answers appear in the back of the book.

> whom
> **What is the address of the artist ~~who~~ Antonio hired?**
>   ^

a. Arriving late for rehearsal, we had no idea who was supposed to dance with whom.

b. The environmental policy conference featured scholars who I had never heard of.

c. Whom did you support in last month's election for student government president?

d. Daniel always gives a holiday donation to whomever needs it.

e. The singers who Natalia selected for the choir attended their first rehearsal last night.

27 Choose adjectives and adverbs with care.

Adjectives modify nouns or pronouns. Adverbs modify verbs, adjectives, or other adverbs. (See 40d and 40e.)

Many adverbs are formed by adding *-ly* to adjectives (*normal, normally; smooth, smoothly*). But don't assume that all words ending in *-ly* are adverbs or that all adverbs end in *-ly*. Some adjectives end in *-ly* (*lovely, friendly*), and some adverbs don't (*always, here, there*). When in doubt, consult a dictionary.

27a Use adjectives to modify nouns.

Adjectives ordinarily precede the nouns they modify (*tall building*). But they can also function as subject complements or object complements, following the nouns they modify.

> **For Multilingual Writers**
>
> In English, adjectives are not made plural to agree with the words they modify: *The red* [not *reds*] *roses were a surprise.*

A subject complement follows a linking verb and completes the meaning of the subject. (See 41b.) When an adjective functions as a subject complement, it describes the subject.

Justice is *blind*.

Verbs such as *smell, taste, look,* and *feel* may be linking verbs. If the word following one of these verbs describes the subject, use an adjective; if the word following the verb modifies the verb, use an adverb.

ADJECTIVE	The detective looked *cautious*.
ADVERB	The detective looked *cautiously* for fingerprints.

The adjective *cautious* describes the detective; the adverb *cautiously* modifies the verb *looked*.

Linking verbs suggest states of being, not actions. Notice, for example, the different meanings of *looked* in the preceding examples. *To look cautious* suggests the state of being cautious; *to look cautiously* is to perform an action in a cautious way.

> ► **The lilacs in our backyard smell especially ~~sweetly~~ this year.**
>
> ^{sweet} appears above *sweetly*

The verb *smell* here suggests a state of being, not an action. Therefore, it should be followed by an adjective, not an adverb.

An object complement follows a direct object and completes its meaning. (See 41b.) When an adjective functions as an object complement, it describes the direct object.

Sorrow makes *us wise*.

Object complements occur with verbs such as *call, consider, create, find, keep,* and *make.* When a modifier follows the direct object of one of these verbs, use an adjective to describe the direct object; use an adverb to modify the verb.

ADJECTIVE	The referee called the plays *perfect.*
ADVERB	The referee called the plays *perfectly.*

The first sentence means that the referee considered the plays to be perfect; the second means that the referee did an excellent job of calling the plays.

27b Use adverbs to modify verbs, adjectives, and other adverbs.

When adverbs modify verbs (or verbals), they nearly always answer the question *When? Where? How? Why? Under what conditions? How often?* or *To what degree?* When adverbs modify adjectives or other adverbs, they usually qualify or intensify the meaning of the word they modify. (See 40e.)

Adjectives are often used incorrectly in place of adverbs in casual or nonstandard speech.

▶ The travel arrangement worked out ~~perfect~~ ^{perfectly} for everyone.

    ^

The adverb *perfectly* modifies the verb *worked out*.

▶ The chance of recovering lost property looks ~~real~~ ^{really} slim.

    ^

Only adverbs can modify adjectives or other adverbs. *Really* intensifies the meaning of the adjective *slim*.

27c Distinguish between *good* and *well*, *bad* and *badly*.

Good is an adjective (*good performance*). *Well* is an adverb when it modifies a verb (*speak well*). The use of the adjective *good* in place of the adverb *well* to modify a verb is nonstandard, although it is common in casual speech.

▶ We were glad that Sanya had done ~~good~~ ^{well} on the CPA exam.

    ^

The adverb *well* modifies the verb *had done*.

Bad is always an adjective and should be used to describe a noun; *badly* is always an adverb and should be used to modify a verb. The adverb *badly* is often used inappropriately to describe a noun, especially following a linking verb.

▶ The sisters felt ~~badly~~ ^{bad} when they realized they had ignored their

    ^

brother.

27d Use comparatives and superlatives with care.

Most adjectives and adverbs have three forms: the positive, the comparative, and the superlative.

POSITIVE	COMPARATIVE	SUPERLATIVE
fast	faster	fastest
friendly	friendlier	friendliest
carefully	more carefully	most carefully
bad	worse	worst
good	better	best

Use the comparative to compare two things, the superlative to compare three or more.

▶ Which of these two protein drinks is ~~best?~~ *better?*

▶ Zhao is the ~~more~~ *most* qualified of the three candidates running for state senator.

To form comparatives and superlatives of most one- and two-syllable adjectives, use the endings *-er* and *-est*: *smooth, smoother, smoothest; easy, easier, easiest.* With longer adjectives, use *more* and *most* (or *less* and *least* for downward comparisons): *exciting, more exciting, most exciting; considerate, less considerate, least considerate.*

Some one-syllable adverbs take the endings *-er* and *-est* (*fast, faster, fastest*), but longer adverbs and all of those ending in *-ly* form the comparative and superlative with *more* and *most* (or *less* and *least*).

The comparative and superlative forms of some adjectives and adverbs are irregular: *good, better, best; well, better, best; bad, worse, worst; badly, worse, worst.*

▶ According to our projections, sales at local businesses will be ~~worser~~ *worse* than those at the chain stores this winter.

Do not use double comparatives or superlatives. When you have added *-er* or *-est* to an adjective or adverb, do not also use *more* or *most* (or *less* or *least*).

► All the polls indicated that Gore was more ~~likelier~~ to win than Bush.
                                           likely
                                            ^

Avoid expressions such as *less perfect*, *very round*, and *most unique*. Either something is unique or it isn't. It is illogical to suggest that absolute concepts come in degrees.

                      unusual
► That is the most ~~unique~~ wedding gown I have ever seen.
                    ^

EXERCISE 27–1   Edit the following sentences to eliminate errors in the use of adjectives and adverbs. If a sentence is correct, write "correct" after it. Answers appear in the back of the book.

                                     well
We weren't surprised by how ~~good~~ the sidecar racing team flowed
                                           ^

through the tricky course.

a. Do you expect to perform good on the nursing board exam next week?

b. With the budget deadline approaching, our office has been handling routine correspondence more slow than we usually do.

c. When I worked in a flower shop, I learned that some flowers smell surprisingly bad.

d. The customer complained that he hadn't been treated nice by the agent on the phone.

e. Of all the smart people in my family, Uncle Roberto is the most cleverest.

28 Choose appropriate verb forms, tenses, and moods in Standard English.

In speech, some people use verb forms and tenses that match a home dialect or variety of English. In writing, use Standard English verb forms unless you are quoting nonstandard speech or using alternative forms for literary effect. (See 17d.)

Except for the verb *be*, all verbs in English have five forms. The following list shows the five forms and provides a sample sentence in which each might appear.

BASE FORM	Usually I (*walk*, *ride*).
PAST TENSE	Yesterday I (*walked*, *rode*).
PAST PARTICIPLE	I have (*walked*, *ridden*) many times before.
PRESENT PARTICIPLE	I am (*walking*, *riding*) right now.
-S FORM	He/she/it (*walks*, *rides*) regularly.

The verb *be* has eight forms instead of the usual five: *be, am, is, are, was, were, being, been.*

Basic verb forms

	REGULAR (HELP)	IRREGULAR (GIVE)	IRREGULAR (BE)*
BASE FORM	help	give	be
PAST TENSE	helped	gave	was, were
PAST PARTICIPLE	helped	given	been
PRESENT PARTICIPLE	helping	giving	being
-S FORM	helps	gives	is

*Be also has the forms *am* and *are*, which are used in the present tense.

28a Choose Standard English forms of irregular verbs.

For all regular verbs, the past-tense and past-participle forms are the same (ending in *-ed* or *-d*), so there is no danger of confusion. This is not true, however, for irregular verbs, such as the following.

BASE FORM	PAST TENSE	PAST PARTICIPLE
go	went	gone
break	broke	broken
fly	flew	flown

The past-tense form always occurs alone, without a helping verb. It expresses action that occurred entirely in the past: *I rode to work yesterday*; *I walked to work last Tuesday*. The past participle is used with a helping verb. It forms the perfect tenses with *has*, *have*, or *had*; it forms the passive voice with *be*, *am*, *is*, *are*, *was*, *were*, *being*, or *been*. (See 40c for a complete list of helping verbs and 28f for a survey of tenses.)

When in doubt about the Standard English forms of irregular verbs, look up the base form of the verb in the dictionary, which also lists any irregular forms. (If no additional forms are listed in the dictionary, the verb is regular, not irregular.)

Common irregular verbs

BASE FORM	PAST TENSE	PAST PARTICIPLE
be	was, were	been
break	broke	broken
bring	brought	brought
choose	chose	chosen
come	came	come
do	did	done
drink	drank	drunk
eat	ate	eaten
find	found	found
give	gave	given
go	went	gone
hang (execute)	hanged	hanged
hang (suspend)	hung	hung
have	had	had
know	knew	known
rise	rose	risen
sing	sang	sung
take	took	taken
teach	taught	taught
write	wrote	written

28b Distinguish among the forms of *lie* and *lay*.

Writers and speakers frequently confuse the various forms of *lie* (meaning "to recline or rest on a surface") and *lay* (meaning "to put or place something").

BASE FORM	PAST TENSE	PAST PARTICIPLE	PRESENT PARTICIPLE
lie ("recline")	lay	lain	lying
lay ("put")	laid	laid	laying

▶ Sue was so exhausted that she ~~laid~~ down for a nap.

   lay

   ^

   The past-tense form of *lie* ("to recline") is *lay*.

▶ The prosecutor ~~lay~~ the pistol on a table close to the jurors.

   laid

   ^

   The past-tense form of *lay* ("to place") is *laid*.

▶ Letters dating from 1915 were ~~laying~~ in a corner of the chest.

   lying

   ^

   The present participle of *lie* ("to rest on a surface") is *lying*.

28c Use -s (or -es) endings on present-tense verbs that have third-person singular subjects.

All singular nouns (*child*, *tree*) and the pronouns *he*, *she*, and *it* are third-person singular; indefinite pronouns such as *everyone* and *neither* are also third-person singular. When the subject of a sentence is third-person singular, its verb has an -*s* or -*es* ending in the present tense, whether the verb is regular or irregular. (See also 22.)

	SINGULAR		PLURAL	
FIRST PERSON	I	know, have, do	we	know, have, do
SECOND PERSON	you	know, have, do	you	know, have, do
THIRD PERSON	he/she/it	knows, has, does	they	know, have, do
	child	knows, has, does	parents	know, have, do
	everyone	knows, has, does		

▶ My neighbor ~~drive~~ *drives* to Marco Island every weekend.

▶ Sulfur dioxide ~~turn~~ *turns* leaves yellow and ~~dissolve~~ *dissolves* marble.

The subjects *neighbor* and *sulfur dioxide* are third-person singular, so the verbs must end in -s.

▶ The female deer tick ~~have~~ *has* a red and brown body.

NOTE: Do not add the -s ending to the verb if the subject is not third-person singular. The writers of the following sentences added -s endings where they don't belong.

▶ I prepares system specifications for every installation.

The pronoun *I* is first-person singular, so its verb does not require the -s.

▶ Parents ~~does~~ have the right to excuse children from the vaccine.

The -s form is used only on present-tense verbs with third-person *singular* subjects.

28d Do not omit -*ed* endings on verbs.

Speakers who do not fully pronounce -*ed* endings sometimes omit them unintentionally in writing. Failure to pronounce -*ed* endings is common in informal speech. For example, the -*ed* ending is not always fully pronounced in frequently used words and phrases such as *asked, fixed, pronounced, supposed to,* and *used to.*

Past tense

Use the ending -*ed* or -*d* to express the past tense of regular verbs. The past tense is used when the action occurred entirely in the past.

▶ In 1998, journalist Barbara Ehrenreich ~~decide~~ *decided* to try to live on minimum wage.

▶ Last summer, my counselor ~~advise~~ *advised* me to ask my graphic arts instructor for help.

Past participles

Past participles are used in three ways: (1) following *have, has,* or *had* to form one of the perfect tenses; (2) following *be, am, is, are, was, were, being,* or *been* to form the passive voice; and (3) as adjectives modifying nouns or pronouns. The perfect tenses are listed in 28f, and the passive voice is discussed in 8a. For a discussion of participles as adjectives, see 42b.

>   asked
> Robin has ~~ask~~ the Office of Student Affairs for more housing staff
>   ^
> for next year.

Has asked is the present perfect tense (*have* or *has* followed by a past participle).

> Though it is not a new phenomenon, domestic violence is now
> publicized
> ~~publicize~~ more than ever.
> ^

Is publicized is a verb in the passive voice (a form of *be* followed by a past participle).

28e Do not omit needed verbs.

Linking verbs, used to link subjects to subject complements, are frequently a form of *be: be, am, is, are, was, were, being, been.* (See 41b.) Some of these forms may be contracted (*I'm, she's, we're, you're, they're*), but they should not be omitted altogether.

>   are
> When we quiet in the evening, we can hear the crickets.
>   ^

Helping verbs, used with main verbs, include forms of *be, do,* and *have* and the modal verbs *can, will, shall, could, would, should, may, might,* and *must.* (See 29a and 40c.) Some helping verbs may be contracted (*he's leaving, we'll celebrate, they've been told*), but they should not be omitted altogether.

>   We've
> ~~We~~ been in Chicago since last Thursday.
> ^

For Multilingual Writers

Some languages do not require a linking verb between a subject and its complement. English, however, requires a verb in every sentence.

▶ Every night, I read a short book to my daughter. When I ~~too busy,~~ her
                                                            am
   older brother reads to her.

EXERCISE 28–1   Edit the following sentences to eliminate problems with -s and -ed verb forms and with omitted verbs. If a sentence is correct, write "correct" after it. Answers appear in the back of the book.

                                    covers
The Pell Grant sometimes ~~cover~~ the student's full tuition.

a. The glass sculptures of the Swan Boats was prominent in the brightly lit lobby.

b. When I get the urge to exercise, I lay down until it passes.

c. Grandmother had drove our new hybrid to the sunrise church service, so we were left with the van.

d. Christos didn't know about Marlo's promotion because he never listens. He always talking.

e. A pile of dirty rags was laying at the bottom of the stairs.

28f Choose the appropriate verb tense.

Tenses indicate the time of an action in relation to the time of the speaking or writing about that action. Tenses are classified as present, past, and future, with simple, perfect, and progressive forms for each.

The most common problem with tenses—confusing shifts from one tense to another—is discussed in section 13. Other problems with tenses are detailed in this section, after the following survey of tenses.

Survey of tenses

Simple tenses (base form or -s form) *For general facts, states of being, and habitual actions*

SIMPLE PRESENT

SINGULAR		PLURAL	
I	walk, ride, am	we	walk, ride, are
you	walk, ride, are	you	walk, ride, are
he/she/it	walks, rides, is	they	walk, ride, are

SIMPLE PAST

SINGULAR		PLURAL	
I	walked, rode, was	we	walked, rode, were
you	walked, rode, were	you	walked, rode, were
he/she/it	walked, rode, was	they	walked, rode, were

SIMPLE FUTURE

I, you, he/she/it, we, they   will walk, ride, be

Perfect tenses (a form of *have* plus past participle) *For an action that was or will be completed at the time of another action*

PRESENT PERFECT

I, you, we, they	have walked, ridden, been
he/she/it	has walked, ridden, been

PAST PERFECT

I, you, he/she/it, we, they   had walked, ridden, been

FUTURE PERFECT

I, you, he/she/it, we, they   will have walked, ridden, been

Progressive forms (a form of *have* plus present participle) *For actions in progress*

PRESENT PROGRESSIVE

I	am walking, riding, being
he/she/it	is walking, riding, being
you, we, they	are walking, riding, being

PAST PROGRESSIVE

I, he/she/it	was walking, riding, being
you, we, they	were walking, riding, being

FUTURE PROGRESSIVE

I, you, he/she/it, we, they   will be walking, riding, being

PRESENT PERFECT PROGRESSIVE

I, you, we, they   have been walking, riding, being

he/she/it   has been walking, riding, being

PAST PERFECT PROGRESSIVE

I, you, he/she/it, we, they   had been walking, riding, being

FUTURE PERFECT PROGRESSIVE

I, you, he/she/it, we, they   will have been walking, riding, being

NOTE: The progressive forms are not normally used with certain verbs, such as *believe*, *know*, and *seem*.

Special uses of the present tense

Use the present tense when expressing general truths, when writing about literature, and when quoting, summarizing, or paraphrasing an author's views.

General truths or scientific principles should be stated in the present tense unless such principles have been disproved.

▶ Galileo taught that the earth ~~revolved~~ around the sun.
                                revolves

When writing about a work of literature, you may be tempted to use the past tense. The convention in the humanities, however, is to describe fictional events in the present tense.

▶ In Masuji Ibuse's *Black Rain*, a child ~~reached~~ for a pomegranate in
                                  reaches

his mother's garden, and a moment later he ~~was~~ dead, killed by the
                                              is

blast of the atomic bomb.

When you are quoting, summarizing, or paraphrasing the author of a nonliterary work, use present-tense verbs such as *writes*, *reports*, or *asserts* to introduce the source. This convention is usually followed even when the author is dead (unless a date or the context specifies the time of writing).

NOTE: Whereas present tense is used in this situation in MLA (Modern Language Association) style, the APA (American Psychological Association) uses past tense or present perfect tense to introduce quotations, summaries, and paraphrases: *wrote, has written; reported, has reported.*

The past perfect tense

The past perfect tense (*had* plus past participle) is used for an action already completed by the time of another past action or for an action already completed at some specific past time.

> Everyone *had spoken* by the time I arrived.

>   had
> ▶ By the time dinner was served, the guest of honor left.
>   ^

> The past perfect tense is needed because the action of leaving was already completed at a specific past time (when dinner was served).

Sequence of tenses with infinitives and participles

An infinitive is the base form of a verb preceded by *to*. (See 42b.) Use the present infinitive to show action at the same time as or later than the action of the verb in the sentence.

>   pay
> ▶ Barb had hoped to ~~have paid~~ the bill by May 1.
>   ^

> The action expressed in the infinitive (*to pay*) occurred later than the action of the sentence's verb (*had hoped*).

Use the perfect form of an infinitive (*to have* followed by the past participle) for an action occurring earlier than that of the verb in the sentence.

>   have joined
> ▶ Dan would like to ~~join~~ the navy, but he could not swim.
>   ^

> The liking occurs in the present; the joining would have occurred in the past.

28g Use the subjunctive mood in the few contexts that require it.

There are three moods in English: the *indicative*, used for facts, opinions, and questions; the *imperative*, used for orders and advice; and the *subjunctive*, used in certain contexts to express wishes, requests, or conditions contrary to fact. For many writers, the subjunctive causes the most problems.

In wishes and *if* clauses expressing conditions contrary to fact, the subjunctive is the past-tense form of the verb; in the case of *be*, it is always *were* (not *was*), even if the subject is singular.

I wish that Jamal drove more slowly late at night.

If I were the committee chair, I would allow the policy change.

NOTE: Do not use the subjunctive mood in *if* clauses expressing conditions that exist or may exist: *If Danielle passes* (not *passed*) *the test, she will become a lifeguard.*

In *that* clauses following verbs such as *ask, insist, recommend,* and *request,* the subjunctive is the base form of the verb.

Dr. Chung insists that her students arrive on time.

EXERCISE 28–2 Edit the following sentences to eliminate errors in verb tense or mood. If a sentence is correct, write "correct" after it. Answers appear in the back of the book.

> had been
> After the path ~~was~~ plowed, we were able to walk in the park.
> ^

a. The palace of Knossos in Crete is believed to have been destroyed by fire around 1375 BCE.

b. Watson and Crick discovered the mechanism that controlled inheritance in all life: the workings of the DNA molecule.

c. When city planners proposed rezoning the waterfront, did they know that the mayor promised to curb development in that neighborhood?

d. Tonight's concert begins at 9:30. If it was earlier, I'd consider going.

e. The math position was filled by the instructor who had been running the tutoring center.

29 Review grammar topics for multilingual writers.

This section offers a brief review of common grammar challenges for multilingual writers.

29a Use modal verbs to express appropriate meaning.

Both native and nonnative speakers of English encounter challenges with verbs. Section 28 provides details about verb forms, tenses, and mood (also see 40c). This section describes the use of modal verbs to express ability, certainty, necessity, permission, obligation, or possibility.

The nine modal verbs — *can, could, may, might, must, shall, should, will,* and *would* — are used with the base forms of verbs. Modals do not change form to indicate tense.

▸ The art museum will ~~launches~~ its fundraising campaign next month.
   ^launch^

▸ We could ~~spoke~~ Portuguese when we were young.
   ^speak^

The modal *could* must be followed by the base form *speak*, not the past tense *spoke*.

Modals and their meanings	
can	
• general ability (present)	Valerie *can sing*. Paolo *can run* the race faster than his brother.
• informal requests or permission	*Can* you *tell* me where the bookstore is?
	You *can borrow* my calculator until Wednesday.
could	
• general ability (past)	Jean *could speak* three languages by age four.
• polite, informal requests or permission	*Could* you *give* me that pen?

170

MODALS AND THEIR MEANINGS (cont.)

---

may

- formal requests or permission
- possibility

May I see the report? Students *may park* only in the yellow zone.

I *may try* to finish my homework tonight, or I *may wake up* early and *finish* it tomorrow.

---

might

- possibility

The population of Kolkata *might reach* six million by 2025.

---

must

- necessity (present or future)
- strong probability or near certainty (present or past)

Employers *must post* a minimum wage poster where employees can view it.

Amy doesn't look well this morning. She *must be* sick. [She is probably sick.] I *must have left* my wallet at home. [I almost certainly left my wallet at home.]

---

should

- suggestions or advice
- obligations or duties
- expectations

Frank *should join* student government. You *should drink* plenty of water every day.

The government *should protect* citizens' rights.

The books *should arrive* soon. [We expect the books to arrive soon.]

---

will

- certainty
- requests
- promises and offers

If you don't leave now, you *will be* late.

Will you *help* me study for my psychology exam?

Jonah *will arrange* the carpool.

---

would

- polite requests

- habitual or repeated actions (in the past)

Would you *help* me carry these books?

I *would like* some coffee. [Polite for *want*.]

Whenever Elena needed help with sewing, she *would call* her aunt.

EXERCISE 29–1   Edit the following sentences to correct errors in the use of verb forms with modals. If a sentence is correct, write "correct" after it. Answers appear in the back of the book.

> We should ~~to~~ order pizza for dinner.

a. A major league pitcher can to throw a baseball more than ninety-five miles per hour.
b. The writing center tutor will helps you revise your essay.
c. A reptile must adjusted its body temperature to its environment.
d. In some states, individuals may renew a driver's license online.
e. My uncle, a cartoonist, could sketched a face in less than a minute.

29b Be familiar with articles and other noun markers.

Articles (*a, an, the*) are part of a category of words known as *noun markers* or *determiners*. Noun markers identify the nouns that follow them. Besides articles, noun markers include possessive nouns (*Elena's, child's*); possessive pronouns/adjectives (*my, your, their*); demonstrative pronouns/adjectives (*this, that*); quantifiers (*all, few, neither, some*); and numbers (*one, twenty-six*).

> ART N
> Felix is reading a book about mythology.

> ART ADJ   N
> We took an exciting trip to Alaska last summer.

When to use *the*

Use *the* with most nouns that the reader can identify specifically. Usually the identity will be clear to the reader for one of the following reasons.

1. The noun has been previously mentioned.

> ► A truck cut in front of our van. When the truck skidded a few seconds later, we almost crashed into it.

2. A phrase or clause following the noun restricts its identity.

    the
▶ Bryce warned me that GPS in his car was not working.
       ^

3. A superlative adjective such as *best* or *most intelligent* makes the noun's identity specific. (See also 27d.)

    the
▶ Brita had best players on her team.
    ^

4. The noun describes a unique person, place, or thing.

       the
▶ During an eclipse, one should not look directly at sun.
       ^

5. The context or situation makes the noun's identity clear.

    the
▶ Please don't slam door when you leave.
    ^

6. The noun is singular and refers to a scientific class or category of items (most often animals, musical instruments, or inventions).

  The tin
▶ ~~Tin~~ whistle is common in traditional Irish music.
  ^

When to use *a* or *an*

Use *a* or *an* with singular count nouns that refer to one unspecific item (not a whole category). *Count nouns* refer to persons, places, things, or ideas that can be counted: *one girl, two girls; one city, three cities; one goose, four geese.*

     a
▶ My professor asked me to bring dictionary to class.
     ^

    an
▶ We want to rent apartment close to the lake.
    ^

When not to use articles

Do not use *a* or *an* with noncount nouns. *Noncount nouns* refer to things or abstract ideas that cannot be counted or made plural: *salt, silver, air, furniture, patience, knowledge.* (See the following chart.)

To express an approximate amount of a noncount noun, use a quantifier such as *some* or *more: some water, enough coffee, less violence.* Do not use articles with nouns that refer to all of something or something in general.

Commonly used noncount nouns

Food and drink

beef, bread, butter, candy, cereal, cheese, cream, meat, milk, pasta, rice, salt, sugar, wine

Nonfood substances

air, cement, coal, dirt, gasoline, gold, paper, petroleum, plastic, rain, silver, snow, soap, steel, wood, wool

Abstract nouns

advice, anger, beauty, confidence, courage, employment, fun, happiness, health, honesty, information, intelligence, knowledge, love, poverty, satisfaction, wealth

Other

biology (and other areas of study), clothing, equipment, furniture, homework, jewelry, luggage, machinery, mail, money, news, poetry, pollution, research, scenery, traffic, transportation, violence, weather, work

---

NOTE: A few noncount nouns (such as *love*) can also be used as count nouns: *He had two loves: music and archery.*

Kindness
► ~~The kindness~~ is a virtue.
  ^

► In some places, ~~the~~ rice is preferred to all other grains.

When to use articles with proper nouns

Do not use articles with most singular proper nouns: *Prime Minister Trudeau, Jamaica, Lake Huron, Ivy Street, Mount Everest.* Use *the* with most plural proper nouns: *the McGregors, the Bahamas, the Finger Lakes, the United States.* Also use *the* with large regions, oceans, rivers, and mountain ranges: *the Sahara, the Indian Ocean, the Amazon River, the Rocky Mountains.* There are, however, many exceptions, especially with geographic names. Note exceptions when you encounter them or consult a native speaker or an ESL dictionary.

29c Overcome certain challenges when writing sentences in English.

Omitted subjects

Some languages do not require a subject in every sentence. Every English sentence, however, needs a subject.

                              She seems
► Your aunt is very energetic. ~~Seems~~ young for her age.
                              ^

EXCEPTION: In commands, the subject *you* is understood but not present in the sentence: *Give me the book.*

The word *it* may be used as the subject of a sentence describing the weather or temperature, stating the time, indicating distance, or suggesting an environmental fact.

Do not omit *it* in such sentences.

It is raining in the valley and snowing in the mountains.

It is 9:15 a.m.

It is three hundred miles to Chicago.

In July, it is very hot in Arizona.

In some English sentences, the subject comes after the verb, and a placeholder called an *expletive* (*there* or *it*) comes before the verb.

EXP   V ┌──── S ────┐   ┌──── S ────┐ V
There are many people here today. (Many people are here today.)

EXP V   ┌── S ──┐   ┌── S ──┐   V
It is important to study daily. (To study daily is important.)

                    there are
▶ As you know, ~~many~~ religious sects in India.
                    ^

Repeated subjects, objects, and adverbs

English does not allow a subject to be repeated in its own clause.

▶ The doctor ~~she~~ advised me to cut down on salt.

Do not add a pronoun even when a word group comes between the subject and the verb.

▶ The car that had been stolen ~~it~~ was found.

Do not repeat an object or an adverb in an adjective clause. Adjective clauses begin with relative pronouns (*who, whom, whose, which, that*) or relative adverbs (*when, where*). Relative pronouns usually serve as subjects or objects in the clauses they introduce; another word in the clause cannot serve the same function.

▶ The cat ran under the car that ~~it~~ was parked on the street.

The relative pronoun *that* is the subject of the adjective clause, so the pronoun *it* cannot be added as a subject.

If the clause begins with a relative adverb, do not use another adverb with the same meaning later in the clause.

▶ The office where I work ~~there~~ is close to home.

The adverb *there* cannot repeat the relative adverb *where*.

29d Become familiar with prepositions that show time and place.

The following chart is limited to three prepositions that show time and place: *at*, *on*, and *in*. Not every possible use is listed in the chart, so don't be surprised when you encounter exceptions and idiomatic uses that you must learn one at a time. For example, in English a person rides *in* a car but *on* a bus, plane, train, or subway.

At, on, and in to show time and place	
Showing time	
AT	*at* a specific time: *at* 7:20, *at* dawn, *at* dinner
ON	*on* a specific day or date: *on* Tuesday, *on* June 4
IN	*in* a part of a 24-hour period: *in* the afternoon, *in* the daytime [but *at* night]
	in a year or month: *in* 2008, *in* July
	in a period of time: finished *in* three hours
Showing place	
AT	*at* a meeting place or location: *at* home, *at* the club
	at the edge of something: sitting *at* the desk
	at the corner of something: turning *at* the intersection
	at a target: throwing the snowball *at* Lucy
ON	*on* a surface: placed *on* the table, hanging *on* the wall
	on a street: the house *on* Spring Street
	on an electronic medium: *on* television, *on* the Internet
IN	*in* an enclosed space: *in* the garage, *in* an envelope
	in a geographic location: *in* San Diego, *in* Texas
	in a print medium: *in* a book, *in* a magazine

EXERCISE 29-2 Edit the following sentences for proper use of articles, nouns, and prepositions and for proper sentence structure. If a sentence is correct, write "correct" after it. Answers appear in the back of the book.

The play begins ~~on~~ 7:30 p.m.
at

a. Freezing rain causes icy glaze on trees.

b. I don't use the subway because am claustrophobic.

c. Recently have been a number of earthquakes in Turkey.

d. Whenever we eat at the café, we sit at a small table on the corner of the room.

e. In the 1990s, entrepreneurs created new online business in record numbers.

PART 6

Punctuation

30 The comma

The comma was invented to help readers. Without it, sentence parts can collide into one another unexpectedly, causing misreadings.

> **CONFUSING**   If you cook Elmer will do the dishes.
>
> **CONFUSING**   While we were eating a rattlesnake approached our campsite.

Add commas in the logical places (after *cook* and *eating*), and suddenly all is clear. No longer is Elmer being cooked, the rattlesnake being eaten.

Various rules have evolved to prevent such misreadings and to guide readers through complex grammatical structures. Those rules are detailed in this section. (Section 31 explains when not to use commas.)

30a Use a comma before a coordinating conjunction joining independent clauses.

When a coordinating conjunction connects two or more independent clauses — word groups that could stand alone as separate sentences — a comma must be placed before the conjunction. There are seven coordinating conjunctions in English: *and, but, or, nor, for, so,* and *yet.*

A comma tells readers that one independent clause has come to a close and that another is about to begin.

▶ The department sponsored a seminar on college survival

skills, and it hosted a barbecue for new students.
 ^

EXCEPTION: If the two independent clauses are short and there is no danger of misreading, the comma may be omitted: *The plane took off and we were on our way.*

NOTE: As a rule, do *not* use a comma with a coordinating conjunction that joins only two words, phrases, or subordinate clauses. (See 31a. See also 30c for commas with coordinating conjunctions joining three or more elements.)

▶ A good money manager controls expenses/ and invests

surplus dollars to meet future needs.

The word group following *and* is not an independent clause; it is the second half of a compound predicate (*controls . . . and invests*).

30b Use a comma after an introductory clause or phrase.

A comma tells readers that the introductory clause or phrase has come to a close and that the main part of the sentence is about to begin. The most common introductory clauses and phrases function as adverbs. Such word groups usually tell when, where, how, why, or under what conditions the main action of the sentence occurred. (See 42a, 42b, and 42e.)

▶ When Irwin was ready to iron, his cat tripped on the cord.
∧

Without the comma, readers may think that Irwin is ironing his cat. The comma signals that *his cat* is the subject of a new clause, not part of the introductory one.

EXCEPTION: The comma may be omitted after a short adverb clause or phrase if there is no danger of misreading: *In no time we were at 2,800 feet.*

Sentences also frequently begin with a participial phrase that functions as an adjective, describing the noun or pronoun immediately following it. The comma tells readers that they are about to learn the identity of the person or thing described; therefore, the comma is usually required even when the phrase is short. (See 42b.)

> ▶ **Buried under layers of younger rocks, the earth's oldest rocks**
> $\wedge$
> **contain no fossils.**

NOTE: Other introductory word groups include transitional expressions and absolute phrases (see 30f).

30c Use a comma between all items in a series.

In a series of three or more items (words, phrases, or clauses), use a comma between all items, including the last two.

> ▶ **Langston Hughes's poetry is concerned with race, justice, and the**
> $\wedge$
> **diversity of the African American experience.**

Although some writers view the last comma in a series as optional, most experts advise using the comma because its omission can result in ambiguity or misreading.

> ▶ **My uncle willed me all of his property, houses, and boats.**
> $\wedge$
>
> Did the uncle will his property *and* houses *and* boats—or simply his property, consisting of houses and boats? If the former meaning is intended, a comma is necessary to prevent ambiguity.

30d Use a comma between coordinate adjectives not joined with *and*.

When two or more adjectives each modify a noun separately, they are coordinate.

> Roberto is a *warm, gentle, affectionate* father.

If the adjectives can be joined with *and*, the adjectives are coordinate, so you should use commas: *warm* and *gentle* and *affectionate* (*warm, gentle, affectionate*).

NOTE: Do not use a comma between cumulative adjectives, those that do not each modify the noun separately.

Three large gray shapes moved slowly toward us.

Cumulative adjectives cannot be joined with *and* (not *three* and *large* and *gray shapes*).

EXERCISE 30–1   Add or delete commas where necessary in the following sentences. If a sentence is correct, write "correct" after it. Answers appear in the back of the book.

> **We gathered our essentials, took off for the great outdoors, and**
> ^
> **ignored the fact that it was Friday the 13th.**

a. The cold impersonal atmosphere of the university was unbearable.

b. An ambulance threaded its way through police cars, fire trucks and irate citizens.

c. The *1812 Overture* is a stirring, magnificent piece of music.

d. After two broken arms, three cracked ribs and one concussion, Ken quit the varsity football team.

e. My cat's pupils had constricted to small black shining slits.

30e Use commas to set off nonrestrictive (nonessential) elements, but not restrictive (essential) elements.

Restrictive (essential) elements

A restrictive element defines or limits the meaning of the word it modifies; it is therefore essential to the meaning of the sentence and is not set off with commas. If you remove a restrictive modifier from a sentence, the meaning changes significantly, becoming more general than you intended.

RESTRICTIVE (NO COMMAS)

The campers need clothes *that are durable.*

Scientists *who study the earth's structure* are called geologists.

The first sentence does not mean that the campers need clothes in general. The intended meaning is more limited: the campers need durable clothes. The second sentence does not mean that scientists in general are called geologists; only those scientists who specifically study the earth's structure are called geologists. The italicized word groups are essential and are therefore not set off with commas.

Nonrestrictive (nonessential) elements

A nonrestrictive modifier describes a noun or pronoun whose meaning has already been clearly defined or limited. Because the modifier contains nonessential or parenthetical information, it is set off with commas. If you remove a nonrestrictive element from a sentence, the meaning does not change dramatically. Some meaning may be lost, but the defining characteristics of the person or thing described remain the same.

NONRESTRICTIVE (WITH COMMAS)

The campers need sturdy shoes, *which are expensive.*

The scientists, *who represented eight different universities,* met to review applications for the prestigious Advancements in Science Award.

In the first sentence, the campers need sturdy shoes, and the shoes happen to be expensive. In the second sentence, the scientists met to review applications for the award; that they represented eight different universities is informative but not critical to the meaning of the sentence. The nonessential information in both sentences is set off with commas.

NOTE: Often it is difficult to tell whether a word group is restrictive or nonrestrictive without seeing it in context and considering the writer's meaning. Both of the following sentences are grammatically correct, but their meanings are slightly different.

The dessert made with fresh raspberries was delicious.

The dessert, made with fresh raspberries, was delicious.

In the first example, the phrase *made with fresh raspberries* tells readers which of two or more desserts the writer is referring to. In the example with commas, the phrase merely adds information about one dessert.

Elements that may be restrictive or nonrestrictive include adjective clauses, adjective phrases, and appositives.

Adjective clauses

Adjective clauses, which usually follow the noun or pronoun they describe, begin with a relative pronoun (*who, whom, whose, which, that*) or with a relative adverb (*when, where*). When an adjective clause is non-restrictive, set it off with commas; when it is restrictive, omit the commas.

NONRESTRICTIVE CLAUSE (WITH COMMAS)

▶ Ed's house, which is located on thirteen acres, was completely
    ∧   ∧
furnished with bats in the rafters and mice in the kitchen.

The adjective clause *which is located on thirteen acres* does not restrict the meaning of *Ed's house*; the information is nonessential and is therefore set off with commas.

RESTRICTIVE CLAUSE (NO COMMAS)

▶ The giant panda / that was born at the San Diego Zoo in 2003 / was

sent to China in 2007.

Because the adjective clause *that was born at the San Diego Zoo in 2003* identifies one particular panda out of many, the information is essential and is therefore not set off with commas.

NOTE: Use *that* only with restrictive (essential) clauses. Many writers prefer to use *which* only with nonrestrictive (nonessential) clauses, but usage varies.

Adjective phrases

Prepositional or verbal phrases functioning as adjectives may be restrictive or nonrestrictive. Nonrestrictive phrases are set off with commas; restrictive phrases are not.

NONRESTRICTIVE PHRASE (WITH COMMAS)

▶ The helicopter, with its million-candlepower spotlight illuminating
  ∧
the area, circled above.
  ∧

The *with* phrase is nonessential because its purpose is not to specify which of two or more helicopters is being discussed. The phrase is not required for readers to understand the meaning of the sentence.

RESTRICTIVE PHRASE (NO COMMAS)

▶ One corner of the attic was filled with newspapers⌿ dating from the
early 1900s.

Dating from the early 1900s restricts the meaning of *newspapers,* so the comma should be omitted.

Appositives

An appositive is a noun or noun phrase that renames a nearby noun. Nonrestrictive appositives are set off with commas; restrictive appositives are not.

NONRESTRICTIVE APPOSITIVE (WITH COMMAS)

▶ Darwin's most important book, *On the Origin of Species,* was the
  ∧   ∧
result of many years of research.

Most important restricts the meaning to one book, so the appositive *On the Origin of Species* is nonrestrictive and should be set off with commas.

$\wedge$
,

RESTRICTIVE APPOSITIVE (NO COMMAS)

▶ The song/ "Viva la Vida/" was blasted out of huge amplifiers at
the concert.

> Once they've read *song*, readers still don't know precisely which song the
> writer means. The appositive following *song* restricts its meaning, so the
> appositive should not be set off with commas.

30f Use commas to set off transitional and parenthetical expressions, absolute phrases, and word groups expressing contrast.

Transitional expressions

Transitional expressions serve as bridges between sentences or parts of sentences. They include conjunctive adverbs such as *however, therefore,* and *moreover* and transitional phrases such as *for example, as a matter of fact,* and *in other words.* (For complete lists of these expressions, see 32b.)

When a transitional expression appears between independent clauses in a compound sentence, it is preceded by a semicolon and is usually followed by a comma. (See 32b.)

▶ Minh did not understand our language; moreover, he was
$\wedge$
unfamiliar with our customs.

When a transitional expression appears at the beginning of a sentence or in the middle of an independent clause, it is usually set off with commas.

▶ Natural foods are not always salt-free; celery, for example, contains
$\wedge$ $\wedge$
more sodium than most people think.

Parenthetical expressions

Expressions that provide only supplemental information and interrupt the flow of a sentence should be set off with commas.

▶ Evolution, as far as we know, doesn't work this way.
⌃ ⌃

Absolute phrases

An absolute phrase consists of a noun followed by a participle or participial phrase. (See 42d.)

┌──────── ABSOLUTE PHRASE ────────┐
│ N   PARTICIPLE │

The sun appearing for the first time in a week, we were at last able to begin the archaeological dig.

▶ Elvis Presley made music industry history in the 1950s, his records
⌃
having sold more than ten million copies.

Word groups expressing contrast

Sharp contrasts beginning with words such as *not*, *never*, and *unlike* are set off with commas.

▶ Unlike Robert, Celia loved dance contests.
⌃

30g Use commas to set off nouns of direct address, the words *yes* and *no*, interrogative tags, and mild interjections.

▶ Forgive me, Angela, for forgetting your birthday.
⌃ ⌃

▶ The film was faithful to the book, wasn't it?
⌃

30h Use commas with expressions such as *he said* to set off direct quotations.

▶ In his "Letter from Birmingham Jail," Martin Luther King Jr.

wrote, "We know through painful experience that freedom is never
∧
voluntarily given by the oppressor; it must be demanded by the

oppressed" (225).

See 34 on the use of quotation marks and 48c on citing literary sources.

30i Use commas with dates, addresses, titles, and numbers.

Dates

In dates, set off the year from the rest of the sentence with a pair of commas.

▶ On December 12, 1890, orders were sent out for the arrest of
∧   ∧
Sitting Bull.

EXCEPTIONS: Commas are not needed if the date is inverted or if only the month and year are given: 15 April 2009; January 2020.

Addresses

The elements of an address or a place name are separated with commas. A zip code, however, is not preceded by a comma.

▶ Please send the package to Greg Tarvin at 708 Spring Street,
∧
Washington, IL 61571.
∧

Titles

If a title follows a name, set off the title with a pair of commas.

▶ Ann Hall, MD, has been appointed to the board of trustees.
    ^   ^

Numbers

In numbers more than four digits long, use commas to separate the numbers into groups of three, starting from the right. In numbers four digits long, a comma is optional.

3,500 [*or* 3500]   100,000   5,000,000

EXERCISE 30-2   This exercise covers the major uses of the comma described in 30a–30e. Add or delete commas where necessary. If a sentence is correct, write "correct" after it. Answers appear in the back of the book.

Even though our brains actually can't focus on two tasks at a time,
                                                                  ^
many people believe they can multitask.

a. Cricket which originated in England is also popular in Australia, South Africa and India.

b. At the sound of the starting pistol the horses surged forward toward the first obstacle, a sharp incline three feet high.

c. After seeing an exhibition of Western art Gerhard Richter escaped from East Berlin, and smuggled out many of his notebooks.

d. Corrie's new wet suit has an intricate, blue pattern.

e. We replaced the rickety, old, spiral staircase with a sturdy, new ladder.

31 Unnecessary commas

Many common misuses of the comma result from a misunderstanding of the major comma rules presented in section 30.

31a Do not use a comma with a coordinating conjunction that joins only two words, phrases, or subordinate clauses.

▶ Ron discovered a leak/and came back to fix it.

The coordinating conjunction *and* links two verbs in a compound predicate: *discovered* and *came*.

▶ We knew that she had won/but that the election was close.

The coordinating conjunction *but* links two subordinate clauses, each beginning with *that*.

31b Do not use a comma to separate a verb from its subject or object.

Commas may appear between these major sentence elements only when a specific rule calls for them.

▶ Zoos large enough to give the animals freedom to roam/are

becoming more popular.

The comma should not separate the subject, *Zoos*, from the verb, *are becoming*.

31c Do not use a comma before the first or after the last item in a series.

▶ Other causes of asthmatic attacks are/stress, change in temperature, and cold air.

▶ Even novels that focus on horror, evil, and alienation/often have themes of spiritual renewal and redemption as well.

31d Do not use a comma between cumulative adjectives, between an adjective and a noun, or between an adverb and an adjective.

▶ In the corner of the closet, we found an old/maroon hatbox.

▶ It was a senseless, dangerous/mission.

▶ Deer are often responsible for severely/damaged crops.

31e Do not use a comma to set off a concluding adverb clause that is essential for meaning.

When adverb clauses introduce a sentence, they are nearly always followed by a comma (see 30b). When they conclude a sentence, however, they are not set off by a comma if their content is essential to the meaning of the earlier part of the sentence. Adverb clauses beginning with *after, as soon as, because, before, if, since, unless, until,* and *when* are usually essential.

▶ Don't visit Paris at the height of the tourist season/unless you have booked hotel reservations.

Without the *unless* clause, the meaning of the sentence might at first seem broader than the writer intended.

When a concluding adverb clause is nonessential, it should be preceded by a comma. Clauses beginning with *although, even though, though,* and *whereas* are usually nonessential.

▶ The lecture seemed to last only a short time, although the clock said
it had gone on for more than an hour.

31f Do not use a comma after a phrase that begins an inverted sentence.

Though a comma belongs after most introductory phrases (see 30b), it does not belong after phrases that begin an inverted sentence. In an inverted sentence, the subject follows the verb, and a phrase that ordinarily would follow the verb is moved to the beginning.

▶ At the bottom of the hill/sat the stubborn mule.

31g Avoid other common misuses of the comma.

Do not use a comma in the following situations.

AFTER A COORDINATING CONJUNCTION (*AND, BUT, OR, NOR, FOR, SO, YET*)

▶ Occasionally TV talk shows are performed live, but/more often they
are taped.

AFTER *SUCH AS* OR *LIKE*

▶ Shade-loving plants such as/begonias, impatiens, and coleus can
add color to a shady garden.

AFTER *ALTHOUGH*

▶ Although/the air was balmy, the water was cold.

BEFORE A PARENTHESIS

▶ Though Sylvia's ACT score was low/(only 24), her application essay
was superior.

TO SET OFF AN INDIRECT (REPORTED) QUOTATION

▶ Samuel Goldwyn once said/that a verbal contract isn't worth the
paper it's written on.

WITH A QUESTION MARK OR AN EXCLAMATION POINT

▶ "Why don't you try it?/" she coaxed. "You can't do any worse than
the rest of us."

EXERCISE 31–1 Delete any unnecessary commas in the following
sentences. If a sentence is correct, write "correct" after it. Answers appear in
the back of the book.

**In his Silk Road Project, Yo-Yo Ma incorporates work by musicians such
as/ Kayhan Kalhor and Richard Danielpour.**

a. After the morning rains cease, the swimmers emerge from their
cottages.
b. Tricia's first artwork was a bright, blue, clay dolphin.
c. Some modern musicians, (trumpeter Jon Hassell is an example) blend
several cultural traditions into a unique sound.
d. Myra liked hot, spicy foods such as, chili, kung pao chicken, and
buffalo wings.
e. On the display screen, was a soothing pattern of light and
shadow.

32 The semicolon and the colon

The semicolon is used to connect major sentence elements of equal grammatical rank. The colon is used primarily to call attention to the words that follow it.

32a Use a semicolon between closely related independent clauses not joined with a coordinating conjunction.

When two independent clauses appear in one sentence, they are usually linked with a comma and a coordinating conjunction (*and, but, or, nor, for, so, yet*). The coordinating conjunction signals the relation between the clauses. If the relation is clear without a conjunction, a writer may choose to connect the clauses with a semicolon instead.

> In film, a low-angle shot makes the subject look powerful; a high-angle shot does just the opposite.

A semicolon must be used whenever a coordinating conjunction has been omitted between independent clauses. To use merely a comma creates a type of run-on sentence known as a *comma splice*. (See 21.)

▶ In 1800, a traveler needed six weeks to get from New York to

Chicago; in 1860, the trip by train took only two days.
      ^

32b Use a semicolon between independent clauses linked with a transitional expression.

Transitional expressions include conjunctive adverbs and transitional phrases (see p. 196).

CONJUNCTIVE ADVERBS

accordingly	furthermore	moreover	still
also	hence	nevertheless	subsequently
anyway	however	next	then
besides	incidentally	nonetheless	therefore
certainly	indeed	now	thus
consequently	instead	otherwise	
conversely	likewise	similarly	
finally	meanwhile	specifically	

TRANSITIONAL PHRASES

after all	even so	in fact
as a matter of fact	for example	in other words
as a result	for instance	in the first place
at any rate	in addition	on the contrary
at the same time	in conclusion	on the other hand

When a transitional expression appears between independent clauses, it is preceded by a semicolon and usually followed by a comma.

▶ Many corals grow very gradually/; in fact, the creation of a coral

reef can take centuries.

When a transitional expression appears in the middle or at the end of the second independent clause, the semicolon goes between the clauses.

▶ Biologists have observed laughter in primates other than humans/;

chimpanzees, however, sound more like they are panting than

laughing.

Transitional expressions should not be confused with the coordinating conjunctions *and, but, or, nor, for, so,* and *yet,* which are preceded by a comma when they link independent clauses. (See 30a.)

32c Use a semicolon between items in a series containing internal punctuation.

▶ Researchers point to key benefits of positive thinking: it leads

to high self-esteem, especially in people who focus on their

achievements/; it helps make social interactions, such as those with
          ^
co-workers, more enjoyable/;and, most important, it results in
                      ^
better sleep and overall health.

Without the semicolons, the reader would have to sort out the major
groupings, distinguishing between important and less important pauses
according to the logic of the sentence. By inserting semicolons at the major
breaks, the writer does this work for the reader.

32d Avoid common misuses of the semicolon.

Do not use a semicolon in the following situations.

BETWEEN A SUBORDINATE CLAUSE AND THE REST OF THE SENTENCE

▶ Although children's literature was added to the National Book Awards

in 1969/, it has had its own award, the Newbery Medal, since 1922.
        ^
BETWEEN AN APPOSITIVE AND THE WORD IT REFERS TO

▶ The scientists were fascinated by the species *Argyroneta aquatica/*,
                                                                  ^
a spider that lives underwater.

TO INTRODUCE A LIST

▶ Some of my favorite celebrities have their own blogs/: Katy Perry,
                                                     ^
Beyoncé, and Zooey Deschanel.

BETWEEN INDEPENDENT CLAUSES JOINED BY *AND, BUT, OR, NOR, FOR,*
SO, **OR** *YET*

▶   Five of the applicants had worked with spreadsheets/, but only one
                                                      ^
    was familiar with database management.

EXCEPTION: If one or both of the independent clauses contain a comma,
you may use a semicolon with a coordinating conjunction between the
clauses.

32e Use a colon after an independent clause to direct attention to a list, an appositive, a quotation, or a summary or an explanation.

A LIST
The daily exercise routine should include at least the following: twenty
knee bends, fifty sit-ups, and five minutes of running in place.

AN APPOSITIVE
My roommate seems to live on two things: snacks and social media.

A QUOTATION
Consider the words of Benjamin Franklin: "There never was a good war
or a bad peace."

A SUMMARY OR AN EXPLANATION
Faith is like love: it cannot be forced.

TIP: For other ways of introducing quotations, see "Introducing quoted
material" in 34d. When an independent clause follows a colon, MLA recommends using a lowercase letter (see 51a) whereas APA says to begin
with a capital letter (see 53a).

32f Follow conventions for colon use.

SALUTATION IN A LETTER Dear Editor:

HOURS AND MINUTES 5:30 p.m.

PROPORTIONS The ratio of women to men was 2:1.

TITLE AND SUBTITLE *The Glory of Hera: Greek Mythology and the Greek Family*

BIBLIOGRAPHIC ENTRIES Boston: Bedford/St. Martin's, 2018

CHAPTER AND VERSE IN SACRED TEXT Luke 2:14, Qur'an 67:3

32g Avoid common misuses of the colon.

A colon must be preceded by a full independent clause. Therefore, avoid using it in the following situations.

BETWEEN A VERB AND ITS OBJECT OR COMPLEMENT

▶ Some important vitamins found in vegetables are̸ vitamin A, thiamine, niacin, and vitamin C.

BETWEEN A PREPOSITION AND ITS OBJECT

▶ The heart's two pumps each consist of̸ an upper chamber, or atrium, and a lower chamber, or ventricle.

AFTER *SUCH AS, INCLUDING,* OR *FOR EXAMPLE*

▶ The NCAA regulates college athletic sports, including̸ basketball, baseball, softball, and football.

EXERCISE 32–1   Edit the following sentences to correct errors in the use of the comma, the semicolon, or the colon. If a sentence is correct, write "correct" after it. Answers appear in the back of the book.

Lifting the cover gently, Luca found the source of the odd sound/: a

marble in the gears.

a. We always looked forward to Thanksgiving in Vermont: it was our only chance to see our Grady cousins.

b. If we have come to fight, we are far too few, if we have come to die, we are far too many.

c. The travel package includes: a round-trip ticket to Athens, a cruise through the Cyclades, and all hotel accommodations.

d. The news article portrays the land use proposal as reckless; although 62 percent of the town's residents support it.

e. Strong black coffee will not sober you up, the truth is that time is the only way to get alcohol out of your system.

33 The apostrophe

The apostrophe indicates possession and marks contractions. In addition, it has a few conventional uses.

33a Use an apostrophe to indicate that a noun is possessive.

Possessive nouns usually indicate ownership, as in *Tim's hat* or *the lawyer's desk*. Frequently, however, ownership is only loosely implied: *the tree's roots, a day's work*. If you are not sure whether a noun is possessive, try turning it into an *of* phrase: *the roots of the tree, the work of a day*. (Pronouns also have possessive forms. See 33b and 33e.)

When to add -'s

1. If the noun does not end in -s, add -'s.

   Luck often propels a rock musician's career.

   The Children's Defense Fund is a nonprofit organization that supports programs for poor and minority children.

2. If the noun is singular and ends in -s or an s sound, add -'s to indicate possession.

   Lois's sister spent last year in India.

   Her article presents an overview of Marx's teachings.

EXCEPTION: To avoid potentially awkward pronunciation, some writers use only the apostrophe with a singular noun ending in -s: *Sophocles'*.

When to add only an apostrophe

If the noun is plural and ends in -s, add only an apostrophe.

   Both diplomats' briefcases were searched by guards.

Joint possession

To show joint possession, use -'s or (-s') with the last noun only; to show individual possession, make all nouns possessive.

   Have you seen Joyce and Greg's new camper?

   Hernando's and Maria's expectations were quite different.

Joyce and Greg jointly own one camper. Hernando and Maria individually have different expectations.

Compound nouns

If a noun is compound, use -'s (or -s') with the last element.

   My father-in-law's memoir about his childhood in Sri Lanka was published in October.

33b Use an apostrophe and -s to indicate that an indefinite pronoun is possessive.

Indefinite pronouns refer to no specific person or thing: *everyone, someone, no one, something.* (See 40b.)

> Someone's raincoat has been left behind.

33c Use an apostrophe to mark omissions in contractions and numbers.

In a contraction, the apostrophe takes the place of one or more missing letters. *It's* stands for *it is, can't* for *cannot.*

> It's a shame that Frank can't go on the tour.

The apostrophe is also used to mark the omission of the first two digits of a year (*the class of '19*) or years (*the '80s generation*).

33d Do not use an apostrophe in certain situations.

Plural of numbers

Do not use an apostrophe in the plural of any numbers.

> Oksana skated nearly perfect figure 8s.
>
> The 1920s are known as the Jazz Age.

Plural of letters

Italicize the letter and use regular type for the *-s* ending.

> Two large *P*s were painted on the door.
>
> He received two *D*s for the first time in his life.

To avoid misreading, you may use an apostrophe with some letters: two *A*'s in biology.

Plural of abbreviations

Do not use an apostrophe to pluralize an abbreviation.

> Harriet has thirty DVDs on her desk.

Plural of words mentioned as words

Generally, omit the apostrophe to form the plural of words mentioned as words. If the word is italicized, the -*s* ending appears in roman (regular) type.

> We've heard enough *maybe*s.

Words mentioned as words may instead appear in quotation marks. When you choose this option, use the apostrophe.

> We've heard enough "maybe's."

33e Avoid common misuses of the apostrophe.

Do not use an apostrophe with nouns that are not possessive or with the possessive pronouns *its, whose, his, hers, ours, yours,* and *theirs.*

>   outpatients
> ► Some ~~outpatient's~~ have special parking permits.
>   ^
>
>   its
> ► Each area has ~~it's~~ own conference room.
>   ^
>
> *It's* means "it is." The possessive pronoun *its* contains no apostrophe despite the fact that it is possessive.

> We attended a reading by Amy Tan, ~~who's~~ *whose* work focuses on the
Chinese immigration experience.

Who's means "who is." The possessive pronoun is *whose*.

EXERCISE 33–1   Edit the following sentences to correct errors in the use of the apostrophe. If a sentence is correct, write "correct" after it. Answers appear in the back of the book.

Our favorite barbecue restaurant is Poor ~~Richards~~ *Richard's* Ribs.

a. This diet will improve almost anyone's health.
b. The innovative shoe fastener was inspired by the designers young son.
c. Each days menu features a different European country's dish.
d. Sue worked overtime to increase her families earnings.
e. Ms. Jacobs is unwilling to listen to students complaints about computer failures.

---

34 Quotation marks

Writers use quotation marks primarily to enclose direct quotations of another person's spoken or written words, with some exceptions.

34a Use quotation marks to enclose direct quotations.

Direct quotations of a person's words, whether spoken or written, must be in quotation marks.

"Twitter," according to social media researcher Jameson Brown, "is the best social network for brand to customer engagement."

Exception: indirect quotations

Do not use quotation marks around indirect quotations. An indirect quotation reports someone's ideas without using that person's exact words. In academic writing, indirect quotation is called *paraphrase* or *summary*. (See 48d.)

> Social media researcher Jameson Brown finds Twitter the best social media tool for companies that want to reach their consumers.

Exception: long quotations

Long quotations of prose or poetry are generally set off from the text by indenting. Quotation marks are not used because the indented format tells readers that the quotation is taken word for word from the source.

> After making an exhaustive study of the historical record, James Horan evaluates Billy the Kid like this:
>> The portrait that emerges of [the Kid] from the thousands of pages of affidavits, reports, trial transcripts, his letters, and his testimony is neither the mythical Robin Hood nor the stereotyped adenoidal moron and pathological killer. Rather Billy appears as a disturbed, lonely young man, honest, loyal to his friends, dedicated to his beliefs, and betrayed by our institutions and the corrupt, ambitious, and compromising politicians in his time. (158)

NOTE: The number in parentheses is a citation handled according to MLA style.

MLA and APA have specific guidelines for what constitutes a long quotation and how it should be indented (see 51a and 53a).

34b Use single quotation marks to enclose a quotation within a quotation.

> Megan Marshall notes that Elizabeth Peabody's school focused on "not merely 'teaching' but 'educating children morally and spiritually as well as intellectually from the first'" (107).

34c Use quotation marks around the titles of short works.

Short works include articles, poems, short stories, songs, television and radio episodes, and chapters or subdivisions of long works.

> James Baldwin's story "Sonny's Blues" tells the story of two brothers who come to understand each other's suffering.

Titles of long works such as books, plays, television and radio programs, films, magazines, and so on are put in italics. (See 37g.)

34d Follow conventions for the use of punctuation with quotation marks.

This section describes the conventions American publishers use in placing various marks of punctuation inside or outside quotation marks. It also explains how to punctuate when introducing quoted material. (For the use of quotation marks in MLA and APA styles, see 48c and 49b. The examples in this section show MLA style.)

Periods and commas

Place periods and commas inside quotation marks.

> "I'm here as part of my service-learning project," I told the classroom teacher. "I'm hoping to become a reading specialist."

This rule applies to single quotation marks as well as double quotation marks. (See 34b.) It also applies to all uses of quotation marks: for quoted material, for titles of works, and for words used as words.

NOTE: In MLA- and APA-style parenthetical in-text citations, the period follows the citation in parentheses.

> James M. McPherson comments, approvingly, that the Whigs "were not averse to extending the blessings of American liberty, even to Mexicans and Indians" (48).

Colons and semicolons

Put colons and semicolons outside quotation marks.

> Harold wrote, "I regret that I am unable to attend the fundraiser for ALS research"; his letter, however, came with a substantial contribution.

Question marks and exclamation points

Put question marks and exclamation points inside quotation marks unless they apply to the whole sentence.

> Dr. Abram's first question on the first day of class was "What three goals do you have for the course?"

> Have you heard the old proverb "Do not climb the hill until you reach it"?

In the first sentence, the question mark applies only to the quoted question. In the second sentence, the question mark applies to the whole sentence.

NOTE: For a quotation that ends with a question mark or an exclamation point, the parenthetical citation and a period should follow the entire quotation.

> Rosie Thomas asks, "Is nothing in life ever straight and clear, the way children see it?" (77).

Introducing quoted material

After a word group introducing a quotation, choose a colon, a comma, or no punctuation at all, whichever is appropriate in context.

Formal introduction   If a quotation is formally introduced, a colon is appropriate. A formal introduction is a full independent clause, not just an expression such as *he writes*.

> Thomas Friedman provides a challenging yet optimistic view of the future: "We need to get back to work on our country and on our planet. The hour is late, the stakes couldn't be higher, the project couldn't be harder, the payoff couldn't be greater" (25).

Signal phrase such as *he explains* If a quotation is introduced with an expression such as *he explains* or *she argues* — or if it is followed by such an expression — a comma is needed. (For the use of signal phrases in MLA and APA, see 49c.)

> Stephen Ambrose notes, "With regard to air travel, Jefferson was a full century ahead of the curve" (53).

> "Unless another war is prevented it is likely to bring destruction on a scale never before held possible and even now hardly conceived," Albert Einstein wrote in the aftermath of the atomic bomb (29).

Blended quotation When a quotation is blended into the writer's own sentence, either a comma or no punctuation is appropriate, depending on the way in which the quotation fits into the sentence structure.

> The future champion could, as he put it, "float like a butterfly and sting like a bee."

> Virginia Woolf wrote in 1928 that "a woman must have money and a room of her own if she is to write fiction" (4).

Beginning of sentence If a quotation appears at the beginning of a sentence, use a comma after it unless the quotation ends with a question mark or an exclamation point.

> "I've always thought of myself as a reporter," American poet Gwendolyn Brooks has stated (162).

> "What is it?" she asked, bracing herself.

Interrupted quotation If a quoted sentence is interrupted by explanatory words, use commas to set off the explanatory words. If two successive quoted sentences from the same source are interrupted by explanatory words, use a comma before the explanatory words and a period after them.

> "Everyone agrees journalists must tell the truth," Bill Kovach and Tom Rosenstiel write. "Yet people are befuddled about what 'the truth' means" (37).

34e Avoid common misuses of quotation marks.

Do not use quotation marks to draw attention to familiar slang, to disown trite expressions, or to justify an attempt at humor.

▶ The economist estimated that 5 percent was only a ~~"ballpark figure."~~

Do not use quotation marks around the title of your own essay.

EXERCISE 34–1 Add or delete quotation marks as needed and make any other necessary changes in punctuation in the following sentences. If a sentence is correct, write "correct" after it. Answers appear in the back of the book.

> Gandhi once said, "An eye for an eye only ends up making the whole
> world blind."

a. As for the advertisement "Sailors have more fun", if you consider chipping paint and swabbing decks fun, then you will have plenty of it.

b. Even after forty minutes of discussion, our class could not agree on an interpretation of Robert Frost's poem "The Road Not Taken."

c. After winning the lottery, Juanita said that "she would give half the money to charity."

d. After the movie, Vicki said, "The reviewer called this flick "trash of the first order." I guess you can't believe everything you read."

e. "Cleaning your house while your kids are still growing," said Phyllis Diller, "is like shoveling the walk before it stops snowing."

---

35 End punctuation

35a The period

Use a period to end all sentences except direct questions or genuine exclamations. Also use periods in abbreviations according to convention.

To end *most* sentences

▶ The professor asked whether talk therapy was more beneficial than

antidepressants̷.
  ^

In *some* abbreviations

Mr.	i.e.	a.m. (or AM)
Ms.	e.g.	p.m. (or PM)
Dr.	etc.	

NOTE: If a sentence ends with a period marking an abbreviation, do not add a second period.

Periods are not used with most other abbreviations.

CA	UNESCO	UCLA	BS	BC
NY	AFL-CIO	IRS	PhD	BCE

35b The question mark

Use a question mark after a direct question.

What is the horsepower of a 777 engine?

Use a period, not a question mark, after an indirect question, one that is reported rather than asked directly.

▶ He asked me who was teaching the psychology course this year̷.
                                                              ^

35c The exclamation point

Use an exclamation point after a sentence that expresses exceptional feeling or deserves special emphasis.

When Gloria entered the room, we all yelled, "Surprise!"

Do not overuse the exclamation point.

▶ **In the fisherman's memory, the fish lives on, increasing in length and weight with each passing year, until at last it is big enough to shade a fishing boat.**

This sentence is emphatic enough without an exclamation point.

36 Other punctuation marks

36a The dash

The dash may be used to set off parenthetical material that deserves special emphasis. When typing, use two hyphens to form a dash (--), with no space before or after the dash.

Use a dash to introduce a list, to signal a restatement or amplification, or to indicate a shift in tone or thought.

> Peter decided to focus on his priorities—applying to graduate school and getting financial aid.

> Kiere took a few steps back, came running full speed, kicked a mighty kick—and missed the ball.

In the first example, the writer could instead have used a colon. The colon is more formal than the dash and not quite as emphatic.

Use a pair of dashes to set off parenthetical material that deserves special emphasis or to set off an appositive that contains commas.

> Everything in the classroom—from the pencils on the desks to the books on the shelves—was in perfect order.

36b Parentheses

Use parentheses to enclose supplemental material, minor digressions, and afterthoughts.

> Nurses record patients' vital signs (temperature, pulse, and blood pressure) several times a day.

Use parentheses to enclose letters or numbers labeling items in a series.

> Regulations stipulated that only the following equipment could be used on the survival mission: (1) a knife, (2) thirty feet of parachute line, (3) a book of matches, (4) two ponchos, (5) an E tool, and (6) a signal flare.

Do not overuse parentheses.

> from
> ▶ Researchers have said that seventeen million ~~(estimates run as~~
>   to
> ~~high as~~ twenty-three million)́ Americans have diabetes.
>   ^

36c Brackets

Use brackets to enclose any words or phrases that you have inserted into an otherwise word-for-word quotation.

> *Audubon* reports that "if there are not enough young to balance deaths, the end of the species [California condor] is inevitable" (4).

The sentence quoted from the *Audubon* article did not contain the words *California condor* (since the context of the full article made clear what species was meant), so the writer needed to add the name in brackets.

The Latin word "sic" in brackets indicates that an error in a quoted sentence appears in the original source.

> According to the review, Nelly Furtado's performance was brilliant, "exceding [sic] the expectations of even her most loyal fans."

Instead of using "sic," the writer could have paraphrased the preceding quotation: *According to the review, even Nelly Furtado's most loyal fans were surprised by the brilliance of her performance.*

TIP: For advice on using "sic" in MLA and APA styles, see 49b.

36d The ellipsis mark

Use an ellipsis mark, three spaced periods, to indicate that you have deleted words from an otherwise word-for-word quotation.

> Shute acknowledges that treatment for autism can be expensive: "Sensory integration therapy . . . can cost up to $200 an hour" (82).

If you delete a full sentence or more in the middle of a quoted passage, use a period before the three ellipsis dots.

> "If we don't properly train, teach, or treat our growing prison population," says Luis Rodríguez, "somebody else will. . . . This may well be the safety issue of the new century" (16).

NOTE: Do not use the ellipsis mark at the beginning or at the end of a quotation. Readers will understand that the quoted material is taken from a longer passage. (If you have cut some words from the end of the final quoted sentence, however, MLA requires an ellipsis mark.)

36e The slash

Use a slash to separate two or three lines of poetry that have been run into your text. Add a space both before and after the slash.

> In the opening lines of "Jordan," George Herbert pokes gentle fun at popular poems of his time: "Who says that fictions only and false hair / Become a verse? Is there in truth no beauty?" (1-2).

Four or more lines of poetry should be handled as an indented quotation.

Use the slash sparingly, if at all, to separate options: *pass/fail, producer/ director*. Put no space around the slash. Avoid using expressions such as *and/or, he/she,* and *his/her*. Instead of using *he/she* and *his/her* to solve sexist language problems, you can usually find more graceful alternatives. (See 17e.)

EXERCISE 36–1 Edit the following sentences to correct errors in punctuation, focusing especially on appropriate use of the dash, parentheses, brackets, the ellipsis mark, and the slash. If a sentence is correct, write "correct" after it. Answers appear in the back of the book.

> Social insects/——bees, for example,/——are able to communicate
> complicated messages to one another.

a. A client left his/her cell phone in our conference room after the meeting.

b. The films we made of Kilauea—on our trip to Hawaii Volcanoes National Park—illustrate a typical spatter cone eruption.

c. Although he was confident in his course selections, Greg chose the pass/ fail option for Chemistry 101.

d. Of three engineering fields, chemical, mechanical, and materials, Keegan chose materials engineering for its application to toy manufacturing.

e. The writer Chitra Divakaruni explained her work with other Indian American immigrants: "Many women who came to Maitri [a women's support group in San Francisco] needed to know simple things like opening a bank account or getting citizenship. . . . Many women in Maitri spoke English, but their English was functional rather than emotional. They needed someone who understands their problems and speaks their language."

PART 7

Mechanics

37 Abbreviations, numbers, and italics

This section describes conventional uses and treatments of abbreviations, numbers, and italics.

37a Use standard abbreviations for titles immediately before and after proper names.

TITLES BEFORE PROPER NAMES	TITLES AFTER PROPER NAMES
Mr. Rafael Zabala	William Albert Sr.
Ms. Nancy Linehan	Valda Coimbra, PhD
Dr. Margaret Simmons	Robert Simkowski, MD
Rev. John Stone	Mia Chin, LLD

Do not abbreviate a title if it is not used with a proper name: *My history professor* (not *prof.*) *is an expert on race relations in South Africa.*

Avoid redundant titles such as *Dr. Amy Day, MD.* Choose one title or the other: *Dr. Amy Day* or *Amy Day, MD.*

37b Use abbreviations only when you are sure your readers will understand them.

Familiar abbreviations for the names of organizations, companies, countries, academic degrees, and common terms, written without periods, are generally acceptable.

CIA	FBI	MD	NAACP
NBA	CEO	PhD	DVD

Talk show host Conan O'Brien is a Harvard graduate with a BA in history.

When using an unfamiliar abbreviation (such as *NASW* for National Association of Social Workers) or a potentially ambiguous abbreviation (such as *AMA*, which can refer to either the American Medical Association or the American Management Association), write the full name followed by the abbreviation in parentheses at the first mention of the name. Then use just the abbreviation throughout the rest of the paper.

37c Units of measurement

Generally, use abbreviations for units when they appear with numerals; spell out the units when they are used alone or when they are used with spelled-out numbers (see also 37f).

METRIC UNITS	US STANDARD UNITS
m, cm, mm	yd, ft, in.
km, kph	mi, mph
kg, g, mg	lb, oz

Results were measured in pounds.

Runners in the 5-km race had to contend with pouring rain.

Use no periods after abbreviations for units of measurement, except the abbreviation for "inch" (*in.*), to distinguish it from the preposition *in*.

37d Plural of abbreviations

To form the plural of most abbreviations, add *-s*, without an apostrophe: *MBAs*. Do not add *-s* to indicate the plural of units of measurement: *mm* (not *mms*), *lb* (not *lbs*), *in.* (not *ins.*).

37e Follow the conventions in your discipline for spelling out or using numerals to express numbers.

Academic styles vary in how they handle numbers in the text of a paper. In the humanities, MLA spells out all numbers below 101 and large round numbers (*forty million*). In the social sciences, APA spells out the numbers one through nine and uses numerals for all other numbers.

If a sentence begins with a number, spell out the number or rewrite the sentence.

> One hundred fifty
> ▶ ~~150~~ children in our program need expensive dental treatment.
>   ^

Rewriting the sentence may be less awkward if the number is long: *In our program, 150 children need expensive dental treatment.*

37f Follow conventions for using numerals in dates, addresses, and so on.

DATES July 4, 1776; 56 BC; CE 30

ADDRESSES 77 Latches Lane, 519 West 42nd Street

PERCENTAGES 55 percent (or 55%)

FRACTIONS, DECIMALS ⅞, 0.047

SCORES 7 to 3, 21–18

STATISTICS average age 37, average weight 180

SURVEYS 4 out of 5

EXACT AMOUNTS OF MONEY $105.37, $106,000

DIVISIONS OF BOOKS volume 3, chapter 4, page 189

DIVISIONS OF PLAYS act 3, scene 3 (or act III, scene iii)

TIME OF DAY 4:00 p.m., 1:30 a.m.

37g Follow conventions for italicizing the titles of works.

Titles of the following types of works should be italicized.

BOOKS *The Color Purple*, *The Round House*

MAGAZINES *Time*, *Scientific American*, *Slate*

NEWSPAPERS the *Baltimore Sun,* the *Orlando Sentinel*

LONG POEMS *The Waste Land, Paradise Lost*

PLAYS *In the Heights, Wicked*

FILMS *Casablanca, Argo*

TELEVISION PROGRAMS *The Voice, Frontline*

RADIO PROGRAMS *All Things Considered*

PODCAST SERIES *Embedded*

MUSICAL COMPOSITIONS *Porgy and Bess*

WORKS OF VISUAL ART *American Gothic*

VIDEO GAMES *Dragon Age, Call of Duty*

DATABASES OR WEBSITES [MLA] *JSTOR, Salon*

SOFTWARE OR APPS [MLA] *Photoshop, Instagram*

The titles of other works — including short stories, essays, episodes of a podcast or radio or TV program, songs, and short poems — are enclosed in quotation marks. (See 34c.)

NOTE: Do not use italics when referring to the Bible, titles of books in the Bible (Genesis, not *Genesis*), or titles of legal documents (the Constitution, not the *Constitution*).

37h Italicize non-English words used in an English sentence.

Shakespeare's Falstaff is a comic character known for both his excessive drinking and his general *joie de vivre*.

EXCEPTION: Do not italicize non-English words that have become a standard part of the English language — "laissez-faire," "fait accompli," "modus operandi," and "per diem," for example.

38 Spelling and the hyphen

A spell checker is a useful tool, but it has limitations. It won't catch words commonly confused (*accept* for *except*) or some typographical (*won* for *own*) or hyphenation errors. You still need to proofread, and you may need to consult a dictionary.

38a Become familiar with the major spelling rules.

i *before* e *except after* c

In general, use *i* before *e* except after *c* and except when sounded like *ay*, as in *neighbor* and *weigh*.

I BEFORE E	relieve, believe, sieve, niece, fierce, frieze
E BEFORE I	receive, deceive, sleigh, freight, eight
EXCEPTIONS	seize, either, weird, height, foreign, leisure

Suffixes

Final silent -e   Generally, drop a final silent *-e* when adding a suffix that begins with a vowel. Keep the final *-e* if the suffix begins with a consonant.

desire, desiring
remove, removable

achieve, achievement
care, careful

Words such as *changeable*, *judgment*, *argument*, and *truly* are exceptions.

Final -y   When adding *-s* or *-d* to words ending in *-y*, ordinarily change *-y* to *-ie* when the *-y* is preceded by a consonant but not when it is preceded by a vowel.

comedy, comedies
dry, dried

monkey, monkeys
play, played

With proper names ending in *-y*, however, do not change the *-y* to *-ie* even if it is preceded by a consonant: *the Doughertys*.

Final consonants If a final consonant is preceded by a single vowel *and* the consonant ends a one-syllable word or a stressed syllable, double the consonant when adding a suffix beginning with a vowel.

> bet, betting   occur, occurrence
> commit, committed

Plurals

-s or -es Add *-s* to form the plural of most nouns; add *-es* to singular nouns ending in *-s*, *-sh*, *-ch*, and *-x*.

> table, tables   church, churches
> paper, papers   dish, dishes

Ordinarily add *-s* to nouns ending in *-o* when the *-o* is preceded by a vowel. Add *-es* when it is preceded by a consonant.

> radio, radios   hero, heroes
> video, videos   tomato, tomatoes

38b Consult the dictionary to determine how to treat a compound word.

The dictionary will tell you whether to treat a compound word as hyphenated (*water-repellent*), as one word (*waterproof*), or as two words (*water table*). If the compound word is not in the dictionary, treat it as two words.

38c Hyphenate two or more words used together as an adjective before a noun.

▶ Today's teachers depend on both traditional textbook material and

  web-delivered content.
    ^

▶ Richa Gupta is not yet a well-known candidate.
                            ^

Generally, do not use a hyphen when such compounds follow the noun.

▶ After our television campaign, Richa Gupta will be well/known.

Do not use a hyphen to connect -*ly* adverbs to the words they modify.

▶ A slowly/moving truck tied up traffic.

38d Hyphenate fractions and certain numbers when they are spelled out.

For numbers written as words, use a hyphen in all fractions (*two-thirds*) and in all forms of compound numbers from twenty-one to ninety-nine (*thirty-five, sixty-seventh*).

38e Use a hyphen with the prefixes *all-, ex-* (meaning "former"), and *self-* and with the suffix *-elect*.

▶ The private foundation is funneling more money into self-help
  ^
  projects.

▶ The Student Senate bylaws require the president-elect to attend all
  ^
  senate meetings before the transfer of office.

38f Check for correct word breaks when words must be divided at the end of a line.

Only words that already contain a hyphen should be broken at the end of a line of text. If your word-processing software automatically breaks words at the ends of lines, disable that setting when writing academic papers.

Email addresses, URLs, and DOIs need special attention when they must break in text or in a bibliographic citation. Do not insert a hyphen. Instead, break an email address after the @ symbol or before a period. For URLs and DOIs, consult the guidelines for MLA (51a) and APA (53a).

EXERCISE 38–1 Edit the following sentences to correct errors in spelling and hyphenation. If a sentence is correct, write "correct" after it. Answers appear in the back of the book.

Émile Zola's first readers were scandalized by his slice-of-life novels.
                                                              ^   ^

a. The Williams sisters were the heros of my entire high school tennis team.

b. The swiftly-moving tugboat pulled alongside the barge and directed it away from the oil spill in the harbor.

c. We managed to get the most desireable seats in the theater.

d. As a livestock veterinarian, she cares for horses, donkies, cows, and other large farm animals.

e. Road-blocks were set up along all the major highways leading out of the city.

---

39 Capitalization

In addition to the rules in this section, a good dictionary can help you decide when to use capital letters.

39a Capitalize proper nouns and words derived from them; do not capitalize common nouns.

Proper nouns and words derived from them are capitalized; common nouns are not. Proper nouns name specific persons, places, and things. All other nouns are common nouns. The following types of words are usually capitalized: names of deities, religions, religious followers, sacred books; words of family relationship used as names; particular places; nationalities and their languages, races, tribes; educational institutions, departments, particular courses; government departments, organizations, political parties; historical movements, periods, events, documents; and trade names.

PROPER NOUNS	COMMON NOUNS
God (used as a name)	a god
Uncle Pedro	my uncle
Father (used as a name)	my father
Lake Superior	a picturesque lake
the South	a southern state
University of Wisconsin	a state university
the Democratic Party	a political party
the Enlightenment	the eighteenth century
Advil	a painkiller

Months, holidays, and days of the week are capitalized: *May, Labor Day, Monday.* The seasons and numbers of the days of the month are not: *summer, the fifth of June.*

EXCEPTION: Capitalize Fourth of July (or July Fourth) when referring to the holiday.

Names of school subjects are capitalized only if they are names of languages: *English, French.* Names of particular courses are capitalized: *Geology 101, Principles of Economics.*

39b Capitalize titles of persons when used as part of a proper name but usually not when used alone.

District Attorney Marshall was ruled out of order.

The district attorney was elected for a two-year term.

Usage varies when the title of an important public figure is used alone: *The president* [or *President*] *vetoed the bill.*

39c Follow conventions for capitalizing titles.

In titles and subtitles found in the text of a paper, all major words—nouns, pronouns, verbs, adjectives, and adverbs—should be capitalized. Minor words—articles, prepositions, and coordinating conjunctions—are not capitalized unless they are the first or last word of a title or subtitle. (In APA style, capitalize all words of four or more letters. See 53a.)

> *The Impossible Theater: A Manifesto*
> *A River Runs through It*
> "I Want to Hold Your Hand"

Titles of works are handled differently in the APA reference list. See "Preparing the list of references" in 53a.

39d Capitalize the first word of a sentence or quoted sentence.

The first word of a sentence should be capitalized. Also capitalize the first word of a quoted sentence within a sentence, but not a quoted phrase.

> Loveless writes, "If failing schools are ever to be turned around, much more must be learned about how schools age as institutions" (25).

> Russell Baker has written that in this country, sports are "the opiate of the masses" (46).

If a quoted sentence is interrupted by explanatory words, do not capitalize the first word after the interruption. (See also 34d.)

> "If you want to go out," he said, "tell me now."

When a sentence appears within parentheses, capitalize the first word unless the parentheses appear within another sentence.

> Early detection of breast cancer increases survival rates. (See table 2.)

> Early detection of breast cancer increases survival rates (see table 2).

39e Know your options when the first word after a colon begins an independent clause.

When a group of words following a colon can stand on its own as a complete sentence, MLA recommends using lowercase for the first word (see 51a) whereas APA calls for capitalizing it (see 53a).

> Clinical trials revealed problems: a high percentage of participants reported severe headaches.

> Clinical trials revealed problems: A high percentage of participants reported severe headaches.

Always use lowercase for a list or an appositive that follows a colon (see 32e).

> Students were divided into two groups: residents and commuters.

EXERCISE 39–1   Edit the following sentences to correct errors in capitalization. If a sentence is correct, write "correct" after it. Answers appear in the back of the book.

> On our trip to the West, we visited the ̶g̶rand ̶canyon and
> the ̶great ̶salt ̶desert.

a. Assistant dean Shirin Ahmadi recommended offering more world language courses.

b. We went to the Mark Taper Forum to see a production of *Angels in America*.

c. Kalindi has an ambitious semester, studying differential calculus, classical hebrew, brochure design, and greek literature.

d. Lydia's Aunt and Uncle make modular houses as beautiful as modernist works of art.

e. We amused ourselves on the long flight by discussing how Spring in Kyoto stacks up against Summer in London.

PART 8

Grammar Basics

40 Parts of speech

Traditional grammar recognizes eight parts of speech: noun, pronoun, verb, adjective, adverb, preposition, conjunction, and interjection. Many words can function as more than one part of speech. For example, the word *paint* can be a noun (*The paint is wet*) or a verb (*Please paint the ceiling next*).

40a Nouns

A noun is the name of a person, place, thing, or concept.

>   N   N   N
> The *lion* in the *cage* growled at the *zookeeper*.

Nouns sometimes function as adjectives modifying other nouns. Because of their dual role, nouns used in this manner may be called *noun/adjectives*.

>   N/ADJ   N/ADJ
> The *leather* notebook was tucked in the *student's* backpack.

40b Pronouns

A pronoun is a word used in place of a noun. Usually the pronoun substitutes for a specific noun, known as its *antecedent*.

>   ANT   PN
> When the *battery* wears down, we recharge *it*.

Although most pronouns function as substitutes for nouns, some can function as adjectives modifying nouns. Such pronouns may be called *pronoun/adjectives*.

> PN/ADJ
> *That* bird was at the same window yesterday morning.

Pronouns are classified in the following ways.

Personal pronouns Personal pronouns refer to specific persons or things. They always function as substitutes for nouns.

Singular: I, me, you, she, her, he, him, it

Plural: we, us, you, they, them

Possessive pronouns Possessive pronouns indicate ownership.

Singular: my, mine, your, yours, her, hers, his, its
Plural: our, ours, your, yours, their, theirs

Some of these possessive pronouns function as adjectives modifying nouns: *my, your, his, her, its, our, their.*

Intensive and reflexive pronouns Intensive pronouns emphasize a noun or another pronoun (The senator *herself* met us at the door). Reflexive pronouns name a receiver of an action identical with the doer of the action (Paula cut *herself*).

Singular: myself, yourself, himself, herself, itself
Plural: ourselves, yourselves, themselves

Relative pronouns Relative pronouns introduce subordinate clauses functioning as adjectives (The writer *who won the award* refused to accept it). The relative pronoun, in this case *who*, also points back to a noun or pronoun that the clause modifies (*writer*). (See 42e.)

who, whom, whose, which, that

The pronouns *whichever, whoever, whomever, what,* and *whatever* are sometimes considered relative pronouns, but they introduce noun clauses and do not point back to a noun or pronoun. (See "Noun clauses" in 42e.)

Interrogative pronouns Interrogative pronouns introduce questions (*Who* is expected to win the election?).

who, whom, whose, which, what

Demonstrative pronouns   Demonstrative pronouns identify or point to nouns. Frequently they function as adjectives (*This* chair is my favorite), but they may also function as substitutes for nouns (*This* is my favorite chair).

this, that, these, those

Indefinite pronouns   Indefinite pronouns (*anybody, anyone, somebody, someone,* etc.) refer to nonspecific persons or things. Most are always singular (*everyone, each*); some are always plural (*both, many*); a few may be singular or plural (see 22e). Most indefinite pronouns function as substitutes for nouns (*Something* is burning), but some can also function as adjectives (*All* campers must check in at the lodge). For a list of indefinite pronouns, see 22e.

Reciprocal pronouns   Reciprocal pronouns (each other, one another) refer to individual parts of a plural antecedent (By turns, the penguins fed *one another*).

TIP: See also pronoun-antecedent agreement (23), pronoun reference (24), distinguishing between pronouns such as *I* and *me* (25), and distinguishing between *who* and *whom* (26).

40c Verbs

The verb of a sentence usually expresses action (*jump, think*) or being (*is, become*). It is composed of a main verb possibly preceded by one or more helping verbs.

MV
The horses *exercise* every day.

HV   MV
The task force report *was* not *completed* on schedule.

HV HV   MV
No one *has been praised* with more passion than our town manager.

Notice that words, usually adverbs, can intervene between the helping verb and the main verb (was *not* completed). (See 40e.)

Helping verbs

There are twenty-three helping verbs in English: forms of *have*, *do*, and *be*, which may also function as main verbs, and nine modals, which function only as helping verbs. *Have*, *do*, and *be* change form to indicate tense; the nine modals do not.

FORMS OF *HAVE*, *DO*, AND *BE*

have, has, had

do, does, did

be, am, is, are, was, were, being, been

MODALS

can, could, may, might, must, shall, should, will, would

The verb phrase *ought to* is often classified as a modal as well.

Main verbs

The main verb of a sentence is always the kind of word that would change form if put into these test sentences:

BASE FORM	Usually I (*cook*, *drive*).
PAST TENSE	Yesterday I (*cooked*, *drove*).
PAST PARTICIPLE	I have (*cooked*, *driven*) many times before.
PRESENT PARTICIPLE	I am (*cooking*, *driving*) right now.
-S FORM	Usually he/she/it (*cooks*, *drives*).

If a word doesn't change form when slipped into the test sentences, you can be certain that it is not a main verb. For example, the noun *revolution*, though it may seem to suggest action, can never function as a main verb. Try to make it behave like one (*Today I revolution . . . Yesterday I revolutioned . . .*) and you'll see why.

When both the past-tense and the past-participle forms of a verb end in -ed, the verb is regular (*cooked*, *cooked*). Otherwise, the verb is irregular (*drove*, *driven*). (See 28a.)

The verb *be* is highly irregular, having eight forms instead of the usual five: the base form *be*; the present-tense forms *am*, *is*, and *are*; the past-tense forms *was* and *were*; the present participle *being*; and the past participle *been*. Helping verbs combine with main verbs to create tenses.

NOTE: Some verbs are followed by words that look like prepositions but are so closely associated with the verb that they are a part of its meaning. These words are known as *particles*. Common verb-particle combinations include *bring up*, *call off*, *drop off*, *give in*, *look up*, *run into*, and *take off*.

TIP: For more information about using verbs, see these sections of the handbook: active verbs (8), subject-verb agreement (22), Standard English verb forms (28a), verb tense and mood (28f and 28g), and modal verbs (29a).

40d Adjectives

An adjective is a word used to modify, or describe, a noun or pronoun. An adjective usually answers one of these questions: Which one? What kind? How many?

ADJ
the *playful* dog [Which dog?]

ADJ   ADJ
cracked old plates [What kind of plates?]

ADJ
nine months [How many months?]

ADJ
qualified applicants [What kind of applicants?]

Adjectives usually precede the words they modify. They may also follow linking verbs, in which case they describe the subject. (See 41b.)

ADJ
The decision was *unpopular*.

The definite article *the* and the indefinite articles *a* and *an* are also classified as adjectives.

ART   ART   ART
A defendant should be judged on *the* evidence provided to *the* jury.

Some possessive, demonstrative, and indefinite pronouns can function as adjectives: *their, its, this, all* (see 40b). And nouns can function as adjectives when they modify other nouns: *apple pie* (the noun *apple* modifies the noun *pie*; see 40a).

TIP: You can find more details about using adjectives in 27.

40e Adverbs

An adverb is a word used to modify, or qualify, a verb (or verbal), an adjective, or another adverb. It usually answers one of these questions: When? Where? How? Why? Under what conditions? To what degree?

Pull *firmly* on the emergency handle. [Pull how?]

Read the text *first* and *then* complete the exercises. [Read when? Complete when?]

Place the flowers *here*. [Place where?]

Adverbs modifying adjectives or other adverbs usually intensify or limit the intensity of the word they modify.

ADV
Be *extremely* kind, and you will have many friends.

ADV
We proceeded *very* cautiously in the dark house.

The words *not* and *never* are classified as adverbs. A word such as *cannot* contains the helping verb *can* and the adverb *not*. The word *can't* contains the helping verb *can* and a contracted form of *not* (see 33c).

TIP: You can find more details about using adverbs in 27b–27d.

40f Prepositions

A preposition is a word placed before a noun or a pronoun to form a phrase that modifies another word in the sentence. The prepositional phrase functions as an adjective or an adverb.

>   P   P   P
> The winding road *to* the summit travels *past* craters *from* an extinct volcano.

To the summit functions as an adjective modifying the noun *road*; *past craters* functions as an adverb modifying the verb *travels*; *from an extinct volcano* functions as an adjective modifying the noun *craters*. (For more on prepositional phrases, see 42a.)

    English has a limited number of prepositions. The most common are included in the following list.

about	below	from	outside	underneath
above	beside	in	over	unlike
across	besides	inside	past	until
after	between	into	plus	unto
against	beyond	like	round	up
along	but	near	since	upon
among	by	next	than	with
around	despite	of	through	within
as	down	off	throughout	without
at	during	on	to	
before	except	onto	toward	
behind	for	out	under	

Some prepositions are more than one word long. *Along with, as well as, in addition to, next to,* and *rather than* are examples.

40g Conjunctions

Conjunctions join words, phrases, or clauses, and they indicate the relation between the elements joined.

Coordinating conjunctions   A coordinating conjunction is used to connect grammatically equal elements. (See 9b and 14a.) The coordinating conjunctions are *and, but, or, nor, for, so,* and *yet.*

> The sociologist interviewed children *but* not their parents.

> Write clearly, *and* your readers will appreciate your efforts.

In the first sentence, *but* connects two noun phrases; in the second, *and* connects two independent clauses.

Correlative conjunctions   Correlative conjunctions come in pairs; they connect grammatically equal elements.

> either . . . or
>
> neither . . . nor
>
> not only . . . but also
>
> whether . . . or
>
> both . . . and

> *Either* the painting was brilliant *or* it was a forgery.

Subordinating conjunctions   A subordinating conjunction introduces a subordinate clause and indicates the relation of the clause to the rest of the sentence. (See 42e.) The most common subordinating conjunctions are *after, although, as, as if, because, before, if, in order that, once, since, so that, than, that, though, unless, until, when, where, whether,* and *while.*

> *When* the fundraiser ends, we expect to have raised more than half a million dollars.

Conjunctive adverbs   Conjunctive adverbs connect independent clauses and indicate the relation between the clauses. They can be used with a semicolon to join two independent clauses in one sentence, or they can be used alone with an independent clause. The most common conjunctive adverbs are *finally, however, nevertheless, similarly, then, therefore,* and *thus.* (For a complete list, see 32b.)

The photographer failed to take a light reading; *therefore*, all the pictures were underexposed.

During the day, the kitten sleeps peacefully. *However*, when night falls, the kitten is ready to play.

Conjunctive adverbs can appear at the beginning or in the middle of a clause.

When night falls, *however*, the kitten is ready to play.

TIP: The ability to distinguish between conjunctive adverbs and coordinating conjunctions will help you avoid run-on sentences and make punctuation decisions (see 21, 30a, and 30f). The ability to recognize subordinating conjunctions will help you avoid sentence fragments (see 20).

40h Interjections

An interjection is a word used to express surprise or emotion (*Oh! Hey! Wow!*).

EXERCISE 40–1 In the sentences below, identify the part of speech of each underlined word or phrase. Answers appear in the back of the book.

>   Adjective   Adjective   Noun
> **Poor** road conditions cause **most** bicycle **accidents**.

a. **No one** **had seen** a full-length computer-generated film **before** 1995's *Toy Story*.

b. Runners who **sleep** more than eight hours **nightly** will see their **performance** improve.

c. Wolverines are thought to be **in** the wolf family; **however**, **they** are closely related to weasels.

d. **Climate** scientists **can** predict global temperature changes, **but** the research has recently been questioned.

e. **This** building **shakes** **when** a train passes by.

41 Sentence patterns

The vast majority of English sentences conform to one of these five patterns:

> subject/verb/subject complement
>
> subject/verb/direct object
>
> subject/verb/indirect object/direct object
>
> subject/verb/direct object/object complement
>
> subject/verb

Adverbial modifiers (single words, phrases, or clauses) may be added to any of these patterns, and they may appear nearly anywhere — at the beginning, in the middle, or at the end.

Predicate is the grammatical term given to the verb plus its objects, complements, and adverbial modifiers.

41a Subjects

The subject of a sentence names whom or what the sentence is about. The simple subject is always a noun or pronoun; the complete subject consists of the simple subject and any words or word groups modifying the simple subject.

The complete subject

To find the complete subject, ask *Who?* or *What?*, insert the verb, and finish the question. The answer is the complete subject.

┌────── COMPLETE SUBJECT ──────┐
The devastating effects of famine can last for many years.

Who or what can last for many years? *The devastating effects of famine.*

┌─────────── COMPLETE SUBJECT ───────────┐
Adventure novels that contain multiple subplots are often made into
successful movies.

Who or what are often made into movies? *Adventure novels that contain
multiple subplots.*

┌─── COMPLETE ───┐
└─── SUBJECT ───┘
In our program, student teachers work full-time for ten months.

Who or what works full-time for ten months? *Student teachers.* Notice that
In our program, student teachers is not a sensible answer to the question. (It is
not safe to assume that the subject always appears first in a sentence.)

The simple subject

To find the simple subject, strip away all modifiers in the complete subject.
This includes single-word modifiers such as *the* and *devastating*, phrases such
as *of famine*, and subordinate clauses such as *that contain multiple subplots*.

┌ SS ┐
The devastating effects of famine can last for many years.

┌ SS ┐
Adventure novels that contain multiple subplots are often made into
successful movies.

A sentence may have a compound subject containing two or more simple subjects joined with a coordinating conjunction such as *and, but,* or *or.*

┌─── SS ───┐   ┌SS┐
Great commitment and a little luck make a successful actor.

Understood subjects

In imperative sentences, which give advice or issue commands, the subject is understood but not actually present in the sentence. The subject of
an imperative sentence is understood to be *you.*

[*You*] Put your hands on the steering wheel.

Subject after the verb

Although the subject ordinarily comes before the verb (*The planes took off*), occasionally it does not. When a sentence begins with *There is* or *There are* (or *There was* or *There were*), the subject follows the verb. In such inverted constructions, the word *There* is an expletive, an empty word serving merely to get the sentence started.

      ┌ SS ┐
There are *eight planes waiting to take off.*

Occasionally a writer will invert a sentence for effect.

      ┌ SS ┐
Joyful is *the child whose school closes for snow.*

Joyful is an adjective, so it cannot be the subject. Turn this sentence around and its structure becomes obvious.

     ┌ SS ┐
The child whose school closes for snow is joyful.

In questions, the subject frequently appears between the helping verb and the main verb.

HV   ┌── SS ──┐ MV
Do *Kenyan marathoners* train year-round?

TIP: The ability to recognize the subject of a sentence will help you edit for fragments (20), subject-verb agreement (22), and correct use of pronouns such as *I* and *me* (25).

EXERCISE 41–1 In the following sentences, underline the complete subject and write *SS* above the simple subject(s). If the subject is an understood *you*, insert *you* in parentheses. Answers appear in the back of the book.

  ┌ SS ┐   ┌ SS ┐
<u>Parents and their children</u> often look alike.

a. The hills and mountains seemed endless, and the snow atop them glistened.

b. In foil fencing, points are scored by hitting an electronic target.

c. Do not stand in the aisles or sit on the stairs.
d. There were hundreds of fireflies in the open field.
e. The evidence against the defendant was staggering.

41b Verbs, objects, and complements

Section 40c explains how to find the verb of a sentence. A sentence's verb is classified as linking, transitive, or intransitive, depending on the kinds of objects or complements the verb can (or cannot) take.

Linking verbs and subject complements

Linking verbs connect the subject to a subject complement, a word or word group that completes the meaning of the subject by renaming or describing it.

If the subject complement renames the subject, it is a noun or noun equivalent (sometimes called a *predicate noun*).

```
                     — S —                    ┐┌ V ┐┌ SC ┐
A phone call requesting personal information may be a scam.
```

If the subject complement describes the subject, it is an adjective or adjective equivalent (sometimes called a *predicate adjective*).

```
        — S —          ┐ V    SC
Last month's temperatures were mild.
```

Whenever they appear as main verbs (rather than helping verbs), the forms of *be*—*be, am, is, are, was, were, being, been*—usually function as linking verbs. In the preceding examples, for instance, the main verbs are *be* and *were*.

Verbs such as *appear, become, feel, grow, look, make, seem, smell, sound,* and *taste* are linking when they are followed by a word or word group that renames or describes the subject.

```
        ┌ S ┐┌ V ┐      SC
As it thickens, the sauce will look unappealing.
```

Transitive verbs and direct objects

A transitive verb takes a direct object, a word or word group that names a receiver of the action.

```
        ┌─── S ────┐   V   ┌─────── DO ───────┐
        The hungry cat clawed the bag of dry food.
```

The simple direct object is always a noun or pronoun, in this case *bag.* To find it, simply strip away all modifiers.

Transitive verbs usually appear in the active voice, with the subject doing the action and a direct object receiving the action. Active-voice sentences can be transformed into passive, with the subject receiving the action. (See 8a.)

Transitive verbs, indirect objects, and direct objects

The direct object of a transitive verb is sometimes preceded by an indirect object, a noun or pronoun telling to whom or for whom the action of the sentence is done.

```
     S   V  IO ┌─ DO ─┐      S ┌─ V ─┐ IO ┌DO┐
     You give her some yarn, and she will knit you a scarf.
```

The simple indirect object is always a noun or pronoun. To test for an indirect object, insert the word *to* or *for* before the word or word group in question. If the sentence makes sense, the word or word group is an indirect object.

You give [to] *her* some yarn, and she will knit [for] *you* a scarf.

An indirect object may be turned into a prepositional phrase using *to* or *for: You give some yarn to her, and she will knit a scarf for you.*

Only certain transitive verbs take indirect objects. Some examples are *ask, bring, find, get, give, hand, lend, make, offer, pay, promise, read, send, show, teach, tell, throw,* and *write.*

Transitive verbs, direct objects, and object complements

The direct object of a transitive verb is sometimes followed by an object complement, a word or word group that renames or describes the object.

> ```
>       S              V        DO   ┌──── OC ────┐
> ```
> People often consider chivalry a thing of the past.

> ```
> ┌─ S ─┐   V      DO  ┌──── OC ────┐
> ```
> The kiln makes clay firm and strong.

When the object complement renames the direct object, it is a noun or pronoun (such as *thing*). When it describes the direct object, it is an adjective (such as *firm* and *strong*).

Intransitive verbs

Intransitive verbs take no objects or complements.

> ```
> ┌──── S ────┐    V
> ```
> The audience laughed.

> ```
> ┌──── S ────┐    V
> ```
> The driver accelerated in the straightaway.

Nothing receives the actions of laughing and accelerating in these sentences, so the verbs are intransitive. Notice that such verbs may or may not be followed by adverbial modifiers. In the second sentence, *in the straightaway* is an adverbial prepositional phrase modifying *accelerated*.

NOTE: The dictionary will tell you whether a verb is transitive or intransitive. Some verbs can be both transitive and intransitive.

TRANSITIVE	Sandra *flew* her small plane over the canyon.
INTRANSITIVE	A flock of migrating geese *flew* overhead.

In the first example, *flew* has a direct object that receives the action: *her small plane*. In the second example, the verb is followed by an adverb (*overhead*), not by a direct object.

42 Subordinate word groups

Subordinate word groups include phrases and clauses. Phrases are subordinate because they lack a subject and a verb; they are classified as prepositional, verbal, appositive, and absolute (see 42a–42d). Subordinate clauses have a subject and a verb, but they begin with a word (such as *although*, *that*, or *when*) that marks them as subordinate (see 42e).

42a Prepositional phrases

A prepositional phrase begins with a preposition such as *at, by, for, from, in, of, on, to,* or *with* (see 40f) and usually ends with a noun or noun equivalent: *on the table, for him, by sleeping late.* The noun or noun equivalent is known as the *object of the preposition.*

Prepositional phrases function as adjectives or as adverbs. As an adjective, a prepositional phrase nearly always appears immediately following the noun or pronoun it modifies.

The hut had *walls of mud.*

Adjective phrases usually answer one or both of the questions *Which one?* and *What kind?* If we ask *Which walls?* or *What kind of walls?* we get a sensible answer: *walls of mud.*

Adverbial prepositional phrases usually modify the verb, but they can also modify adjectives or other adverbs. When a prepositional phrase modifies the verb, it can appear nearly anywhere in a sentence.

James *walked* his dog *on a leash.*

Sabrina *will in time adjust* to life in Ecuador.

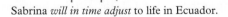

During a mudslide, the terrain *can change* drastically.

If a prepositional phrase is movable, you can be certain that it is adverbial.

> *In the cave*, the explorers found well-preserved prehistoric drawings.

> The explorers found well-preserved prehistoric drawings *in the cave*.

Adverbial word groups usually answer one of these questions: When? Where? How? Why? Under what conditions? To what degree?

> James walked his dog *how? On a leash.*

> Sabrina will adjust to life in Ecuador *when? In time.*

> The terrain can change drastically *under what conditions? During a mudslide.*

In questions and subordinate clauses, a preposition may appear after its object.

> *What* are you afraid *of?*

> We avoided the bike trail *that* John had warned us *about.*

42b Verbal phrases

A verbal is a verb form that does not function as the verb of a clause. Verbals include infinitives (the word *to* plus the base form of the verb), present participles (the *-ing* form of the verb), and past participles (the verb form usually ending in *-d, -ed, -n, -en,* or *-t*). (See 28a and 40c.)

INFINITIVE	PRESENT PARTICIPLE	PAST PARTICIPLE
to dream	dreaming	dreamed
to choose	choosing	chosen
to build	building	built
to grow	growing	grown

Instead of functioning as the verb of a clause, a verbal functions as an adjective, a noun, or an adverb.

ADJECTIVE   *Broken* promises cannot be fixed.

NOUN   Constant *complaining* becomes wearisome.

ADVERB   Can you wait *to celebrate*?

Verbals with objects, complements, or modifiers form verbal phrases.

In my family, *singing loudly* is more appreciated than *singing well*.

Governments exist *to protect the rights of minorities*.

Like verbals, verbal phrases function as adjectives, nouns, or adverbs. Verbal phrases are ordinarily classified as participial, gerund, and infinitive.

Participial phrases

Participial phrases always function as adjectives. Their verbals are either present participles (such as *dreaming, asking*) or past participles (such as *stolen, reached*).

Participial phrases frequently appear immediately following the noun or pronoun they modify.

Congress shall make no *law abridging the freedom of speech or of the press*.

Participial phrases are often movable. They may precede the word they modify.

Being a weight-bearing joint, the *knee* is among the most frequently injured.

They may also appear at some distance from the word they modify.

Last night we saw a *play* that affected us deeply, *written with profound insight into the lives of immigrants*.

Gerund phrases

Gerund phrases are built around present participles (verb forms that end in *-ing*), and they always function as nouns: usually as subjects, subject complements, direct objects, or objects of a preposition.

┌──── S ────┐
Rationalizing a fear can eliminate it.

┌──────── SC ────────┐
The key to good sauce is browning the mushrooms.

┌──── DO ────┐
Lizards usually enjoy sunning themselves.

The American Heart Association has documented the benefits of diet

┌──────── OBJ OF PREP ────────┐
and exercise in reducing the risk of heart attack.

Infinitive phrases

Infinitive phrases, usually constructed around *to* plus the base form of the verb (*to call*, *to drink*), can function as nouns, as adjectives, or as adverbs. When functioning as a noun, an infinitive phrase may appear in almost any noun slot in a sentence, usually as a subject, subject complement, or direct object.

┌──────── S ────────┐
To live without health insurance is risky.

┌──────────── DO ────────────┐
The orchestra wanted to make its premier season memorable.

Infinitive phrases functioning as adjectives usually appear immediately following the noun or pronoun they modify.

The Nineteenth Amendment gave women the *right to vote*.

The infinitive phrase modifies the noun *right*. Which right? *The right to vote*.

Adverbial infinitive phrases usually qualify the meaning of the verb, telling when, where, how, why, under what conditions, or to what degree an action occurred.

Volunteers *rolled up* their pants *to wade through the flood waters.*

NOTE: In some constructions, the infinitive is unmarked; that is, the *to* does not appear.

Graphs and charts can help researchers [*to*] *present complex data.*

42c Appositive phrases

Appositive phrases describe nouns or pronouns. Instead of modifying nouns or pronouns, however, appositive phrases rename them. In form they are nouns or noun equivalents.

Bloggers, *conversationalists at heart,* are the online equivalent of radio talk show hosts.

Appositives are said to be "in apposition to" the nouns or pronouns they rename. *Conversationalists at heart* is in apposition to the noun *Bloggers.*

42d Absolute phrases

An absolute phrase modifies a whole clause or sentence, not just one word. It consists of a noun or noun equivalent usually followed by a participial phrase.

Her words reverberating in the hushed arena, the senator urged the crowd to support her former opponent.

42e Subordinate clauses

Subordinate clauses are patterned like sentences, having subjects and verbs and sometimes objects or complements. But they function within sentences as adjectives, adverbs, or nouns. They cannot stand alone as complete sentences.

A subordinate clause usually begins with a subordinating conjunction or a relative pronoun. The chart on page 249 classifies these words according to the kinds of clauses (adjective, adverb, or noun) they introduce.

Adjective clauses

Adjective clauses modify nouns or pronouns, usually answering the question *Which one?* or *What kind?* Most adjective clauses begin with a relative pronoun (*who, whom, whose, which,* or *that*). In addition to introducing the clause, the relative pronoun points back to the noun that the clause modifies.

The coach chose *players who would benefit from intense drills.*

A *book that goes unread* is a writer's worst nightmare.

Relative pronouns are sometimes "understood."

The things [*that*] *we cherish most* are the things [*that*] *we might lose.*

Occasionally an adjective clause is introduced by a relative adverb, usually *when, where,* or *why.*

The aging actor returned to the *stage where he had made his debut as Hamlet half a century earlier.*

The parts of an adjective clause are often arranged as in sentences (subject/verb/object or complement).

$$\text{S} \quad \text{V} \quad \text{DO}$$
Sometimes it is our closest friends who disappoint us.

Frequently, however, the object or complement appears first, out of the normal order of subject/verb/object.

$$\text{DO} \quad \text{S} \quad \text{V}$$
They can be the very friends whom we disappoint.

Words that introduce subordinate clauses

Words introducing adjective clauses

Relative pronouns: that, which, who, whom, whose
Relative adverbs: when, where, why

Words introducing adverb clauses

Subordinating conjunctions: after, although, as, as if, because, before, even though, if, in order that, once, since, so that, than, that, though, unless, until, when, where, whether, while

Words introducing noun clauses

Relative pronouns: which, who, whom, whose
Other pronouns: what, whatever, whichever, whoever, whomever
Other subordinating words: how, if, that, when, whenever, where, wherever, whether, why

---

TIP: For punctuation of adjective clauses, see 30e.

Adverb clauses

Adverb clauses modify verbs, adjectives, or other adverbs, usually answering one of these questions: When? Where? Why? How? Under what conditions? To what degree? They always begin with a subordinating conjunction (such as *after, although, because, that, though, unless,* or *when*). (For a complete list, see the chart above.)

When the sun went down, the hikers *prepared* their camp.

Adverb clauses are usually movable when they modify a verb. In the preceding example, for instance, the adverb clause can be moved without affecting the meaning of the sentence.

The hikers prepared their camp *when the sun went down.*

When an adverb clause modifies an adjective or an adverb, it is not movable; it must appear next to the word it modifies. In the following examples, the *when* clause modifies the adjective *Uncertain,* and the *than* clause modifies the adverb *better.*

Uncertain *when the baby would be born,* Ray and Leah stayed close to home.

Jackie can dance better *than I can walk.*

Noun clauses

A noun clause functions just like a single-word noun, usually as a subject, a subject complement, a direct object, or an object of a preposition. It usually begins with one of the following words: *how, if, that, what, whatever, when, whenever, where, wherever, whether, which, whichever, who, whoever, whom, whomever, whose, why.*

  ┌──────── S ─────────┐
Whoever leaves the house last must double-lock the door.

        ┌──────────── DO ─────────────┐
Copernicus argued that the sun is the center of the universe.

The subordinating word introducing the clause may or may not play a significant role in the clause. In the preceding examples, *Whoever* is the subject of its clause, but *that* does not perform a function in its clause.

As with adjective clauses, the parts of a noun clause may appear in normal order (subject/verb/object or complement) or out of their normal order.

      S   V ┌─ DO ─┐
Loyalty is what keeps a friendship strong.

        DO   S V
New Mexico is where we live.

EXERCISE 42–1 Underline the subordinate clauses in the following sentences. Tell whether each clause is an adjective clause, an adverb clause, or a noun clause and how it is used in the sentence. Answers appear in the back of the book.

Show the committee the latest draft <u>before you print the final report.</u>

(Adverb clause modifying "Show")

a. The city's electoral commission adjusted the voting process so that every vote would count.

b. A marketing campaign that targets baby boomers may not appeal to young professionals.

c. After the Tambora volcano erupted in the southern Pacific in 1815, no one realized that it would contribute to the "year without a summer" in Europe and North America.

d. The concept of peak oil implies that at a certain point there will be no more oil to extract from the earth.

e. Details are easily overlooked when you are rushing.

43 Sentence types

Sentences are classified in two ways: according to their structure (simple, compound, complex, and compound-complex) and according to their purpose (declarative, imperative, interrogative, and exclamatory).

43a Sentence structures

Depending on the number and the types of clauses they contain, sentences are classified as simple, compound, complex, or compound-complex.

Clauses come in two varieties: independent and subordinate. An independent clause contains a subject and a predicate, and it either stands alone or could stand alone as a sentence. A subordinate clause also contains a subject and a predicate, but it functions within a sentence as an adjective, an adverb, or a noun; it cannot stand alone. (See 42e.)

Simple sentences

A simple sentence is one independent clause with no subordinate clauses.

┌──────────────── INDEPENDENT CLAUSE ────────────────┐
Without a passport, Eva could not visit her grandparents in Hungary.

A simple sentence may contain compound elements—a compound subject, verb, or object, for example—but it does not contain more than one full sentence pattern. The following sentence is simple because its two verbs (*comes in* and *goes out*) share a subject (*Spring*).

┌──────────── INDEPENDENT CLAUSE ────────────┐
Spring comes in like a lion and goes out like a lamb.

Compound sentences

A compound sentence is composed of two or more independent clauses with no subordinate clauses. The independent clauses are usually joined with a comma and a coordinating conjunction (*and, but, or, nor, for, so, yet*) or with a semicolon. (See 14a.)

      INDEPENDENT   INDEPENDENT
┌──── CLAUSE ────┐   ┌──────── CLAUSE ────────┐
The car broke down, but a rescue van arrived within minutes.

┌──── INDEPENDENT CLAUSE ────┐ ┌ INDEPENDENT CLAUSE ┐
A shark was spotted near shore; people left immediately.

Complex sentences

A complex sentence is composed of one independent clause with one or more subordinate clauses. (See 42e.)

                          SUBORDINATE
                     ┌──── CLAUSE ────┐
ADJECTIVE   The pitcher who won the game is a rookie.

                     SUBORDINATE
                ┌── CLAUSE ──┐
ADVERB   If you leave late, take a cab home.

                     SUBORDINATE
                ┌──── CLAUSE ────┐
NOUN   What matters most to us is a quick commute.

Compound-complex sentences

A compound-complex sentence contains at least two independent clauses and at least one subordinate clause. The following sentence contains two independent clauses, each of which contains a subordinate clause.

```
┌── INDEPENDENT CLAUSE ──┐      ┌── INDEPENDENT CLAUSE
         ┌── SUB CL ──┐                               ┌──
Tell the doctor how you feel, and she will decide whether
──────────────────────────┐
──── SUB CL ────┐
you can go home.
```

43b Sentence purposes

Writers use declarative sentences to make statements, imperative sentences to issue requests or commands, interrogative sentences to ask questions, and exclamatory sentences to make exclamations.

DECLARATIVE	The echo sounded in our ears.
IMPERATIVE	Love your neighbor.
INTERROGATIVE	Did the better team win tonight?
EXCLAMATORY	We're here to save you!

EXERCISE 43–1 Identify the following sentences as simple, compound, complex, or compound-complex. Identify the subordinate clauses and classify them according to their function: adjective, adverb, or noun. (See 42e.) Answers appear in the back of the book.

The deli in Courthouse Square was crowded with lawyers at lunchtime.

(Simple)

a. Fires that are ignited in dry areas spread especially quickly.
b. The early Incas were advanced; they used a calendar and developed a decimal system.
c. Elaine's jacket was too thin to block the wintry air.
d. Before we leave for the station, we always check the Amtrak website.
e. Decide when you want to leave, and I will be there to pick you up.

PART 9

Researched Writing

44 Thinking like a researcher; gathering sources

A college research assignment asks you to pose questions worth exploring, read widely in search of possible answers, interpret what you read, draw reasoned conclusions, and support those conclusions with evidence. In short, it asks you to enter a research conversation by being *in* conversation with other writers and thinkers who have explored and studied your topic. As you listen to and learn from the voices already in the conversation, you'll find entry points where you can add your own insights and ideas.

44a Manage the project.

When you begin a research project, you will need to understand the assignment, choose a direction, and ask questions about your topic. The following tips will help you manage the beginning phase of research.

Managing time

When you receive your assignment, set a realistic schedule of deadlines. Think about how much time you might need for each step of your project. One student created a calendar to map out her tasks for a research paper, keeping in mind that some tasks might overlap or need to be repeated.

Sample calendar for a research assignment

2	3	4	5	6	7	8
	Receive and analyze the assignment.	Pose questions you might explore. ⟶	Talk with a reference librarian; plan a ⟶ search strategy.	Start research log.	Settle on a topic; narrow the focus.	Revise research questions. Locate sources. ⟶
9	**10**	**11**	**12**	**13**	**14**	**15**
Read, take notes, and ⟶ compile a working bibliography.				Draft a working thesis and an outline.	Draft the paper. ⟶	
16	**17**	**18**	**19**	**20**	**21**	**22**
⟶ Draft the paper. ⟶			Visit the writing center for feedback.	Do additional ⟶ research if needed.		
23	**24**	**25**	**26**	**27**	**28**	**29**
Ask peers for feedback. Revise the paper; ⟶ if necessary, revise the thesis.				Prepare a list of ⟶ works cited.		Proof-read the final draft. ⟶
30	**31**					
Proof-read the final draft. ⟶	Submit the final draft.					

Getting the big picture

As you consider a possible research topic, take time to read a few sources. Ask yourself questions such as these:

- What aspects of the topic are generating the most debate?
- Why and how are people disagreeing?
- Which approaches seem worth exploring?

44b Pose questions worth exploring.

Every research project starts with questions. Try using the journalist's questions — *Who? What? When? Where? Why?* and *How?* — to form research questions for your project.

- **How** can nutritional labels be redesigned so that they inform rather than confuse consumers?

- **Why** are boys diagnosed with attention deficit disorder more often than girls are?

- **What** happens to the arts without public funding?

Choosing a focused question

If your initial question is too broad given the length of the paper you plan to write, look for ways to narrow and focus your question.

TOO BROAD	FOCUSED
What are the benefits of higher tariffs on imported cars?	How will higher tariffs on imported cars create new auto industry jobs and make US carmakers more profitable?

Choosing a debatable question

Your research paper will be more interesting to both you and your audience if you ask a question that yields more than a statement of fact and that engages readers in a debate.

TOO FACTUAL	DEBATABLE
What percentage of state police departments use body cameras?	How has the widespread use of body cameras changed encounters between officers and civilians?

Choosing a question grounded in evidence

For most college courses, the central argument of a research paper should be grounded in evidence, not in personal preferences or opinions.

TOO DEPENDENT ON PERSONAL OPINION	GROUNDED IN EVIDENCE
Do medical scientists have the right to experiment on animals?	How have technical breakthroughs made medical experiments on animals increasingly unnecessary?

Writing for an audience

In developing your research question, follow your curiosity, but keep in mind how you'll engage readers, too. A good strategy is to ask a debatable question that puts you in the middle of a research conversation that both you and your audience care about. You can test how engaging your question is by trying to articulate possible ways you might answer it. If you can think of only one answer, chances are that your audience's engagement level will be low. Show your readers why the question needs to be asked and why the answer matters to them.

Testing a research question

Before you dive too deep in your search for sources, test your research question by asking the following questions. Strive for a research question that allows you to answer *yes* in all cases.

- Does the question allow you to enter into a research conversation that you care about?
- Can you show your audience why the question needs to be asked and why the answer matters?
- Is the question flexible enough to allow for many possible answers?
- Is the question focused, debatable, and grounded?

Enter a research conversation

A college research project asks you to be in conversation with writers and researchers who have studied your topic—responding to their ideas and arguments and contributing your own insights to move the conversation forward. As you ask preliminary research questions, you may wonder where and how to step into a research conversation.

1 **Identify the experts and ideas in the conversation.** Ask: Who are the major writers and most influential people researching your topic? What are their credentials? What positions have they taken? How and why do the experts disagree?

2 **Identify any gaps in the conversation.** What is missing? Where are the gaps in the existing research? What questions haven't been asked yet? What positions need to be challenged?

3 **Try using a sentence guide,** which acts as a fill-in sentence starter to help you find a point of entry. (See page 300 for more sentence guides.)

- *On one side of the debate is position X. On the other side is Y, but there is a middle position.*

- *The conventional view about the problem needs to be challenged because _____.*

- *Key details in this debate that have been overlooked are _____.*

- *Researchers have drawn conclusion X from the evidence, but one could also draw conclusion Y.*

44c Map out a search strategy.

Before you search for sources, think about what kinds of sources might be appropriate for your project. Considering the kinds of sources you need will help you develop a search strategy — a systematic plan for locating sources.

No single search strategy works for every topic. For some topics, it may be useful to search for information in newspapers, government publications, and websites. For others, the best sources might be scholarly journals, books, research reports, and specialized reference works. Still other topics might be enhanced by field research — interviews, surveys, or observation.

With the help of a librarian, the two students whose research essays appear in this handbook each constructed a search strategy appropriate for her research question.

Researcher Sophie Harba (Full paper: 51b)

Research question Should the government enact laws to regulate healthy eating choices?

Search strategy

- Search the web to locate current news, government publications, and information from organizations that focus on government regulation of food

- Check a library database for current peer-reviewed research articles

- Use the library catalog to search for a recently published book that was cited by a source

Researcher   April Wang (Full paper: 52b)

Research question   How can technology facilitate a shift to student-centered learning?

Search strategy

- Search Google Scholar and *CQ Researcher* to see which aspects of the question are generating debate

- View a TED talk to deepen understanding of education technology

- Use specialized databases related to education and technology to search for studies and articles

---

Distinguishing between primary and secondary sources

As you search for sources, determine whether you are looking at a primary or a secondary source. **Primary sources** include original documents such as letters, diaries, films, legislative bills, laboratory studies, field research reports, speeches, and eyewitness accounts. **Secondary sources** are commentaries on primary sources—another writer's opinions about or interpretation of a primary source. Although a primary source is not necessarily more reliable than a secondary source, it has the advantage of being a firsthand account. You can better evaluate what a secondary source says if you have read any primary sources it discusses.

44d Search efficiently; master a few shortcuts to finding good sources.

You can save yourself time by becoming an efficient searcher of library databases and the web.

Using the library

The website hosted by your college library links to databases and other references containing articles, studies, and reports written by key researchers. Use your library's resources, designed for academic researchers, to find the most authoritative sources for your project.

Using bibliographies and citations as shortcuts

Scholarly books and articles list the works the author has cited, usually at the end. These lists are useful shortcuts to additional reliable sources on your topic. Following the trail of citations may lead you to helpful sources by those experts or the organizations they represent.

Using the web

When conducting searches, use terms that are as specific as possible. The keywords you use will determine the quality of the results you see. You can refine your search by date or domain. Use clues in what you find (such as websites of organizations or government agencies that seem informative) to refine your search.

44e Write a research proposal.

One effective way to manage your project and focus your thinking is to write a research proposal. A proposal gives you an opportunity to look back—to remind yourself why you chose your topic—and to look forward—to predict any difficulties or obstacles that might arise during your project.

The following questions will help you organize your proposal.

- **Research question.** What question will you be exploring? Why does this question need to be asked? What do you hope to learn from the project?

- **Research conversation.** What have you learned so far about the debate or specific research conversation you will enter? What entry point have you found to offer your own insights and ideas?

- **Search strategy.** What kinds of sources will you use to explore your question? What sources will be most useful, and why? How will you locate a variety of sources (primary/secondary, textual/visual)?

- **Research challenges.** What challenges, if any, do you anticipate (locating sufficient sources, managing the project, finding a position to take)? What resources are available to help you meet these challenges?

44f Conduct field research, if appropriate.

Your own field research can enhance or be the focus of a writing project. For a composition class, for example, you might interview a local politician about a current issue, such as the initiation of a city bike-share program. For a sociology class, you might conduct a survey regarding campus trends in community service.

NOTE: Colleges and universities often require researchers to submit projects to an institutional review board (IRB) if the research involves human subjects outside a classroom setting. Before administering a survey or conducting other fieldwork, check with your instructor to see if IRB approval is required.

Interviewing

Interviews can often shed new light on a topic. Look for an expert who has firsthand knowledge of the subject, or seek out a key participant whose personal experience will provide a valuable perspective on your topic. Ask open questions that lead to facts, anecdotes, and vivid details that will add a meaningful dimension to your paper.

USING SOURCES RESPONSIBLY: When quoting your source (the interviewee), be accurate and fair. Do not change the meaning of your interviewee's words or take them out of context.

Go beyond a Google search

You might start with Google to gain an overview of your topic, but relying on the popular search engine to choose your sources isn't a research strategy. Good research involves going beyond the information available from a quick Google search. To locate reliable, authoritative sources, be strategic about *how* and *where* to search.

1 **Familiarize yourself with the research conversation.** Identify the current debate about the topic you have chosen and the most influential writers and experts in the debate. Where is the research conversation happening? In scholarly sources? Government agencies? The popular media?

2 **Generate keywords to focus your search.** Use specific words and combinations to search. Add words such as *debate, disagreements, proponents*, or *opponents* to track down the various positions in the research conversation. Use a journalist's questions—*Who? What? When? Where? Why? How?*—to refine a search.

3 **Search discipline-specific databases available through your school library** to locate carefully chosen scholarly (peer-reviewed) content that doesn't appear in search results on the open web. Use databases such as JSTOR and Academic Search Premier, designed for academic researchers, to locate sources in the most influential publications.

4 **If your topic has been in the news, try *CQ Researcher***, available through most college libraries. Its brief articles provide pro/con arguments on current controversies in criminal justice, law, environment, technology, health, and education.

5 **Explore the Pew Research Center** (pewresearch.org), which sponsors original research and nonpartisan discussions of findings and trends in a wide range of academic fields.

Conducting a survey

For some topics, you may find it useful to survey opinions or practices through a written questionnaire, a phone or email poll, or questions posted on a social media site. Many people resist long questionnaires, so for a good response rate, limit your questions with your purpose in mind.

Surveys with yes/no questions or multiple-choice options can be completed quickly, and the results are easy to tally, but you may also want to ask a few open-ended questions to invite more individual responses.

45 Managing information; taking notes responsibly

An effective researcher is a good record keeper. Whether you decide to keep records on paper or on a computer or mobile device, you will need methods for managing information: maintaining a working bibliography (see 45a), keeping track of source materials (see 45b), and taking notes without plagiarizing your sources (see 45c).

45a Maintain a working bibliography.

Keep a record of sources you read or view. This record, called a *working bibliography*, will help you keep track of publication information for the sources you might use so that you can easily refer to them as you write and compile a list of works cited. The format of this list will depend on the documentation style you are using (for MLA style, see 51a; for APA style, see 53a). (See 46e for advice on using your working bibliography as the basis for an annotated bibliography.)

Information to collect for a working bibliography

For an article

- All authors of the article
- Title and subtitle of the article
- Title of the journal, magazine, or newspaper
- Date; volume, issue, and page numbers
- Date you accessed the source (for an online source that lists no publication date)

For an article retrieved from a database (in addition to the preceding information)

- Name of the database
- Accession number or other number assigned by the database
- Digital object identifier (DOI), if there is one
- URL of the database home page or of the journal's home page, if there is no DOI

For a web source (including video, audio, and multimedia)

- All authors, editors, or composers of the source
- Title and subtitle of the source
- Title of the longer work, if the source is contained in a longer work
- Title of the website
- Print publication information for the source, if available
- Online page or paragraph numbers, if the source provides them
- Date of online publication or latest update
- Sponsor or publisher of the site
- Date you accessed the source (for an undated source)
- URL or permalink for the page on which the source appears

→

INFORMATION TO COLLECT FOR A WORKING BIBLIOGRAPHY (*cont.*)

For an entire book

- All authors; any editors or translators
- Title and subtitle
- Edition, if not the first
- Publisher and date

45b Keep track of source materials.

Save a copy of each potential source as you conduct your research. Many database services will allow you to email, text, save, or print citations or full texts, and you can easily download, copy, or take screen shots of information from the web.

Working with photocopies, printouts, or files—as opposed to relying on memory or hastily written notes—lets you annotate the source as you read. You also reduce the chances of unintentional plagiarism since you will be able to compare your use of a source in your paper with the actual source, not just with your notes.

45c As you take notes, avoid unintentional plagiarism.

Plagiarism, using someone's words or ideas without giving credit, is often accidental. After spending so much time thinking through your topic and reading sources, it's easy to forget where a helpful idea came from or that the idea wasn't yours to begin with. Even if you half-copy an author's sentences—either by mixing the author's phrases with your own without using quotation marks or by plugging your synonyms into the author's sentence structure—you are plagiarizing.

Take notes responsibly

1 **Understand the ideas in the source.** Ask: What is the argument? What is the evidence? Present the source in your own words, rather than repeating the author.

2 **Keep the source close by to check for accuracy,** but resist the temptation to look at the source as you take notes—except when you are quoting.

3 **Use quotation marks around any borrowed words or phrases.** Copy the words exactly and keep complete bibliographic information for each source.

4 **Use labels** to indicate a *summary* of the text or its data or a *paraphrase* of the author's words. (See 48d.)

5 **Develop a system** to distinguish your insights and ideas from those of the source. Some researchers use a color-coding system.

Summarizing and paraphrasing ideas and quoting exact language are three ways of taking notes without unintentionally plagiarizing.

- **Summarizing:** A summary, written in your own words, condenses information and captures main ideas, reducing a chapter to a short paragraph or a paragraph to a single sentence.

- **Paraphrasing:** Like a summary, a paraphrase is written in your own words, but it restates information in roughly the same number of words as the original source, using different sentence structure.

- **Quoting:** A quotation consists of the exact words from a source. Put all quoted material in quotation marks.

When summarizing and paraphrasing, start by determining the purpose and meaning of the source. Focus on the overall ideas in the source rather than the individual words.

Make sure that any summary, paraphrase, or quotation in your notes includes information about where the words and ideas came from so that you can easily integrate and document the source.

TIP: For more information on how to summarize, paraphrase, and quote effectively, see 48c and 48d.

46 Evaluating sources

You will often locate far more potential sources on your topic than you will have time to read. Your challenge then is to determine what kinds of sources you need—and what you need these sources to do—and to select a reasonable number of trustworthy sources. This kind of decision making is referred to as *evaluating sources*.

Avoid plagiarizing from the web

1 **Understand what plagiarism is.** When you use another author's intellectual property (language, visuals, or ideas) in your own writing without giving proper credit, you commit a kind of academic theft called *plagiarism*.

2 **Treat online sources as someone else's intellectual property.** Language, data, or images that you find on the web must be cited, even if the material is in the public domain (which includes older works no longer protected by copyright law), is publicly accessible on free sites or social media, or is on a government website.

3 **Keep track of words and ideas borrowed from sources.** When you copy and paste passages from online sources, put quotation marks around any text that you have copied. Develop a system for distinguishing your words and ideas from anything you've summarized, paraphrased, or quoted.

4 **Create a complete bibliographic entry for each source** to keep track of publication information. From the start of your research project, maintain accurate records for all online sources you read or view.

46a Evaluate the reliability and usefulness of a source.

The following questions will help you judge the reliability and usefulness of sources you might use to support your research project.

Relevance Is the source clearly related to your research topic and your argument? Will your readers understand why you've included the source in your paper? How will the source help you clarify or support your position?

Currency How recent is the source? Is the information up to date? Does your research topic require current information? Will your research benefit from consulting older sources, including primary sources from a historical period?

Credibility Where does the source come from? What are the author's credentials? How accurate and trustworthy is the information? If the source is authored by an organization, what research has the organization done to support its claims? Are the source's ideas and research cited by other authorities?

Bias Does the author endorse political or religious views that could affect objectivity? Is evidence and counterevidence presented in a fair and objective way? Is the author engaging in a scholarly debate or giving a personal point of view?

Determining if a source is scholarly

Scholarly sources are written by experts for a knowledgeable audience and usually go into more depth than books and articles written for a general audience. (Scholarly sources are sometimes called *refereed* or *peer-reviewed* because the work is evaluated by experts in the field before publication.) To determine if a source is scholarly, look for the following:

- Formal language and presentation
- Authors who are academics or scientists
- Footnotes or a bibliography documenting the works cited in the source
- Original research and interpretation (rather than a summary of other people's work)

Detect false and misleading sources

Sources can distort information or spread misinformation by taking information out of context or by promoting opinions as facts. As you evaluate sources, determine authenticity: Can the information be verified? Is the source reliable? You can verify facts and quotations by reading multiple sources and gathering a variety of perspectives. Because information and misinformation live side by side on the web, you need to read critically to determine the truth.

1 **Consider the source.** Is more than one source covering the topic? Is the author anonymous or named? What can you learn about the author's credentials and the mission of a site from checking the "About Us" tab? Does the site present only one side of an issue? Be skeptical if the source is the only one reporting the story.

2 **Examine the source's language and visual clues.** Does the headline use sensational (shocking or emotional) language? Is the language of the source offensive? Is the screen cluttered with ALL CAPS and unprofessional web design?

3 **Question the seriousness of the source.** Is it possible that the source is satirical and humorous and is not intended to be read as factual?

4 **Fact-check the information.** Can the facts be objectively verified? If the conclusions of a research study are cited, find the study to verify; if an authority is quoted, research the original source of the quotation, if possible, to see whether the quotation was taken out of context. Also, be skeptical if a source reports a research study but doesn't quote the study's principal investigator or other respected researchers.

5 **Pay attention to the URL.** Established news organizations have standard domain names. Fake sites often use web addresses that imitate the addresses of real sites, such as "Newslo" or "com.co," and package information with misinformation to make the site look authentic. Among the more credible sites are those sponsored by higher education (.edu), nonprofit groups (.org), and government agencies (.gov).

6 **Note your biases.** If an article makes you angry or challenges your beliefs, or if it confirms your beliefs by ignoring evidence to the contrary, take notice, and try to be as objective as possible. Learn about an issue from reliable sources and from multiple perspectives.

46b Consider how sources might contribute to your research project.

How you plan to use sources will affect how you evaluate them. As you evaluate a source, ask yourself what you learned from it. Did it support your position? Did it challenge your thinking? Consider how a source will inform, support, or counter your argument.

Sources can have a range of functions in a paper. You can use them to

- Provide background information or context
- Explain terms or concepts
- Provide evidence for your argument
- Lend authority to your argument
- Offer counterarguments to your argument

46c Read with an open mind and a critical eye.

As you begin reading the sources you have chosen, keep an open mind. Do not let your personal beliefs prevent you from considering new ideas and opposing viewpoints. Be curious about the wide range of positions in the research conversation you are entering.

When you read critically, you are examining an author's assumptions, assessing evidence, and weighing conclusions. Ask questions such as these:

- What is the author's central claim or thesis?
- How does the author support this claim—with relevant and sufficient evidence or with just a few anecdotes or emotional examples?
- Are statistics consistent with those you encounter in other sources? Have they been used fairly? Does the author explain where the statistics come from?
- Are any of the author's assumptions questionable?
- Does the author consider opposing arguments and refute them persuasively?

46d Assess web sources with special care.

Before using a web source in your paper, make sure you know who created the material and for what purpose. Sources with reliable information can stand up to scrutiny. As you evaluate sources, ask questions about their reliability and purpose.

Evaluating a website: Checking reliability

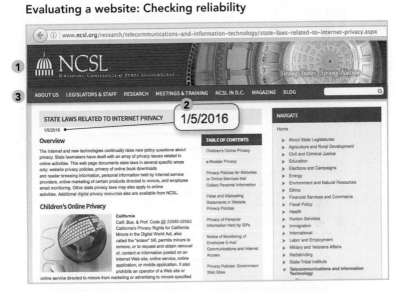

1 This page on Internet monitoring and workplace privacy appears on a website sponsored by the National Conference of State Legislatures. The NCSL is a bipartisan group that functions as a clearinghouse of ideas and research of interest to state lawmakers. It is also a lobby for state issues before the US government. The URL ending .org marks this sponsor as a nonprofit organization.

2 A clear date of publication shows currency.

3 An "About Us" page confirms that this is a credible organization whose credentials can be verified.

Evaluating a website: Checking purpose

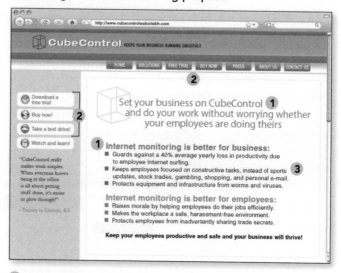

1 The site is sponsored by a company that specializes in employee-monitoring software.

2 Repeated links for trial downloads and purchase suggest the site's intended audience: consumers seeking to purchase software (probably not researchers seeking detailed information about employees' use of the Internet in the workplace).

3 The site appears to provide information and even shows statistics from studies, but ultimately the purpose of the site is to sell a product.

46e Construct an annotated bibliography.

An annotated bibliography is a list of sources with notes about each source. Constructing an annotated bibliography doesn't just help you remember which sources you've consulted; it also offers you an opportunity to reflect on *how* and *why* your most promising sources will help you answer your research question. See the writing guide on page 278 for help.

SAMPLE ANNOTATED BIBLIOGRAPHY ENTRY (MLA STYLE)

Resnik, David. "Trans Fat Bans and Human Freedom." *American Journal of Bioethics*, vol. 10, no. 3, Mar. 2010, pp. 27–32.

Student records publication information using MLA style.

Student presents the author's argument and chooses verbs— *argues, claims, explains*—to summarize the key ideas.

Student establishes the source as strong and reliable.

In this scholarly article, bioethicist David Resnik argues that bans on unhealthy foods threaten our personal freedom. He claims that researchers don't have enough evidence to know whether banning trans fats will save lives or money; all we know is that such bans restrict dietary choices. Resnik explains why most Americans oppose food restrictions, noting our multiethnic and regional food traditions as well as our resistance to government limitations on personal freedoms. He acknowledges that few people would miss eating trans fats, but he fears that bans on such substances could lead to widespread restrictions on red meat, sugary sodas, and other foods known to have harmful effects. Resnik offers a well-reasoned argument, but he goes too far by insisting that all proposed food restrictions will do more harm than good. This article contributes important perspectives on American resistance to government intervention in food choice and counters arguments in other sources that support the idea of food legislation to advance public health.

Student indicates the type of source and gives the author's name and credentials.

Summary sentences show the student's understanding of the author's main points.

Evaluation sentences show the student's understanding of how the source contributes to her research.

How to write an annotated bibliography

Creating an annotated bibliography gives you an opportunity to summarize, evaluate, and record publication information for your sources before drafting your research paper. You summarize each source to understand its main ideas; you evaluate each source for accuracy, quality, and relevance. Finally, you reflect, asking yourself how the source will contribute to your research project.

Key features

- **The list of sources, arranged in alphabetical order by author,** includes complete bibliographic information for each source.

- **A brief annotation or note for each source,** typically one hundred to two hundred words, is written in paragraph form and contains a summary and an evaluation.

- **The summary** of each source states the work's main ideas and key points briefly and accurately. The summary is written in the present tense, third person, directly and concisely. Summarizing helps you test your understanding of a source and restate its meaning responsibly.

- **The evaluation** of the source's role and usefulness in your project includes an assessment of the source's strengths and limitations, the author's qualifications and expertise, and the function of the source in your project. Evaluating a source helps you analyze how the source fits into your project and separate the source's ideas from your own.

Writing your annotated bibliography

For each source, begin by brainstorming responses to questions such as the following:

- What is the purpose of the source? Who is the author's intended audience?
- What is the author's thesis? What evidence supports the thesis?
- What qualifications and expertise does the author bring? Does the author have any biases or make any questionable assumptions?
- Why do you think this source is useful for your project?
- How does this source relate to the other sources in your bibliography?

The following tips can help you draft one or more entries in your annotated bibliography.

- Arrange the sources in alphabetical order by author (or by title for works with no author).
- Provide consistent bibliographic information for each source. For the exact bibliographic format, see 50b (MLA) or 52b (APA).
- Start your summary by identifying the thesis and purpose of the source as well as the credentials of the source's author.
- Keep your research question in mind. How does this source contribute to your project? How does it help you take your place in the conversation?

Ask reviewers for specific feedback. Here are some questions to guide their comments.

- Is each source summarized clearly? Have you identified the author's main idea?
- For each source, have you made a clear judgment about how and why the source is useful for your project?
- Have you used quotation marks around exact words from a source?

47 Writing a research paper

▸ Testing your thesis, 281
▸ Template for organizing a researched argument, 282

Once you have read a range of sources, considered your topic from different perspectives, and chosen an entry point into a research conversation, you are ready to focus your research paper by forming a thesis statement and supporting that thesis with well-organized evidence.

47a Form a working thesis statement.

A thesis statement expresses your informed answer to your research question — an answer about which people might disagree. Start by developing a working thesis statement to help you narrow your ideas and clarify your purpose. As your ideas develop, you'll revise your working thesis to make it more specific and focused.

Here, for example, is one student writer's research question and working thesis.

SOPHIE HARBA'S RESEARCH QUESTION

Should state governments enact laws to regulate healthy eating choices?

A good starting point because it provides an answer to the research question, but it doesn't show readers why the thesis matters.

WORKING THESIS

State governments have the responsibility to regulate healthy eating choices because of the rise of chronic diseases.

REVISED THESIS

In the name of public health and safety, state governments have the responsibility to shape health policies and to regulate healthy eating choices, especially since doing so offers a potentially large social benefit for a relatively small cost.

Revised thesis is sharper and more specific, announces a cle position, and shows readers why the positio matters.

The thesis usually appears at the end of the introductory paragraph. To read Harba's thesis in the context of her entire paper, see 51b.

> **Testing your thesis**
>
> Keep the following guidelines in mind to develop an effective thesis statement for your research project.
>
> - A thesis should be your answer to a question and should take a position that needs to be argued and supported. It should not be a statement of fact or a description. Make sure that your position is debatable by anticipating opposing viewpoints and counterpositions.
>
> - A thesis should match the scope of the research project. If your thesis is too broad, explore a subtopic of your original topic. If your thesis is too narrow, ask a research question that has more than one simple answer.
>
> - A thesis should be focused. Avoid vague words such as *interesting* or *good*. Use concrete language and make sure your thesis lets readers know your position.
>
> - A thesis should stand up to the "So what?" test (see p. 8). Ask yourself why readers should be interested in your essay and care about your thesis.

47b Organize your ideas.

The body of your paper will consist of evidence in support of your thesis. Try sketching an informal plan to focus and organize your ideas. Sophie Harba, for example, used this simple, informal plan to outline the structure of her argument.

INFORMAL OUTLINE

- Debates about the government's role in regulating food have a long history in the United States.

- Some experts argue that we should focus on the dangers of unhealthy eating habits and on preventing chronic diseases linked to diet.

- But food regulations are not a popular solution because many Americans object to government restrictions on personal choice.

- Food regulations designed to prevent chronic disease don't ask Americans to give up their freedom; they ask Americans to see health as a matter of public good.

There is no right or wrong way to organize a researched argument. A fairly typical way for research writers to proceed is shown below, but of course you should consider your own assignment, purpose, and audience as you organize and develop your work.

48 Citing sources; avoiding plagiarism

▸ Understand the MLA and APA systems of documentation, 283
▸ How to be a responsible research writer, 285

In a research paper, you draw on the work of other writers, and you must document their contributions by citing your sources. Sources are cited for two reasons:

1. to tell readers where your information comes from — so that they can assess its reliability and, if interested, find and read the original source

2. to give credit to the writers from whom you have borrowed words and ideas

You must include a citation when you quote from a source, when you summarize or paraphrase, and when you borrow facts that are not common knowledge. Borrowing another writer's language, sentence structure, or ideas without proper acknowledgment is plagiarism.

The only exception is common knowledge — widely available information that your readers may know or could easily locate in any number of general sources. When in doubt about what is or isn't common knowledge, acknowledge your source.

Writing for an audience

You demonstrate your credibility, your *ethos,* by choosing the most trustworthy, reliable sources and showing readers how to find them. When your citations guide readers quickly to the sources of a quoted, paraphrased, or summarized idea, you show respect for your audience's interest in your research. Ask yourself two questions: How can I make my documentation useful to my readers? What would readers need to know to find the source themselves?

48a Understand what plagiarism is.

When you use another author's intellectual property (words, ideas, or visuals) in your own writing without giving proper credit, you commit a serious academic offense called *plagiarism.*

In general, these three acts are considered plagiarism:

1. failing to cite quotations and borrowed ideas
2. failing to enclose borrowed language in quotation marks
3. failing to put summaries and paraphrases in your own words

Definitions of plagiarism vary; it's a good idea to find out how your school defines academic dishonesty.

48b Understand the MLA and APA systems of documentation.

Although various academic disciplines use their own style for citing sources, all disciplines cite sources for the same reasons — to acknowledge the contributions of others and to show readers where they can find the sources for themselves.

The Bedford Handbook describes two commonly used documentation styles:

Modern Language Association (MLA) in section 50

American Psychological Association (APA) in section 52

MLA is often used in humanities courses such as composition, literature, and film and media studies. APA is the choice for social science courses such as psychology, sociology, and criminal justice; at times it is used in business, education, and the natural sciences as well.

The MLA and APA styles require you to acknowledge your sources by using in-text citations — citations placed in parentheses within the body of your paper — to indicate the source of a particular quotation, paraphrased or summarized statement, or fact. The in-text citations point readers to a list of works cited or list of references at the end of your paper.

Understand how the MLA system works

In MLA style, you use parenthetical citations within the text of your paper to credit your sources and to refer your readers to a more detailed citation of the source in the works cited list at the end of your paper. There is a direct connection between the in-text citation and the alphabetical listing in your Works Cited.

Here, briefly, is how the MLA citation system works.

IN-TEXT CITATION

A signal phrase names the author and gives credentials. Writer includes a page number after cited material.

Bioethicist David Resnik emphasizes that such policies "open the door to excessive government control over food, which could restrict dietary choices, interfere with cultural, ethnic, and religious traditions, and exacerbate socioeconomic inequalities" (31).

The in-text citation point readers to th works cited p at the end of paper.

ENTRY IN THE LIST OF WORKS CITED WITH COMPLETE BIBILIOGRAPHIC INFORMATION

Resnik, David. "Trans Fat Bans and Human Freedom." *The American Journal of Bioethics*, vol. 10, no. 3, Mar. 2010, pp. 27–32.

Be a responsible research writer

Using good citation habits is the best way to avoid plagiarizing sources and to demonstrate that you are a responsible researcher.

1 **Cite your sources as you write drafts.** Don't wait until your final draft is complete to add citations. Include a citation when you quote from a source, when you summarize or paraphrase, and when you borrow facts that are not common knowledge.

2 **Place quotation marks around direct quotations,** both in your notes and in your drafts.

3 **Check each quotation, summary, and paraphrase against the source** to make certain you aren't misrepresenting the source. For paraphrases, be sure that your language and sentence structure differ from those in the original passage.

4 **Provide a full citation in your list of works cited.** It is not sufficient to cite a source only in the body of your paper; you must also provide complete publication information for each source in a list of works cited.

Understand how the APA system works

APA recommends an author-date system of citations. The date is important because disciplines that use APA style value current research. APA style requires the use of the past tense or the present perfect tense in signal phrases introducing cited material: Bell (2010) reported, Bell (2010) has argued.

Here, briefly, is how the APA citation system works.

IN-TEXT CITATION

A signal phrase names the author and gives the date. Writer includes page numbers for a paginated source.

Bell (2010) reported that students engaged in this kind of learning performed better on both project-based assessments and standardized texts (pp. 39–40).

ENTRY IN THE LIST OF REFERENCES

At the end of the paper, a list of references gives complete publication information.

Bell, S. (2010). Project-based learning for the 21st century: Skills for the future. *The Clearing House, 83*(2), 39–43.

48c Use quotation marks around borrowed language.

To indicate that you are using a source's exact phrases or sentences, you must enclose them in quotation marks unless they have been set off from the text by indenting (see 49b). To omit the quotation marks is to claim — falsely — that the language is your own, as in the following example. Such an omission is plagiarism even if you have cited the source.

ORIGINAL SOURCE

Although these policies may have a positive impact on human health, they open the door to excessive government control over food, which could restrict dietary choices, interfere with cultural, ethnic, and religious traditions, and exacerbate socioeconomic inequalities.

—David Resnik, "Trans Fat Bans and Human Freedom," p. 31

PLAGIARISM

Bioethicist David Resnik points out that policies to ban trans fats may protect human health, but they open the door to excessive government control over food, which could restrict dietary choices and interfere with cultural, ethnic, and religious traditions (31).

The highlighted words are directly from the original.

BORROWED LANGUAGE IN QUOTATION MARKS (MLA STYLE)

Bioethicist David Resnik points out that policies to ban trans fats may protect human health, but they "open the door to excessive government control over food, which could restrict dietary choices, interfere with cultural, ethnic, and religious traditions, and exacerbate socioeconomic inequalities" (31).

48d Put summaries and paraphrases in your own words.

A summary condenses information from a source; a paraphrase conveys the information using roughly the same number of words as the original source. When you summarize or paraphrase, it is not enough to name the source. You must restate the source's meaning using your own words and sentence structure. Half-copying the author's sentences either by using the author's phrases in your own sentences without quotation marks or by plugging synonyms into the author's sentence structure (sometimes called patchwriting) is a form of plagiarism.

The first paraphrase of the following source is plagiarized, even though the source is cited, because the paraphrase borrows too much of its language from the original. The highlighted strings of words have been copied exactly (without quotation marks). In addition, the writer has closely echoed the sentence structure of the source, merely substituting some synonyms (*interfere with lifestyle choices* for *paternalistic intervention into lifestyle choices*, for example).

ORIGINAL SOURCE

[A]ntiobesity laws encounter strong opposition from some quarters on the grounds that they constitute paternalistic intervention into lifestyle choices and enfeeble the notion of personal responsibility. Such arguments echo those made in the early days of tobacco regulation.

—Michelle M. Mello et al., "Obesity—the New Frontier of Public Health Law," p. 2602

PLAGIARISM: UNACCEPTABLE BORROWING

Health policy experts Mello and others argue that antiobesity laws encounter strong opposition from some quarters because they interfere with lifestyle choices and decrease the feeling of personal responsibility. These arguments mirror those made in the early days of tobacco regulation (2602).

The paraphrase borrows too much language from the original and follows its sentence structure too closely.

To avoid plagiarizing an author's language, resist the temptation to look at the source while you are summarizing or paraphrasing. After you have read the passage you want to paraphrase, set the source aside. Ask yourself: What is the author's meaning? In your own words, state your understanding of the author's ideas. Then return to the source and check that you haven't used the author's language or sentence structure or misrepresented the author's ideas.

ACCEPTABLE PARAPHRASE (MLA STYLE)

As health policy experts Mello and others point out, opposition to food and beverage regulation is similar to the opposition to early tobacco legislation: the public views the issue as one of personal responsibility rather than one requiring government intervention (2602).

The student uses her own language and sentence structure.

49 Integrating sources

Quotations, summaries, paraphrases, and facts will help you develop your argument, but they cannot speak for you. You need to find a balance between the words of your sources and your own voice, so that readers always know who is speaking in your paper. You can use several strategies to integrate sources into your paper while maintaining your own voice.

- Use sources as concisely as possible so that your own thinking and voice aren't lost (49a and 49b).

- Use signal phrases to avoid dropping quotations into your paper without indicating the boundary between your words and the source's words (49c).

- Use language that shows readers how each source supports your argument and how the sources relate to one another (49d).

49a Summarize and paraphrase effectively.

In your academic writing, keep the emphasis on your ideas and your language.

Summarizing

When you summarize a source, you express another writer's ideas in your own words, condensing the author's key points and using fewer words than the author.

WHEN TO SUMMARIZE

- When a passage is lengthy and you want to condense a chapter to a short paragraph or a paragraph to a sentence

- When you want to state the source's main ideas simply and briefly in your own words

- When you want to compare arguments or ideas from various sources

- When you want to provide readers with an understanding of the source's argument before you respond to it or launch your own

Paraphrasing

When you paraphrase, you express an author's ideas in your own words and sentence structure, using approximately the same number of words and details as in the source.

WHEN TO PARAPHRASE

- When the ideas and information are important but the author's exact words are not needed

- When you want to restate the source's ideas in your own words

- When you need to simplify and explain a technical or complicated source

EXERCISE 49–1   Summarize the following passage from a research source. Then paraphrase the same source. Use MLA-style in-text citation.

> Until recently, school-readiness skills weren't high on anyone's agenda, nor was the idea that the youngest learners might be disqualified from moving on to a subsequent stage. But now that kindergarten serves as a gate-keeper, not a welcome mat, to elementary school, concerns about school preparedness kick in earlier and earlier. A child who's supposed to read by the end of kindergarten had better be getting ready in preschool.
>
> Source: Erika Christakis, "How the New Preschool Is Crushing Kids," *The Atlantic*, Jan./Feb. 2016, p. 18.

49b Use quotations effectively.

When you quote a source, you borrow some of the author's exact words and enclose them in quotation marks. Quotation marks show your readers that both the idea and the words belong to the author.

WHEN TO USE QUOTATIONS

- When language is especially vivid or expressive

- When exact wording is needed for technical accuracy

- When it is important to let the debaters of an issue explain their positions in their own words

- When the words of an authority lend weight to an argument

- When the language of a source is the topic of your discussion

Paraphrase effectively

A paraphrase shows your readers that you understand a source and can explain it to them. When you choose to paraphrase a passage, you use the information and ideas of a source for your own purpose—to provide background information, explain a concept, or advance your argument—and yet maintain your voice. It is challenging to write a paraphrase that isn't a word-for-word translation of the original source and doesn't imitate the source's sentence structure. These strategies will help you paraphrase effectively. The examples in this box are in MLA style.

1 **Understand the source.** Identify the source's key points and argument. Test your understanding by asking questions: What is being said? Why and how is it being said? Look up words you don't know to help you understand whole ideas, not just the words.

Original

People's vision of the world has broadened with the advent of global media such as television and the Internet. Those thinking about going elsewhere can see what the alternatives are and appear to have fewer inhibitions about resettling.

—Darrell M. West, *Brain Gain: Rethinking U.S. Immigration Policy*, Brookings Institution Press, 2011, p. 5

Student's notes

—*TV and Internet have opened our eyes, our minds*

—*We can imagine making big moves (country to country) as we never could before; the web offers a preview*

—*"resettling" = moving to a new location, out of the familiar region*

—*Lessens the anxiety about starting over in a new place*

Use your own vocabulary and sentence structure to convey the source's information. Check to make sure there is no overlap in vocabulary or sentence structure with the original.

> Since TV and the web can offer a preview of life in other places, people feel less uncertainty and anxiety about making moves from one area of the world to another.

 Use a signal phrase to identify the source (*According to X,* or *X argues that* _____).

> West argues that since TV and the web can offer a preview of life in other places, people feel less uncertainty and anxiety about making moves from one area of the world to another.

 Include a citation to give credit to the source. Even though the words are yours, you need to give credit for the idea. Here, the author's name and the page number on which the original passage appeared are listed.

> West argues that since TV and the web can offer a preview of life in other places, people feel less uncertainty and anxiety about making moves from one area of the world to another (5).

NOTE: If you choose to use exact language from the source in a paraphrase, be sure to put quotation marks around any borrowed words or phrases.

> West argues that since TV and the web can offer a preview of life in other places, people "have fewer inhibitions" about making moves from one area of the world to another (5).

Limiting your use of quotations

Keep the emphasis on your own ideas. It is not always necessary to quote full sentences from a source. Often you can integrate words or phrases from a source into your own sentence structure. (MLA is shown below; for APA, see page 403.)

> Resnik acknowledges that his argument relies on the "slippery slope" fallacy, but he insists that "social and political pressures" regarding food regulations make his concerns valid (31).

Using the ellipsis mark

To condense a quoted passage, you can use the ellipsis mark—a series of three spaced periods—to indicate that you have omitted words. What remains must be grammatically complete.

> In Mississippi, legislators passed "a ban on bans—a law that forbids . . . local restrictions on food or drink" (Conly A23).

The writer has omitted the words *municipalities to place*, which appear before *local restrictions* in the original source, to condense the quoted material.

If you want to omit one or more full sentences, use a period before the ellipsis.

> Legal scholars Gostin and Gostin argue that "individuals have limited willpower to defer immediate gratification for longer-term health benefits. . . . A person understands that high-fat foods or a sedentary lifestyle will cause adverse health effects, or that excessive spending or gambling will cause financial hardship, but it is not always easy to refrain" (217).

Ordinarily, do not use an ellipsis mark at the beginning or at the end of a quotation. Your readers will understand that you have taken the quoted material from a longer passage. The only exception occurs when you have dropped words at the end of the final quoted sentence. In such cases, use the ellipsis before the closing quotation mark and parenthetical reference.

USING SOURCES RESPONSIBLY: Make sure omissions and ellipsis marks do not distort the meaning of your source.

Using brackets

Brackets allow you to insert your own words into quoted material to clarify a confusing reference or to keep a sentence grammatical in your context. (MLA is shown below; for APA, see page 409.)

> Neergaard and Agiesta argue that "a new poll finds people are split on how much the government should do to help [find solutions to the national health crisis]—and most draw the line at attempts to force healthier eating."

In this example, the writer inserted words in brackets to clarify the meaning of *help*.

To indicate an error such as a misspelling in a quotation, insert "sic," in brackets, right after the error.

Setting off long quotations

When you quote more than four typed lines of prose or more than three lines of poetry, set off the quotation by indenting it one-half inch from the left margin.

Long quotations should be introduced by an informative sentence, usually followed by a colon. Quotation marks are unnecessary because the indented format tells readers that the passage is taken word for word from the source. (MLA is shown below; for APA, see page 406.)

> In response to critics who claim that laws aimed at stopping us from eating whatever we want are an assault on our freedom of choice, Conly offers a persuasive counterargument:
>
> > [L]aws aren't designed for each one of us individually. Some of us can drive safely at 90 miles per hour, but we're bound by the same laws as the people

who can't, because individual speeding laws aren't practical. Giving up a little liberty is something we agree to when we agree to live in a democratic society that is governed by laws. (A23)

NOTE: At the end of an indented quotation, the parenthetical citation goes outside the final mark of punctuation.

49c Use signal phrases to integrate sources.

Whenever you include a paraphrase, summary, or direct quotation of another writer's work in your paper, prepare your readers for it with introductory words called a *signal phrase*. A signal phrase usually names the author of the source and provides some context for the source material—such as the author's credentials—and helps readers distinguish your ideas from those of the source.

When you write a signal phrase, choose a verb that fits with the way you are using the source. Are you, for example, using the source to support a claim or refute a belief?

WEAK VERB	Lorrine Goodwin, a food historian, says, " . . . "
STRONGER VERB (MLA)	Lorrine Goodwin, a food historian, rejects the claim: " . . . "
STRONGER VERB (APA)	Lorrine Goodwin, a food historian, has rejected the claim: ". . . "

NOTE: MLA style calls for using verbs in the present or present perfect tense (*argues, has argued*) to introduce source material unless you include a date that specifies the time of the original author's writing. APA style calls for using verbs in the past tense or present perfect tense (*explained, has explained*) to introduce source material. In APA style, use the present tense only for discussing the applications or effects of your own results (*the data suggest*) or knowledge that has been clearly established (*researchers agree*).

Using signal phrases in MLA papers

To avoid monotony, try to vary both the language and the placement of your signal phrases.

Model signal phrases

Michael Pollan, who has written extensively about Americans' unhealthy eating habits, argues that . . .

As health policy experts Mello and others point out, ". . ."

Marion Nestle, New York University professor of nutrition and public health, notes, ". . ."

Bioethicist David Resnik acknowledges that his argument . . .

In response to critics, Conly offers a persuasive counterargument: ". . ."

Verbs in signal phrases

acknowledges	comments	endorses	points out
adds	compares	explains	reasons
admits	confirms	grants	refutes
agrees	contends	illustrates	rejects
argues	declares	implies	reports
asserts	denies	insists	responds
believes	disputes	notes	suggests
claims	emphasizes	observes	writes

Using signal phrases in APA papers

To avoid monotony, try to vary both the language and the placement of your signal phrases.

Model signal phrases

In the words of Mitra (2013), ". . ."

Bell (2010) has noted that. . .

Donista-Schmidt and Zuzovsky (2014) pointed out that . . .

USING SIGNAL PHRASES IN APA PAPERS (*cont.*)

". . . ," claimed Çubukçu (2012, Introduction section).

Horn and Staker (2011) have offered a compelling argument for this view: ". . ."

Verbs in signal phrases

admitted	contended	pointed out
agreed	declared	reasoned
argued	denied	refuted
asserted	emphasized	rejected
believed	explained	reported
claimed	insisted	responded
compared	noted	suggested
confirmed	observed	wrote

Marking boundaries

Readers need to move smoothly from your words to the words of a source. Avoid dropping a quotation into the text without warning. Provide a clear signal phrase, including at least the author's name, to indicate the boundary between your words and the source's words. The signal phrase is highlighted in the second example. (MLA is shown below; for APA, see page 403.)

DROPPED QUOTATION

Laws designed to prevent chronic disease by promoting healthier food and beverage consumption also have potential economic benefits. "[A] 1% reduction in the intake of saturated fat across the population would prevent more than 30,000 cases of coronary heart disease annually and would save more than a billion dollars in health care costs" (Nestle 7).

QUOTATION WITH SIGNAL PHRASE

Laws designed to prevent chronic disease by promoting healthier food and beverage consumption also have potential economic benefits. Marion Nestle,

New York University professor of nutrition and public health, notes that "a 1% reduction in the intake of saturated fat across the population would prevent more than 30,000 cases of coronary heart disease annually and would save more than a billion dollars in health care costs" (7).

Establishing authority

The first time you mention a source, include in the signal phrase the author's title, credentials, or experience to help your readers recognize the source's authority and your own credibility (*ethos*) as a responsible researcher who has located reliable sources. Signal phrases are highlighted in the next two examples. (MLA is shown below; for APA, see page 406.)

SOURCE WITH NO CREDENTIALS

No clues given about the source's authority.

Michael Pollan notes that "[t]he Centers for Disease Control estimates that fully three quarters of US health care spending goes to treat chronic diseases, most of which are preventable and linked to diet: heart disease, stroke, type 2 diabetes, and at least a third of all cancers."

SOURCE WITH CREDENTIALS

Authority is suggested in the signal phrase.

Journalist Michael Pollan, who has written extensively about Americans' unhealthy eating habits, notes that "[t]he Centers for Disease Control estimates that fully three quarters of US health care spending goes to treat chronic diseases, most of which are preventable and linked to diet: heart disease, stroke, type 2 diabetes, and at least a third of all cancers."

Introducing summaries and paraphrases

Introduce most summaries and paraphrases with a signal phrase that names the author and places the material in the context of your argument. Readers will then understand that everything between the signal phrase and the parenthetical citation summarizes or paraphrases the cited source. (MLA is shown on the following page; for APA, see page 410.)

To improve public health, advocates such as Bowdoin College philosophy professor Sarah Conly contend that it is the government's duty to prevent people from making harmful choices whenever feasible and whenever public benefits outweigh the costs. In response to critics who claim that laws aimed at stopping us from eating whatever we want are an assault on our freedom of choice, Conly asserts that "laws aren't designed for each one of us individually" (A23).

> Without the signal phrase, readers might think that only the quotation at the end is being cited, when the whole paragraph is based on the source.

There are times, however, when a summary or a paraphrase does not require a signal phrase naming the author. When the context makes clear where the cited material begins, you may omit the signal phrase and include the author's last name in parentheses.

Integrating statistics and other facts

When you cite a statistic or another specific fact, a signal phrase is often not necessary. Readers usually will understand that the citation refers to the statistic or fact and not the whole paragraph.

Seventy-five percent of Americans are opposed to laws that restrict or put limitations on access to unhealthy foods (Neergaard and Agiesta).

Putting source material in context

Readers should not have to guess why source material appears in your paper. A signal phrase can help you connect your own ideas and those of another writer by clarifying how the source will contribute to your paper.

If you use another writer's words, you must explain how they relate to your argument. Quotations don't speak for themselves; you must create a context for readers. Sandwich each quotation between sentences of your own, introducing the quotation with a signal phrase and following it with interpretive comments that link the quotation to your paper's argument. (MLA is shown below; for APA, see pages 409–410.)

QUOTATION WITH EFFECTIVE CONTEXT (QUOTATION SANDWICH)

In response to critics who claim that laws aimed at stopping us from eating whatever we want are an assault on our freedom of choice, Conly offers a persuasive counterargument:

> Quotation is introduced with a signal phrase naming the author.

Long quotation is set off from the text; quotation marks are omitted.

[L]aws aren't designed for each one of us individually. Some of us can drive safely at 90 miles per hour, but we're bound by the same laws as the people who can't, because individual speeding laws aren't practical. Giving up a little liberty is something we agree to when we agree to live in a democratic society that is governed by laws. (A23)

Analysis connects the source to the student's argument.

As Conly suggests, we need to change our either/or thinking (either we have complete freedom of choice *or* we have government regulations and lose our freedom) and instead need to see health as a matter of public good, not individual liberty.

Using sentence guides to integrate sources

You build your credibility (*ethos*) by accurately representing the ideas of others and by integrating these ideas into your paper. An important way to present the ideas of others before agreeing or disagreeing with them is to use sentence guides. These guides act as academic sentence starters; they show you how to use signal phrases in sentences to make clear to your reader whose ideas you're presenting—your own or those you have encountered in a source.

Presenting others' ideas. As an academic writer, you will be expected to demonstrate your understanding of a source by summarizing the views or arguments of its author. The following language will help you to do so:

X argues that _____.

X and Y emphasize the need for _____.

NOTE: The examples in this box are shown in MLA style. If you were writing in APA style, you would include the year of publication after the source's name and typically use past tense or present perfect tense (*emphasized* or *has emphasized*).

Presenting direct quotations. To introduce the exact words of a source because their accuracy and authority are important for your argument, you might try phrases like these:

X describes the problem this way: "_____"

Y argues in favor of the policy, pointing out that "_____."

Presenting alternative ideas. At times you will have to synthesize the ideas of multiple sources before you introduce your own.

USING SENTENCE GUIDES TO INTEGRATE SOURCES (*cont.*)

While X and Y have asked an important question, Z suggests that we should be asking a different question: _____.

X has argued that Y's research findings rest upon questionable assumptions _____ and _____.

Presenting your own ideas by agreeing or extending. You may agree with the author of a source but want to add your own voice to extend the point or go deeper. The following phrases could be useful:

X's argument is convincing because _____.

Y claimed that _____. But isn't it also true that _____?

Presenting your own ideas by disagreeing and questioning. College writing assignments encourage you to show your understanding of a subject but also to question or challenge ideas and conclusions about the subject. This language can help:

X's claims about _____ are misguided.

Y insists that _____, but perhaps she is asking the wrong question.

Presenting and countering objections to your argument. To anticipate objections that readers might make, try the following sentence guides:

Not everyone will endorse this argument; some may argue instead that

_____.

Some will object to this proposal on the grounds that _____.

49d Synthesize sources.

When you synthesize multiple sources in a research paper, you create a conversation about your research topic. You show readers that your argument is based on your analysis and integration of ideas and is not just a series of quotations and paraphrases strung together. Your synthesis will show how your sources relate to one another; one source may support, extend, or counter the ideas of another. Not every source has to "speak" to another in a research paper, but readers should understand how each source functions in your argument.

Considering how sources relate to your argument

Before you integrate sources and show readers how they relate to one another, consider how each one might contribute to your own argument. As student writer Sophie Harba became more informed about her research topic, she asked herself these questions: What have I learned from my sources? Which sources might support my ideas or illustrate the points I want to make? What counterarguments do I need to address to strengthen my position? She annotated a passage from one of her sources—a nonprofit group's assertion that our choices about food are skewed by marketing messages.

STUDENT NOTES ON THE ORIGINAL SOURCE

useful factual information

The food and beverage industry spends approximately $2 billion per year marketing to children.

—"Facts on Junk Food"

could use this to counter the point about personal choice in Mello

Placing sources in conversation

You can show readers how the ideas of one source relate to those of another by connecting and analyzing the ideas in your own voice. After all, you've done the research and thought through the issues, so you should control the conversation. The thread of your argument should be easy to identify and to understand, with or without your sources.

Student writer Sophie Harba sets up her synthesis with a question.

A signal phrase indicates how the source contributes to Harba's argument and shows that the idea that follows is not her own.

SAMPLE SYNTHESIS (MLA STYLE)

Why is the public largely resistant to laws that would limit unhealthy choices or penalize those choices with so-called fat taxes? Many consumers and civil rights advocates find such laws to be an unreasonable restriction on individual freedom of choice. As health policy experts Mello and others point out, opposition to food and beverage regulation is similar to the opposition to early tobacco legislation: the public views the issue as one of personal responsibility rather than one requiring

Student writer

Source 1

Harba
interprets a
paraphrased
source.

government intervention (2602). In other words, if a person
eats unhealthy food and becomes ill as a result, that is his
or her choice. But those who favor legislation claim that
freedom of choice is a myth because of the strong influence
of food and beverage industry marketing on consumers'
dietary habits. According to one nonprofit health advocacy
group, food and beverage companies spend roughly two
billion dollars per year marketing directly to children.

Student writer

Source 2

Harba uses
a source to
support her
counterargument.

As a result, kids see nearly four thousand ads per year
encouraging them to eat unhealthy food and drinks
("Facts"). As was the case with antismoking laws passed in
recent decades, taxes and legal restrictions on junk food
sales could help to counter the strong marketing messages
that promote unhealthy products.

Student writer

Harba extends
the argument
and follows
it with an
interpretive
comment.

The United States has a history of state and local
public health laws that have successfully promoted a
particular behavior by punishing an undesirable behavior.
The decline in tobacco use as a result of antismoking
taxes and laws is perhaps the most obvious example.
Another example is legislation requiring the use of seat
belts, which have significantly reduced fatalities in car
crashes. One government agency reports that seat belt use
saved an average of more than fourteen thousand lives per
year in the United States between 2000 and 2010 (United
States, Dept. of Transportation, Natl. Highway Traffic Safety
Administration 231). Perhaps seat belt laws have public
support because the cost of wearing a seat belt is small,
especially when compared with the benefit of saving
fourteen thousand lives per year.

Source 3

Student writer

In this synthesis, Harba uses her own analysis to shape the conversation
among her sources. She does not simply string quotations together or
allow them to overwhelm her writing. She guides her readers through a
conversation about a variety of laws that could promote and have promoted public health. She finds points of intersection among her sources,

acknowledges the contributions of others in the research conversation, and shows readers, in her own voice, how the various sources support her argument.

To see an example of a synthesis paragraph in an APA paper, see page 407. Look for the marginal annotation that includes the words "synthesis paragraph."

When synthesizing sources, ask yourself the following questions:

- How do your sources address your research question?

- How do your sources speak to one another?

- Have you varied the function of sources—to provide background, to explain concepts, to lend authority, and to anticipate counterarguments?

- Do you connect and analyze sources in your own voice?

- Is your own argument easy to identify and to understand, with or without your sources?

50 Documenting sources in MLA style

In English and other humanities classes, you may be asked to use the MLA (Modern Language Association) system for documenting sources, which is set forth in the *MLA Handbook*, 8th edition (MLA, 2016).

MLA recommends in-text citations that refer readers to a list of works cited. A typical in-text citation names the author of the source, often in a signal phrase, and gives a page number in parentheses. At the end of the paper, the list of works cited provides publication information about the source; the list is alphabetized by authors' last names (or by titles for works without authors). There is a direct connection between the in-text citation and the alphabetical listing. In the following example, that connection is highlighted in orange.

IN-TEXT CITATION

Bioethicist David Resnik emphasizes that such policies, despite their potential to make our society healthier, "open the door to excessive government control over food, which could restrict dietary choices, interfere with cultural, ethnic, and religious traditions, and exacerbate socioeconomic inequalities" (31).

ENTRY IN THE LIST OF WORKS CITED

Resnik, David. "Trans Fat Bans and Human Freedom." *The American Journal of Bioethics*, vol. 10, no. 3, Mar. 2010, pp. 27–32.

For a list of works cited that includes this entry, see 51b.

50a MLA in-text citations

MLA in-text citations are made with a combination of signal phrases and parenthetical references. A signal phrase introduces information taken from a source (a quotation, summary, paraphrase, or fact); usually the signal phrase includes the author's name. The parenthetical reference comes after the cited material, often at the end of the sentence. It includes at least a page number (except for unpaginated sources, such as those found on the web). In the models in this section, the elements of the in-text citation are highlighted in orange.

IN-TEXT CITATION

Resnik acknowledges that his argument relies on "slippery slope" thinking, but he insists that "social and political pressures" regarding food regulation make his concerns valid (31).

Readers can look up the author's last name in the alphabetized list of works cited, where they will learn the work's title and other publication information. If readers decide to consult the source, the page number will take them straight to the cited passage.

List of MLA in-text citation models

List of MLA works cited models

List of **MLA works cited** models (*cont.*)

General guidelines for signal phrases and page numbers

Items 1–5 explain how the MLA system usually works for all sources — in print, on the web, in other media, and with or without authors and page numbers. Items 6–25 give variations on the basic guidelines.

1. Author named in a signal phrase   Ordinarily, introduce the material being cited with a signal phrase that includes the author's name. In addition to preparing readers for the source, the signal phrase allows you to keep the parenthetical citation brief.

> According to Lorine Goodwin, a food historian, nineteenth-century reformers who sought to purify the food supply were called "fanatics" and "radicals" by critics who argued that consumers should be free to buy and eat what they want (77).

The signal phrase *According to Lorine Goodwin* names the author; the parenthetical citation gives the number of the page on which the quoted words may be found.

Notice that the period follows the parenthetical citation. When a quotation ends with a question mark or an exclamation point, leave the end punctuation inside the quotation mark and add a period at the end of your sentence, after the parenthetical citation.

> Burgess asks a critical question: "How can we think differently about food labeling?" (51).

2. Author named in parentheses   If you do not give the author's name in a signal phrase, put the last name in parentheses with the page number (if the source has one). Use no punctuation between the name and the page number: (Moran 351).

> According to a nationwide poll, 75% of Americans are opposed to laws that restrict or put limitations on access to unhealthy foods (Neergaard and Agiesta).

3. Author unknown   If a source has no author, the works cited entry will begin with the title. In your in-text citation, either use the complete title in a signal phrase or use a short form of the title in parentheses. Titles of books and other long works are italicized; titles of articles and other short works are put in quotation marks.

> As a result, kids see nearly four thousand ads per year encouraging them to eat unhealthy food and drinks ("Facts").

NOTE: If the author is a corporation or a government agency, see items 8 and 16.

4. Page number unknown   Do not include the page number if a work lacks page numbers, as is the case with many web sources. Do not use page numbers from a printout from a website. (When the pages of a web source are stable, as in PDF files, supply a page number in your in-text citation.)

> Michael Pollan points out that "cheap food" actually has "significant costs—to the environment, to public health, to the public purse, even to the culture."

If a source has numbered paragraphs or sections, use "par." (or "pars.") or "sec." (or "secs.") in the parentheses: (Smith, par. 4). Notice that a comma follows the author's name.

5. One-page source   If the source is one page long, it is a good idea to include the page number; without it readers may not know where your citation ends or, worse, may not realize that you have provided a citation at all.

NO PAGE NUMBER IN CITATION

Sarah Conly uses John Stuart Mill's "harm principle" to argue that citizens need their government to intervene to prevent them from taking harmful actions—such as driving too fast or buying unhealthy foods—out of ignorance of the harm they can do. But government intervention may overstep in the case of food choices.

PAGE NUMBER IN CITATION

Sarah Conly uses John Stuart Mill's "harm principle" to argue that citizens need their government to intervene to prevent them from taking harmful actions—such as driving too fast or buying unhealthy foods—out of ignorance of the harm they can do (A23). But government intervention may overstep in the case of food choices.

Variations on the general guidelines

This section describes the MLA guidelines for handling a variety of situations not covered in items 1–5.

6. Two authors Name the authors in a signal phrase, as in the following example, or include their last names in the parenthetical reference: (Gostin and Gostin 214).

> As legal scholars Gostin and Gostin explain, "[I]nterventions that do not pose a truly significant burden on individual liberty" are justified if they "go a long way towards safeguarding the health and well-being of the populace" (214).

7. Three or more authors In a parenthetical citation, give the first author's name followed by "et al." (Latin for "and others"). In a signal phrase, give the first author's name followed by "and others."

> The clinical trials were extended for two years, and only after results were reviewed by an independent panel did the researchers publish their findings (Blaine et al. 35).

> Researchers Blaine and others note that clinical trial results were reviewed by an independent panel (35).

8. Organization as author When the author is a corporation or an organization, name that author either in the signal phrase or in the parenthetical citation. (For a government agency as author, see item 16.)

> The American Diabetes Association estimates that the cost of diagnosed diabetes in the United States in 2012 was $245 billion.

In the list of works cited, the American Diabetes Association is treated as the author and alphabetized under *A*. When you give the organization name in the text, spell out the name; when you use it in parentheses, abbreviate common words in the name: "Assn.," "Dept.," "Natl.," "Soc.," and so on.

> The cost of diagnosed diabetes in the United States in 2012 was estimated at $245 billion (Amer. Diabetes Assn.).

9. Authors with the same last name If your list of works cited includes works by two or more authors with the same last name, include the author's first name in the signal phrase or first initial in the parentheses.

> One approach to the problem is to introduce nutrition literacy at the K-5 level in public schools (E. Chen 15).

10. Two or more works by the same author Mention the title of the work in the signal phrase or include a short version of the title in the parentheses.

> The American Diabetes Association tracks trends in diabetes across age groups. In 2012, more than 200,000 children and adolescents had diabetes ("Fast"). Because of an expected dramatic increase in diabetes in young people over the next forty years, the association encourages "strategies for implementing childhood obesity prevention programs and primary prevention programs for youth at risk of developing type 2 diabetes" ("Number").

Titles of articles and other short works are placed in quotation marks; titles of books and other long works are italicized.

In the rare case when both the author's name and a short title must be given in parentheses, separate them with a comma.

> Researchers have estimated that "the number of youth with type 2 [diabetes] could quadruple and the number with type 1 could triple" by 2050, "with an increasing proportion of youth with diabetes from minority populations" (Amer. Diabetes Assn., "Number").

11. Two or more works in one citation To cite more than one source in the parentheses, list the authors (or titles) in alphabetical order and separate them with semicolons.

> The prevalence of early-onset type 2 diabetes has been well documented (Finn 68; Sharma 2037; Whitaker 118).

12. Repeated citations from the same source When you are writing about a single work, you do not need to include the author's name each time you quote from or paraphrase the work. After you mention the author's name at the beginning of your paper, you may include just the page number in your parenthetical citations.

> In Susan Glaspell's short story "A Jury of Her Peers," two women accompany their husbands and a county attorney to an isolated house where a farmer named John Wright has been choked to death in his bed with a rope. The chief suspect is Wright's wife, Minnie, who is in jail awaiting trial. The sheriff's wife, Mrs. Peters, has come along to gather some personal items for Minnie, and Mrs. Hale has joined her. Early in the story, Mrs. Hale sympathizes with Minnie and objects to the way the male investigators are "snoopin' round and criticizin' " her kitchen (249). In contrast, Mrs. Peters shows respect for the law, saying that the men are doing "no more than their duty" (249).

In a paper with multiple sources, if you are citing a source more than once in a paragraph, you may omit the author's name after the first mention in the paragraph as long as it is clear that you are still referring to the same source.

13. Encyclopedia or dictionary entry   When an encyclopedia or dictionary entry does not have an author, it will be alphabetized in the list of works cited under the word or entry that you consulted (see item 23 in 50b). Either in your text or in your parenthetical citation, mention the word or entry and give the number of the page on which the entry may be found.

> The word *crocodile* has a complex etymology ("Crocodile" 139).

14. Entire work   Use the author's name in a signal phrase or a parenthetical citation. There is no need to use a page number.

> Pollan explores the issues surrounding food production and consumption from a political angle.

15. Selection in an anthology or a collection   Put the name of the author of the selection (not the editor of the anthology) in the signal phrase or the parentheses.

> In "Love Is a Fallacy," the narrator's logical teachings disintegrate when Polly declares that she should date Petey because "[h]e's got a raccoon coat" (Shulman 372).

In the list of works cited, the work is alphabetized under *Shulman*, the author of the story, not under the name of the editor of the anthology. (See item 29 in 50b.)

Shulman, Max. "Love Is a Fallacy." *Current Issues and Enduring Questions*, edited by
    Sylvan Barnet and Hugo Bedau, 11th ed., Bedford/St. Martin's, 2017, pp. 365–72.

16. Government document   When a government agency is the author, you will alphabetize the entry in the list of works cited under the name of the government, such as *United States* or *Great Britain* (see item 56 in 50b). For this reason, you must name the government as well as the agency in your in-text citation.

> One government agency reports that seat belt use saved an average of more than fourteen thousand lives per year in the United States between 2000 and 2010 (United States, Dept. of Transportation, Natl. Highway Traffic Safety Administration 231).

17. Historical document   For a historical document, such as the Constitution of the United States or the Canadian Charter of Rights and Freedoms, provide the document title, neither italicized nor in quotation marks, along with relevant article and section numbers. In parenthetical citations, use abbreviations such as "art." and "sec."

> While the Constitution provides for the formation of new states (art. 4, sec. 3), it does not explicitly allow or prohibit the secession of states.

Cite other historical documents as you would any other work, by the first element in the works cited entry (see item 57 in 50b).

18. Legal source   For a legislative act (law) or court case, name the act or case either in a signal phrase or in parentheses. Italicize the names of cases but not the names of acts. (See also items 58 and 59 in 50b.)

> The Jones Act of 1917 granted US citizenship to Puerto Ricans.

> In 1857, Chief Justice Roger B. Taney declared in *Dred Scott v. Sandford* that blacks, whether enslaved or free, could not be citizens of the United States.

19. Visual such as a table, a chart, or another graphic To cite a visual that has a figure number in the original source, use the abbreviation "fig." and the number in place of a page number in your parenthetical citation: (Manning, fig. 4). If you refer to the figure in your text, spell out the word "figure."

To cite a visual that appears in a print source without a figure number, use the visual's title or a description in your text and cite the author and page number as for any other source.

For a visual not in a print source, identify the visual in your text and then in parentheses use the first element in the works cited entry: the artist's or photographer's name or the title of the work. (See items 51–55 in 50b.)

> Photographs such as *Woman Aircraft Worker* (Bransby) and *Women Welders* (Parks) demonstrate the US government's attempt to document the contributions of women during World War II.

20. Personal communication and social media Cite personal letters, personal interviews, email messages, and social media posts by the name listed in the works cited entry, as you would for any other source. Identify the type of source in your text if you think it is necessary for clarity. (See items 60–64 in 50b.)

21. Web source Your in-text citation for a source from the web should follow the same guidelines as for other sources. If the source lacks page numbers but has numbered paragraphs, sections, or divisions, use those numbers with the appropriate abbreviation in your parenthetical citation: "par.," "sec.," "ch.," "pt.," and so on. Do not add such numbers if the source itself does not use them; simply give the author or title in your in-text citation.

> Sanjay Gupta, CNN chief medical correspondent, explains that "limited access to fresh, affordable, healthy food" is one of America's most pressing health problems.

22. Indirect source (source quoted in another source) When a writer's or a speaker's quoted words appear in a source written by someone else, begin the parenthetical citation with the abbreviation "qtd. in." In the following example, Gostin and Gostin are the authors of the source given in the works cited list; their work contains a quotation by Beauchamp.

> Public health researcher Dan Beauchamp has said that "public health practices are communal in nature, and concerned with the well-being of the community as a whole and not just the well-being of any particular person" (qtd. in Gostin and Gostin 217).

Literary works and sacred texts

Literary works and sacred texts are usually available in a variety of editions. Your list of works cited will specify which edition you are using, and your in-text citation will usually consist of a page number from the edition you consulted (see item 23). When possible, give enough information—such as book parts, play divisions, or line numbers—so that readers can locate the cited passage in any edition of the work (see items 24 and 25).

23. Literary work without parts or line numbers   Many literary works, such as most short stories and many novels and plays, do not have parts or line numbers. In such cases, simply cite the page number.

> At the end of Kate Chopin's "The Story of an Hour," Mrs. Mallard drops dead upon learning that her husband is alive. In the final irony of the story, doctors report that she has died of a "joy that kills" (25).

24. Verse play or poem   For verse plays, give act, scene, and line numbers that can be located in any edition of the work. Use arabic numerals and separate the numbers with periods.

> In Shakespeare's *King Lear,* Gloucester learns a profound lesson from a tragic experience: "A man may see how this world goes / with no eyes" (4.2.148–49).

For a poem, cite the part, stanza, and line numbers, if it has them, separated by periods.

> The Green Knight claims to approach King Arthur's court "because the praise of you, prince, is puffed so high, / And your manor and your men are considered so magnificent" (1.12.258–59).

For poems that are not divided into numbered parts or stanzas, use line numbers. For the first reference, use the word "lines": (lines 5-8). Thereafter use just the numbers: (12-13).

25. Sacred text When citing a sacred text such as the Bible or the Qur'an, name the edition you are using in your works cited entry (see item 33 in 50b). In your parenthetical citation, give the book and then the chapter and verse (or their equivalent), separated with a period. Common abbreviations for books of the Bible are acceptable.

> Consider the words of Solomon: "If your enemy is hungry, give him bread to eat; and if he is thirsty, give him water to drink" (*Oxford Annotated Bible,* Prov. 25.21).

The title of a sacred work is italicized when it refers to a specific edition of the work, as in the preceding example. If you refer to the book in a general sense in your text, neither italicize it nor put it in quotation marks.

> The Bible and the Qur'an provide allegories that help readers understand how to lead a moral life.

50b MLA list of works cited

Your list of works cited, which you will place at the end of your paper, guides readers to the sources you have quoted, summarized, and paraphrased. Ask yourself: *What would readers need to know to find this source for themselves?* Usually, you will provide basic information common to most sources, such as author, title, publisher, publication date, and location (page numbers or URL, for example).

Throughout this section of the book, you'll find models organized by type (article, book, website, multimedia source, and so on). But even if you aren't sure exactly what type of source you have (*Is this a blog post or an article?*), you can follow two general principles:

Gather key publication information about the source—the citation elements.

Organize the basic information about the source using what MLA calls "containers."

The author's name and the title of the work are needed for many (though not all) sources and are the first two pieces of information to gather. For the remaining pieces of information, you might find it helpful to think about whether the work is contained within one or more larger works. Some sources are self-contained. Others are nested in larger containers.

☐ Self-contained

a *book*
a *film*

One container

an *article* in a scholarly journal
a *poem* in a collection of poetry
a *video* posted to YouTube
a *fact sheet* on a government website

Two containers

an *article* in a journal within a database (JSTOR etc.)
an *episode* from a TV series within a streaming service (Netflix etc.)

Keep in mind that most sources won't include all of the following pieces of information, so gather only those that are relevant to and available for your source.

Author.		
Title of source.		
Title of container,		Title of container 2,
Other contributors,		Other contributors,
Version (or edition),	*If there is a second container, gather the same information for it (if available).*	Version (or edition),
Volume and issue numbers,	→	Volume and issue numbers,
Publisher,		Publisher,
Date,		Date,
Location (page numbers, URL, DOI, etc.).		Location.

WORKS CITED ENTRY, ONE CONTAINER (SELECTION IN AN ANTHOLOGY)

··········· container 1 ·················
author   title of selection   title of collection

Eisenberg, Deborah. "Some Other, Better Otto." *New American Stories,* edited by

location
contributor   publisher   year   (pages)

Ben Marcus, Vintage Books, 2015, pp. 94–136.

WORKS CITED ENTRY, TWO CONTAINERS (ARTICLE IN A JOURNAL IN A DATABASE)

author   title of article

Coles, Kimberly Anne. "The Matter of Belief in John Donne's Holy Sonnets."

··············· container 1 ·················
journal   volume,   location   database
title   issue   date   (pages)   title

Renaissance Quarterly, vol. 68, no. 3, Fall 2015, pp. 899–931. *JSTOR,*

········ container 2 ········
location
(DOI)

doi:10.1086/683855.

Once you've gathered the relevant and available information about a source, you will organize the elements using the list above as your guideline. Note the punctuation after each element in that list. In this section you will find many examples of how elements and containers are combined to create works cited entries.

▸ List of MLA works cited models, 306–307
▸ General guidelines for the works cited list, 320

General guidelines for listing authors

The formatting of authors' names in items 1–11 applies to all sources — books, articles, websites — in print, on the web, or in other media. For more models of specific source types, see items 12–64.

1. Single author

author: last
name first   title (book)   publisher   year

Bowker, Gordon. *James Joyce: A New Biography*. Farrar, Straus and Giroux, 2012.

2. Two authors

first author: second author:
last name first   in normal order   title (book)

Gourevitch, Philip, and Errol Morris. *Standard Operating Procedure*.

      publisher   year

Penguin Books, 2008.

3. Three or more authors   Name the first author followed by "et al." (Latin for "and others"). For in-text citations, see item 7 in 50a.

first author: "et al." for
last name first   other authors   title (book)

Zumeta, William, et al. *Financing American Higher Education in the Era of Globalization*.

      publisher   year

Harvard Education Press, 2012.

4. Organization or company as author

author: organization
name, not abbreviated   title (book)   publisher   year

Human Rights Watch. *World Report of 2015: Events of 2014*. Seven Stories Press, 2015.

Your in-text citation also should treat the organization as the author (see item 8 in 50a).

5. No author listed

                 newspaper title   descriptive
      article title   (city in brackets)   date   page(s)   label

"Policing Ohio's Online Courses." *Plain Dealer* [Cleveland], 9 Oct. 2012, p. A5. Editorial.

                      title of TV
      episode title   show   producer   network year

"Fast Times at West Philly High." *Frontline*, produced by Debbie Morton, PBS, 2012.

NOTE: In web sources, often the author's name is available but is not easy to find. It may appear at the end of a web page, in tiny print, or on another page of the site, such as the home page. Also, an organization or a government may be the author (see items 4 and 56).

General guidelines for the works cited list

In the list of works cited, include only sources that you have quoted, summarized, or paraphrased in your paper. MLA's guidelines apply to a wide variety of sources. You can adapt the guidelines and models in this section to source types you encounter in your research.

Gathering information and organizing entries

The elements needed for a works cited entry are the following:

- The author (if a work has one)
- The title
- The title of the larger work in which the source is located, if it is contained in a larger work (MLA calls the larger work a "container"—a collection, a journal, a magazine, a website, and so on)
- As much of the following information as is available about the source and the container:

  Editor, translator, director, performer

  Version or edition

  Volume and issue numbers

  Publisher

  Date of publication

  Location of the source: page numbers, URL, DOI, and so on

Not all sources will require every element. See specific models in this section for more details.

Authors

- Arrange the list alphabetically by authors' last names or by titles for works with no authors.
- For the first author, list the last name first, followed by a comma and the first name. Put a second author's name in normal order (first name followed by last name). For three or more authors, use "et al." after the first author's name.
- Spell out "editor," "translator," "edited by," and so on.

GENERAL GUIDELINES FOR THE WORKS CITED LIST, (*cont.*)

Titles

- In titles of works, capitalize all words except articles (*a, an, the*), prepositions, coordinating conjunctions, and the *to* in infinitives—unless the word is first or last in the title or subtitle.

- Use quotation marks for titles of articles and other short works. Place single quotation marks around a quoted term or a title of a short work that appears within an article title; italicize a term or title that is normally italicized.

- Italicize titles of books and other long works. If a book title contains another title that is normally italicized, neither italicize the internal title nor place it in quotation marks. If the title within the title is normally put in quotation marks, retain the quotation marks and italicize the entire book title.

Publication information

- Do not give the place of publication for a book publisher.

- Use the complete version of publishers' names, except for terms such as "Inc." and "Co."; retain terms such as "Books" and "Press." For university publishers, use "U" and "P" for "University" and "Press."

- For a book, take the name of the publisher from the title page (or from the copyright page if it is not on the title page). For a website, the publisher might be at the bottom of a page or on the "About" page. If a work has two or more publishers, separate the names with slashes.

- If the title of a website and the publisher are the same or similar, give the title of the site but omit the publisher.

Dates

- For a book, give the most recent year found on the title page or the copyright page. For a web source, use the copyright date or the most recent update date. Use the complete date as listed in the source.

- Abbreviate all months except May, June, and July and give the date in inverted form: 13 Mar. 2019.

- If the source has no date, give your date of access at the end: Accessed 24 Feb. 2019.

GENERAL GUIDELINES FOR THE WORKS CITED LIST, *(cont.)*

Page numbers

- For most articles and other short works, give page numbers when they are available, preceded by "pp." (or "p." for only one page).
- Do not use the page numbers from a printout of a web source.
- If a short work does not appear on consecutive pages, give the number of the first page followed by a plus sign: 35+.

URLs and DOIs

- Give a permalink or a DOI (digital object identifier) if a source has one.
- If a source does not have a permalink or a DOI, include the full URL for the source (omitting the protocol, such as http://).
- If a database provides only a URL that is long and complicated and if your readers are not likely to be able to use it to access the source, your instructor may allow you to use the URL for the database home page (such as go.galegroup.com). Check with your instructor.
- For open databases and archives, such as Google Books, give the complete URL for the source. (See item 25b.)
- If a URL or a DOI must be divided across lines, break it before a period or a hyphen or before or after any other mark of punctuation. Do not add a hyphen.

6. Two or more works by the same author or group of authors First alphabetize the works by title (ignoring the article *A*, *An*, or *The* at the beginning of a title). Use the author's name or authors' names for the first entry; for subsequent entries, use three hyphens and a period. The three hyphens must stand for exactly the same name or names that appear in the first entry.

García, Cristina. *Dreams of Significant Girls*. Simon and Schuster, 2011.

---. *The Lady Matador's Hotel*. Scribner, 2010.

Agha, Hussein, and Robert Malley. "The Arab Counterrevolution." *The New York Review of Books*, 29 Sept. 2011, www.nybooks.com/articles/2011/09/29/arab-counterrevolution.

---. "This Is Not a Revolution." *The New York Review of Books*, 8 Nov. 2012, www
.nybooks.com/articles/2012/11/08/not-revolution.

7. Editor or translator Begin with the editor's or translator's name.
After the name, add "editor" or "translator." Use "editors" or "translators" for two or more (see also items 2 and 3 for how to handle multiple
contributors).

first editor: last second editor:
 name first in normal order   title (book)

Horner, Avril, and Anne Rowe, editors. *Living on Paper: Letters from Iris Murdoch, 1934–1995.*

   publisher year

 Princeton UP, 2016.

8. Author with editor or translator Begin with the name of the author.
Place the editor's or translator's name after the title.

 author: last
 name first   title (book)   translator:
                in normal order

Ullmann, Regina. *The Country Road: Stories.* Translated by Kurt Beals,

    publisher   year

 New Directions Publishing, 2015.

9. Graphic narrative or other illustrated work If a work has both an
author and an illustrator, the order in your citation will depend on which
of those persons you emphasize in your paper.

Gaiman, Neil. *The Sandman: Overture.* Illustrated by J. H. William III, DC Comics, 2015.

Wenzel, David, illustrator. *The Hobbit.* By J. R. R. Tolkien, Ballantine Books, 2012.

10. Author using a pseudonym (pen name) or screen name Give the
author's name as it appears in the source (the pseudonym), followed by
the author's real name, if available, in parentheses.

Grammar Girl (Mignon Fogarty). "Lewis Carroll: He Loved to Play with Language."
 QuickandDirtyTips.com, 21 May 2015, www.quickanddirtytips.com/education
 /grammar/lewis-carroll-he-loved-to-play-with-language.

Pauline. Comment on "Is This the End?" *The New York Times*, 25 Nov. 2012, nyti
 .ms/1BRUvqQ.

Answer the basic question "Who is the author?"

Problem: Sometimes when you need to cite a source, it's not clear who the author is. This is especially true for sources on the web and other nonprint sources, which may have been created by one person and uploaded by a different person or an organization. Whom do you cite as the author in such a case? How do you determine who *is* the author?

Example: The video "Surfing the Web on the Job" (see below) was uploaded to YouTube by CBSNewsOnline. Is the person or organization that uploads the video the author of the video? Not necessarily.

Strategy: After you view or listen to the source a few times, ask yourself whether you can tell who is chiefly responsible for creating the content in the source. It could be an organization. It could be an identifiable individual. This video consists entirely of reporting by Daniel Sieberg, so in this case the author is Sieberg.

Surfing the Web on The Job

CBSNewsOnline · 42,491 videos

▶ Subscribe | 85,736

Uploaded on Nov 12, 2009
As the Internet continues to emerge as a critical facet of everyday life, CBS News' Daniel Sieberg reports that companies are cracking down on employees' personal Web use.

Citation: To cite the source, you would use the basic MLA guidelines for a video found on the web (item 42).

author: last name first   title of video   website title   upload information

Sieberg, Daniel. "Surfing the Web on the Job." *YouTube*, uploaded by CBSNewsOnline,

upload date   URL

12 Nov. 2009, www.youtube.com/watch?v=1wLhNwY-enY.

11. Author quoted by another author (indirect source)   If one of your sources uses a quotation from another source and you'd like to use the quotation, provide a works cited entry for the source in which you found the quotation. In your in-text citation, indicate that the quoted words appear in the source (see item 22 in 50a).

Articles and other short works

▸ Citation at a glance: Article in an online journal, 327
▸ Citation at a glance: Article from a database, 328

12. Basic format for an article or other short work

a. Print

author:
last name first   article title   journal title   volume, issue

Tilman, David. "Food and Health of a Full Earth." *Daedalus*, vol. 144, no. 4,

date   page(s)

Fall 2015, pp. 5–7.

b. Web

author:
last name first   title of short work

Nelson, Libby. "How Schools Will Be Different without No Child Left Behind."

title of website   date   URL

Vox, 11 Dec. 2015, www.vox.com/2015/12/11/9889350/every-student

-succeeds-act-schools.

c. Database   If a database provides a DOI or a permalink, use that at the end of your citation. If it provides only a URL that is long and complicated and if your readers may not be able to access it, your instructor may allow you to use the URL for the database home page (such as go .galegroup.com). Check with your instructor.

first author: last name first | second author: in normal order | article title

Meyer, Michaela D. E., and Megan M. Wood. "Sexuality and Teen Television: Emerging

journal title

Adults Respond to Representations of Queer Identity on *Glee*." *Sexuality and*

volume, issue | date | page(s) | database title | URL

Culture, vol. 17, no. 3, Sept. 2013, pp. 434–48. *Academic OneFile*, go.galegroup

.com/ps/i.do?p=PPGB&sw=w&u=mlin_n_merrcol&v=2.1&id=GALE%7CA343054749

&it=r&asid=c78658b5b509de7c41177489da8e89ce.

13. Article in a journal

a. Print

author: last name first | article title | journal title

Matchie, Thomas. "Law versus Love in *The Round House*." *The Midwest Quarterly*,

volume, issue | date | page(s)

vol. 56, no. 4, Summer 2015, pp. 353–64.

b. Online journal

author: last name first | article title

Butler, Janine. "Where Access Meets Multimodality: The Case of ASL Music Videos."

journal title | volume, issue | date | URL

Kairos, vol. 21, no. 1, Fall 2016, kairos.technorhetoric.net/21.1/topoi/butler

/index.html.

c. Database

author: last name first | article title | journal title

Maier, Jessica. "A 'True Likeness': The Renaissance City Portrait." *Renaissance Quarterly*,

volume, issue | date | page(s) | database title | DOI

vol. 65, no. 3, Fall 2012, pp. 711–52. *JSTOR*, doi:10.1086/668300.

Citation at a glance

Article in an online journal MLA

To cite an article in an online journal in MLA style, include the following elements:

1 Author(s) of article
2 Title and subtitle of article
3 Title of journal
4 Volume and issue numbers

5 Date of publication (including month or season, if any)
6 Page number(s) of article, if given
7 Location of source (DOI, permalink, or URL)

ONLINE JOURNAL ARTICLE

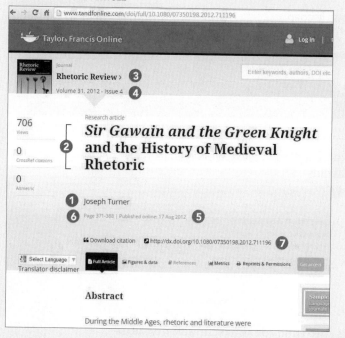

WORKS CITED ENTRY FOR AN ARTICLE IN AN ONLINE JOURNAL

Turner, Joseph. "*Sir Gawain and the Green Knight* and the History of Medieval Rhetoric."

Rhetoric Review, vol. 31, no. 4, 17 Aug. 2012, pp. 371-88, doi:10.1080/07350198

.2012.711196.

For more on citing online articles in MLA style, see item 12.

Citation at a glance

Article from a database `MLA`

To cite an article from a database in MLA style, include the following elements:

1 Author(s) of article
2 Title and subtitle of article
3 Title of journal, magazine, or newspaper
4 Volume and issue numbers (for journal)

5 Date of publication (including month or season, if any)
6 Page number(s) of article, if any
7 Name of database
8 DOI or permalink, if available; otherwise, complete URL or shortened URL of database (see item 12c)

DATABASE RECORD

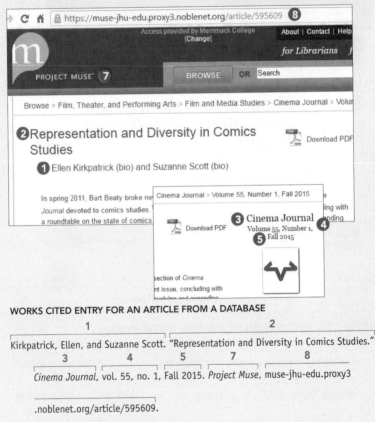

WORKS CITED ENTRY FOR AN ARTICLE FROM A DATABASE

       1   2

Kirkpatrick, Ellen, and Suzanne Scott. "Representation and Diversity in Comics Studies."

    3   4   5   7   8

Cinema Journal, vol. 55, no. 1, Fall 2015. *Project Muse*, muse-jhu-edu.proxy3

.noblenet.org/article/595609.

For more on citing articles from a database in MLA style, see items 12 and 13.

14. Article in a magazine

author: last name first | article title | magazine title | date | page(s)

Bryan, Christy. "Ivory Worship." *National Geographic*, Oct. 2012, pp. 28–61.

author: last name first | article title | magazine title | date | page(s)

Vick, Karl. "The Stateless Statesman." *Time*, 15 Oct. 2012, pp. 32–37.

author: last name first | article title | website title | date | URL

Leonard, Andrew. "The Surveillance State High School." *Salon*, 27 Nov. 2012, www.salon

.com/2012/11/27/the_surveillance_state_high_school.

15. Article in a newspaper
If the city of publication is not obvious from the title of the newspaper, include the city in brackets after the newspaper title (see item 5).

author: last name first | article title | newspaper title

Bray, Hiawatha. "As Toys Get Smarter, Privacy Issues Emerge." *The Boston Globe*,

date | page(s)

10 Dec. 2015, p. C1.

author: last name first | article title | website title

Crowell, Maddy. "How Computers Are Getting Better at Detecting Liars." *The Christian*

date | URL

Science Monitor, 12 Dec. 2015, www.csmonitor.com/Science/Science-Notebook

/2015/1212/How-computers-are-getting-better-at-detecting-liars.

16. Editorial
Cite as you would a source with no author (see item 5) and use the label "Editorial" at the end (and before any database information).

"City's Blight Fight Making Difference." *The Columbus Dispatch*, 17 Nov. 2015,
www.dispatch.com/content/stories/editorials/2015/11/17/1-citys-blight
-fight-making-difference.html. Editorial.

17. Letter to the editor   Use the label "Letter" at the end of the entry (and before any database information). If the letter has no title, place the label directly after the author's name.

Fahey, John A. "Recalling the Cuban Missile Crisis." *The Washington Post*, 28 Oct. 2012,
    p. A16. Letter. *LexisNexis Library Express*, www.lexisnexis.com/hottopics
    /Inpubliclibraryexpress.

18. Comment on an online article   For the use of a screen name and a real name (if known), see item 10. After the name, include "Comment on" followed by the title of the article and publication information for the article.

author:
screen name   article title

pablosharkman. Comment on " 'We All Are Implicated': Wendell Berry Laments a

                                                website title

    Disconnection from Community and the Land." *The Chronicle of Higher Education*,

    date   URL

    23 Apr. 2012, chronicle.com/article/In-Jefferson-Lecture-Wendell/131648.

19. Book review   Name the reviewer and the title of the review, if any, followed by "Review of" and the title and author of the work reviewed. Add publication information for the publication in which the review appears. If the review has no author and no title, begin with "Review of" and alphabetize the entry by the first principal word in the title of the work reviewed.

Della Subin, Anna. "It Has Burned My Heart." Review of *The Lives of Muhammad*,
    by Kecia Ali. *London Review of Books*, 22 Oct. 2015, www.lrb.co.uk/v37/n20
    /anna-della-subin/it-has-burned-my-heart.

Spychalski, John C. Review of *American Railroads—Decline and Renaissance in the
    Twentieth Century*, by Robert E. Gallamore and John R. Meyer. *Transportation
    Journal*, vol. 54, no. 4, Fall 2015, pp. 535–38. *JSTOR*, doi:10.5325
    /transportationj.54.4.0535.

20. Film review or other review   Name the reviewer and the title of the review, if any, followed by "Review of" and the title and the writer or director of the work reviewed. Add publication information for the publication in which the review appears. If the review has no author and no title, begin with "Review of" and alphabetize the entry by the first principal word in the title of the work reviewed.

Lane, Anthony. "Human Bondage." Review of *Spectre*, directed by Sam Mendes. *The New Yorker*, 16 Nov. 2015, pp. 96–97.

Savage, Phil. "*Fallout 4* Review." Review of *Fallout 4*, by Bethesda Game Studios. *PC Gamer*, Future Publishing, 8 Nov. 2015, www.pcgamer.com/fallout-4-review.

21. Performance review Name the reviewer and the title of the review, if any, followed by "Review of" and the title of the work reviewed. After the title, add the author or director of the work, if relevant. Add publication information for the publication in which the review appears. If the review has no author and no title, begin with "Review of" and alphabetize the entry by the first principal word in the title of the work reviewed.

Stout, Gene. "The Ebullient Florence + the Machine Give KeyArena a Workout." Review of *How Big How Blue How Beautiful Odyssey*. *The Seattle Times*, 28 Oct. 2015, www.seattletimes .com/entertainment/music/the-ebullient-florence-the-machine-give-keyarena-a-workout.

22. Interview Begin with the person interviewed, followed by the title of the interview (if there is one). If the interview does not have a title, include the word "Interview" after the interviewee's name. If you wish to include the name of the interviewer, put it after the title of the interview.

Weddington, Sarah. "Sarah Weddington: Still Arguing for *Roe*." Interview by Michele Kort. *Ms.*, Winter 2013, pp. 32–35.

Putin, Vladimir. Interview. By Charlie Rose. *Charlie Rose: The Week*, PBS, 19 June 2015.

Akufo, Rosa. Personal interview. 11 Apr. 2016.

23. Article in a dictionary or an encyclopedia (including a wiki) List the author of the entry (if there is one), the title of the entry, and publication information for the reference work. Include page numbers for a print source as you would for a selection in a collection (see item 29).

Durante, Amy M. "Finn Mac Cumhail." *Encyclopedia Mythica*, 17 Apr. 2011, www .pantheon.org/articles/f/finn_mac_cumhail.html.

"House Music." *Wikipedia*, 16 Nov. 2015, en.wikipedia.org/wiki/House_music.

24. Letter in a collection

a. Print Begin with the writer of the letter, the words "Letter to" and the recipient, and the date of the letter. Add the title of the collection and other publication information. Add the page range at the end.

Murdoch, Iris. Letter to Raymond Queneau. 7 Aug. 1946. *Living on Paper: Letters from Iris Murdoch, 1934–1995*, edited by Avril Horner and Anne Rowe, Princeton UP, 2016, pp. 76–78.

b. Web After information about the letter writer, recipient, and date (if known), give the name of the website or archive, italicized; the publisher of the site; and the URL.

Oblinger, Maggie. Letter to Charlie Thomas. 31 Mar. 1895. *Prairie Settlement: Nebraska Photographs and Family Letters, 1862–1912*, Library of Congress / American Memory, memory.loc.gov/cgi-bin/query/r?ammem/ps:@ field(DOCID+l306)#l3060001.

Books and other long works

▸ Citation at a glance: Book, 333
▸ Citation at a glance: Selection from an anthology or a collection, 336

25. Basic format for a book

a. Print book or e-book If you have used an e-book, indicate "e-book" or the specific reader (using the abbreviation "ed." for "edition") before the publisher's name.

author: last name first | book title | publisher | year

Porter, Max. *Lanny*. Graywolf Press, 2019.

Beard, Mary. *SPQR: A History of Ancient Rome*. Nook ed., Liveright Publishing, 2015.

Citation at a glance

Book MLA

To cite a print book in MLA style, include the following elements:

1 Author(s)
2 Title and subtitle
3 Publisher
4 Year of publication (latest year)

TITLE PAGE

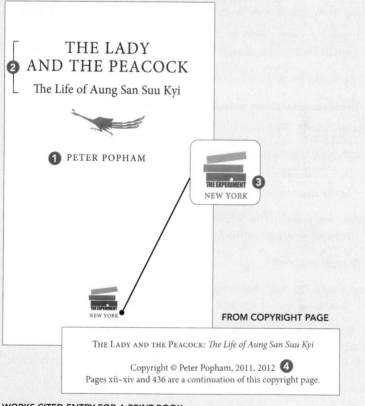

FROM COPYRIGHT PAGE

THE LADY AND THE PEACOCK: *The Life of Aung San Suu Kyi*

Copyright © Peter Popham, 2011, 2012 **4**
Pages xii–xiv and 436 are a continuation of this copyright page.

WORKS CITED ENTRY FOR A PRINT BOOK

```
   1                          2                               3          4
```
Popham, Peter. *The Lady and the Peacock: The Life of Aung San Suu Kyi*. The Experiment, 2012.

For more on citing books in MLA style, see items 25–32.

25. Basic format for a book (cont.)

b. Web Give whatever print publication information is available for the work, followed by the title of the website and the URL.

author: last name first   book title   translator: in normal order

Piketty, Thomas. *Capital in the Twenty-First Century*. Translated by Arthur Goldhammer,

publisher   year   website title   URL

    Harvard UP, 2014. *Google Books*, books.google.com/books?isbn=0674369556.

26. Parts of a book

a. Foreword, introduction, preface, or afterword

author of foreword: last name first   book part   book title

Bennett, Hal Zina. Foreword. *Shimmering Images: A Handy Little Guide to Writing Memoir*,

author of book: in normal order   publisher   year   page(s)

    by Lisa Dale Norton, St. Martin's Griffin, 2008, pp. xiii-xvi.

Sullivan, John Jeremiah. "The Ill-Defined Plot." Introduction. *The Best American Essays 2014*, edited by Sullivan, Houghton Mifflin Harcourt, 2014, pp. xvii-xxvi.

b. Chapter in a book

Rizga, Kristina. "Mr. Hsu." *Mission High: One School, How Experts Tried to Fail It, and the Students and Teachers Who Made It Triumph*, Nation Books, 2015, pp. 89–114.

27. Book in a language other than English

Capitalize the title according to the conventions of the book's language. If your readers are not familiar with the language of the book, include a translation of the title in brackets.

Vargas Llosa, Mario. *El sueño del celta* [*The Dream of the Celt*]. Alfaguara Ediciones, 2010.

28. Entire anthology or collection

An anthology is a collection of works on a common theme, often with different authors for the selections and usually with an editor for the entire volume.

editor: last name first   title of anthology   publisher   year

Marcus, Ben, editor. *New American Stories*. Vintage Books, 2015.

29. One selection from an anthology or a collection

author of   title of   title of   editor(s) of
selection   selection   anthology   anthology

Sayrafiezadeh, Saïd. "Paranoia." *New American Stories,* edited by Ben Marcus,

publisher   year   page(s)

Vintage Books, 2015, pp. 3–29.

30. Two or more selections from an anthology or a collection

Provide an entry for the entire anthology (see item 28) and a shortened entry for each selection. Alphabetize the entries by authors' or editors' last names. Here, the Eisenberg and Sayrafiezadeh selections appear in Marcus's anthology, *New American Stories.*

author of   title of   editor(s) of
selection   selection   anthology   page(s)

Eisenberg, Deborah. "Some Other, Better Otto." Marcus, pp. 94–136.

editor of   title of
anthology   anthology   publisher   year

Marcus, Ben, editor. *New American Stories*. Vintage Books, 2015.

author of   title of   editor(s) of
selection   selection anthology page(s)

Sayrafiezadeh, Saïd. "Paranoia." Marcus, pp. 3–29.

31. Edition other than the first

If the book has a translator or an editor in addition to the author, give the name of the translator or editor before the edition number (see item 8 for a book with an editor or a translator).

Eagleton, Terry. *Literary Theory: An Introduction*. 3rd ed., U of Minnesota P, 2008.

32. Multivolume work

Include the total number of volumes at the end of the entry, using the abbreviation "vols." If the volumes were published over several years, give the inclusive dates of publication.

author: last   book   editor(s): in   inclusive   total
name first   title   normal order   publisher   dates   volumes

Stark, Freya. *Letters*. Edited by Lucy Moorehead, Compton Press, 1974–82. 8 vols.

Citation at a glance

Selection from an anthology or a collection `MLA`

To cite a selection from an anthology in MLA style, include the following elements:

1 Author(s) of selection
2 Title and subtitle of selection
3 Title and subtitle of anthology
4 Editor(s) of anthology
5 Publisher
6 Year of publication
7 Page number(s) of selection

TITLE PAGE OF ANTHOLOGY

FIRST PAGE OF SELECTION

CHAPTER 3

Technology's Quiet Revolution **②**
for Women

Isobel Coleman **①**

[THE UNFINISHED
REVOLUTION
③
VOICES FROM THE GLOBAL FIGHT
FOR WOMEN'S RIGHTS
]

EDITED BY MINKY WORDEN **④**

the eve of Egypt's January 2011 revolution, I happened to be in
iro, having dinner with Gamila Ismail, a longtime Egyptian
l activist who had spent decades opposing the Mubarak
"What will happen tomorrow?" I asked her, referring to the

n 2011, Newsweek named her as one of "150 Women Who Shake the World."

41 ●——— 41 **⑦**

⑤
Seven Stories Press
NEW YORK

FROM COPYRIGHT PAGE

⑥
Copyright © 2012 by Minky Worden
Individual chapters © 2012 by each author

7

Seven Stories Press
NEW YORK

WORKS CITED ENTRY FOR A SELECTION FROM AN ANTHOLOGY

1 ——————— 2 —————————————— 3 ———

Coleman, Isobel. "Technology's Quiet Revolution for Women." *The Unfinished Revolution:*

4 ———— 5 ——

Voices from the Global Fight for Women's Rights, edited by Minky Worden, Seven

6 —— 7 ——

Stories Press, 2012, pp. 41-49.

For more on citing selections from anthologies in MLA style, see items 28–30.

32. Multivolume work *(cont.)*

If you cite only one volume in your paper, include the volume number before the publisher and give the date of publication for that volume. After the date, give the total number of volumes.

author: last name first | book title | editor(s): in normal order | volume cited | publisher | date of volume | total volumes

Stark, Freya. *Letters*. Edited by Lucy Moorehead, vol. 5, Compton Press, 1978. 8 vols.

33. Sacred text   Give the title of the edition (taken from the title page), italicized; the editor's or translator's name (if any); and publication information. Add the name of the version, if there is one, before the publisher.

The Oxford Annotated Bible with the Apocrypha. Edited by Herbert G. May and Bruce
      M. Metzger, Revised Standard Version, Oxford UP, 1965.

The Qur'an: Translation. Translated by Abdullah Yusuf Ali, Tahrike Tarsile Qur'an, 2001.

34. Dissertation

Kidd, Celeste. *Rational Approaches to Learning and Development*. 2013. U of Rochester,
      PhD dissertation.

Abbas, Megan Brankley. *Knowing Islam: The Entangled History of Western Academia
      and Modern Islamic Thought*. 2015. Princeton U, PhD dissertation. *DataSpace*,
      arks.princeton.edu/ark:/88435/dsp016682x6260.

Websites and parts of websites

► Citation at a glance: Work from a website, **339**

35. An entire website

a. Website with author or editor

author or editor: last name first | title of website | publisher

Railton, Stephen. *Mark Twain in His Times*. Stephen Railton / U of Virginia Library,

update date | URL

      2012, twain.lib.virginia.edu.

Halsall, Paul, editor. *Internet Modern History Sourcebook.* Fordham U, 4 Nov. 2011,
    legacy.fordham.edu/halsall/index.asp.

b. Website with organization as author

organization · title of website

Transparency International. *Transparency International: The Global Coalition against*

· · · date · · · URL

Corruption, 2015, www.transparency.org.

c. Website with no author Begin with the title of the site.

The Newton Project. U of Sussex, 2016, www.newtonproject.sussex.ac.uk/prism.php?id=1.

d. Website with no title Use the label "Home page" or another appropriate description in place of a title.

Bae, Rebecca. Home page. Iowa State U, 2015, www.engl.iastate.edu
    /rebecca-bae-directory-page.

36. Work from a website The titles of short works, such as articles or individual web pages, are placed in quotation marks. Titles of long works, such as books and reports, are italicized.

author: last name first · · · title of short work · · · title of website

Gallagher, Sean. "The Last Nomads of the Tibetan Plateau." *Pulitzer Center on Crisis*

· · · date · · · URL

Reporting, 25 Oct. 2012, pulitzercenter.org/reporting/china-glaciers-global

-warming-climate-change-ecosystem-tibetan-plateau-grasslands-nomads.

title of article · · · title of website

"Social and Historical Context: Vitality." *Arapesh Grammar and Digital Language Archive*

· · · publisher · · · URL

Project, Institute for Advanced Technology in the Humanities, www.arapesh

access date for undated site

.org/socio_historical_context_vitality.php. Accessed 22 Mar. 2016.

Citation at a glance

Work from a website MLA

To cite a work from a website in MLA style, include the following elements:

1 Author(s) of work, if any
2 Title and subtitle
3 Title of website
4 Publisher of website (unless it is the same as the title of site)
5 Update date
6 URL of page (or of home page of site)
7 Date of access (if no update date on site)

INTERNAL PAGE FROM A WEBSITE

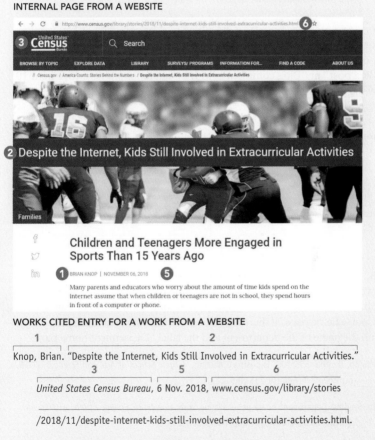

WORKS CITED ENTRY FOR A WORK FROM A WEBSITE

```
        1                              2
```
Knop, Brian. "Despite the Internet, Kids Still Involved in Extracurricular Activities."
```
                3              5             6
```
United States Census Bureau, 6 Nov. 2018, www.census.gov/library/stories

/2018/11/despite-internet-kids-still-involved-extracurricular-activities.html.

For more on citing sources from websites in MLA style, see item 36.

36. Work from a website *(cont.)*

first author: last name first · et al. for other authors · title of long work

Byndloss, D. Crystal, et al. *In Search of a Match: A Guide for Helping Students Make*

title of website · update date · URL

Informed College Choices. Ford Foundation, Apr. 2015, fordfoundcontentthemes

.blob.core.windows.net/media/2607/in_search_of_a_match.pdf.

37. Blog post or comment

Cite a blog post or comment as you would a work from a website (see item 36), with the title of the post or comment in quotation marks. If the post or comment has no title, use the label "Blog post" or "Blog comment" (with no quotation marks). (See item 10 for the use of screen names.)

author: last name first · title of blog post · title of blog · publisher · update date

Eakin, Emily. "*Cloud Atlas*'s Theory of Everything." *NYR Daily*, NYREV, 2 Nov. 2012,

URL

www.nybooks.com/daily/2012/11/02/ken-wilber-cloud-atlas.

author: screen name · label · title of blog post · title of blog · publisher

mitchellfreedman. Comment on "*Cloud Atlas*'s Theory of Everything." *NYR Daily*, NYREV,

date · URL

3 Nov. 2012, www.nybooks.com/daily/2012/11/02/ken-wilber-cloud-atlas.

38. Academic course or department home page

Cite as a work from a website (see item 36). For a course home page, begin with the instructor and the title of the course or page, without quotation marks or italics. (Use "Course home page" if there is no title.) For a department home page, begin with the name of the department and the label "Department home page."

Masiello, Regina. 355:101: Expository Writing. *Rutgers School of Arts and Sciences*, 2016,
wp.rutgers.edu/courses/55-355101.

Film Studies. Department home page. *Wayne State University, College of Liberal Arts and Sciences*, 2016, clas.wayne.edu/FilmStudies.

Audio, visual, and multimedia sources

39. Podcast

author: last
name first   podcast title   website title   publisher

Tanner, Laura. "Virtual Reality in 9/11 Fiction." *Literature Lab*, Department of English,

URL

    Brandeis U, www.brandeis.edu/departments/english/literaturelab/tanner.html.

date of access
for undated site

    Accessed 14 Feb. 2016.

McDougall, Christopher. "How Did Endurance Help Early Humans Survive?" *TED*
    Radio Hour, NPR, 20 Nov. 2015, www.npr.org/2015/11/20/455904655
    /how-did-endurance-help-early-humans-survive.

40. Film Generally, begin the entry with the title, followed by the director and lead performers, as in the first example. If your paper emphasizes one or more people involved with the film, you may begin with those names, as in the second example.

film title   director

Birdman or (The Unexpected Virtue of Ignorance). Directed by Alejandro González

major performers

    Iñárritu, performances by Michael Keaton, Emma Stone, Zach Galifianakis,

distributor   release date

    Edward Norton, and Naomi Watts, Fox Searchlight, 2014.

director: last
name first   film title   major performers

Scott, Ridley, director. *The Martian*. Performances by Matt Damon, Jessica Chastain,

distributor   release date

    Kristen Wiig, and Kate Mara, Twentieth Century Fox, 2015.

41. Supplementary material accompanying a film Begin with the title of the supplementary material, in quotation marks, and the names of any important contributors, as for a film. End with information about the film, as in item 40, and about the location of the supplementary material.

"Sweeney's London." Produced by Eric Young. *Sweeney Todd: The Demon Barber of Fleet
    Street*, directed by Tim Burton, DreamWorks, 2007, disc 2.

42. Video or audio from the web   Cite video or audio that you accessed on the web as you would a work from a website (see item 36), with the title of the video or audio in quotation marks.

author: last
name first   title of video   website
                                               title   upload
                                                               information   date

Lewis, Paul. "Citizen Journalism." *YouTube*, uploaded by TEDx Talks, 14 May 2011,
                         URL

    www.youtube.com/watch?v=9APO9_yNbcg.

author: last
name first   title of video   website title

Fletcher, Antoine. "The Ancient Art of the Atlatl." *Russell Cave National Monument*,
                    narrator   publisher   date   URL

    narrated by Brenton Bellomy, National Park Service, 12 Feb. 2014, www.nps.gov

    /media/video/view.htm?id=C92C0D0A-1DD8-B71C-07CBC6E8970CD73F.

author: last
name first   title of video   website
                                               title   date   URL

Burstein, Julie. "Four Lessons in Creativity." *TED*, Feb. 2012, www.ted.com/talks

    /julie_burstein_4_lessons_in_creativity.

43. Video game   List the developer or author of the game (if any); the title, italicized; the version, if there is one; and the distributor and date of publication. If the game can be played on the web, add information as for a work from a website (see item 36).

Firaxis Games. *Sid Meier's Civilization Revolution*. Take-Two Interactive, 2008.

Edgeworld. Atom Entertainment, 1 May 2012, www.kabam.com/games/edgeworld.

44. Computer software or app   Cite as a video game (see item 43), giving whatever information is available about the version, distributor, and date.

Venmo. Version 7.4.0, PayPal, 2017.

45. Television or radio episode or program If you are citing an episode of a program, begin with the title of the episode, in quotation marks. Then give the title of the program, italicized; relevant information about the program, such as the writer, director, performers, or narrator; the episode number (if any); the network; and the date of broadcast.

For a program you accessed on the web, after the information about the program give the network, the original broadcast date, and the URL. If you are citing an entire program (not an episode or a segment) or an episode that has no title, begin your entry with the title of the program, italicized.

title of episode / program title / narrator (host or speaker)
"Federal Role in Support of Autism." *Washington Journal,* narrated by Robb Harleston,

network / broadcast date
C-SPAN, 1 Dec. 2012.

The Daily Show with Trevor Noah. Comedy Central, 18 Nov. 2015.

title of episode / program title / narrator / episode / publisher
"The Cathedral." *Reply All,* narrated by Sruthi Pinnamaneni, episode 50, Gimlet Media,

date of posting / URL
7 Jan. 2016, gimletmedia.com/episode/50-the-cathedral.

46. Transcript Cite the source (interview, radio or television program, video, and so on), and add the label "Transcript" at the end of the entry.

"How Long Can Florida's Citrus Industry Survive?" *All Things Considered,* narrated by
   Greg Allen, NPR, 27 Nov. 2015, www.npr.org/templates/transcript/transcript
   .php?storyId=457424528. Transcript.

"The Economics of Sleep, Part 1." *Freakonomics Radio,* narrated by Stephen J. Dubner,
   9 July 2015, freakonomics.com/2015/07/09/ the-economics-of-sleep-part-1-full
   -transcript. Transcript.

Cite a source reposted from another source

Problem: Some sources that you find online, particularly on blogs or on video-sharing sites, did not originate with the person who uploaded or published the source online. In such a case, how do you give proper credit to the source?

Example: Say you need to cite President John F. Kennedy's inaugural address. You have found a video on YouTube that provides footage of the address (see image). The video was uploaded by PaddyIrishMan2 on October 29, 2006. But clearly, PaddyIrishMan2 is not the author of the video or of the address.

JFK Inaugural Address 1 of 2

PaddyIrishMan2 · 12 videos

▶ Subscribe ‹ 403

Uploaded on Oct 29, 2006
President John F. Kennedy's inaugural address, January 20th 1961.

Vice President Johnson, Mr. Speaker, Mr. Chief Justice, President Eisenhower, Vice President Nixon, President Truman, reverend clergy, fellow citizens, we observe today not a victory of party, but a celebration of freedom — symbolising an end, as well as a beginning — signifying renewal, as well as change. For I have sworn before you and Almighty God the same solemn oath our forebears prescribed nearly a century and three quarters ago.

Strategy: Start with what you know. The source is a video that you viewed on the web. For this particular video, John F. Kennedy is the speaker and the author of the inaugural address. PaddyIrishMan2 is identified as the person who uploaded the source to YouTube.

Citation: To cite the source, you can follow the basic MLA guidelines for a video found on the web (see item 42).

| author/speaker: last name first | title of video | website title | upload information |

Kennedy, John F. "JFK Inaugural Address: 1 of 2." *YouTube*, uploaded by PaddyIrishMan2,

| upload date | URL |

29 Oct. 2006, www.youtube.com/watch?v=xEOiPY7XGBo.

NOTE: If your work calls for a primary source, you should try to find the original source of the video; a reference librarian can help.

344

47. Live performance   Begin with the title of the work performed, italicized (unless it is named by form, number, and key). Then give the author or composer of the work; relevant information such as the director, the choreographer, the conductor, or the major performers; the theater, ballet, or opera company, if any; the theater and location; and the date of the performance.

The Draft. By Peter Snoad, directed by Diego Arciniegas, Hibernian Hall, Boston,
    10 Sept. 2015.

Symphony no. 4 in G. By Gustav Mahler, conducted by Mark Wigglesworth,
    performances by Juliane Banse and Boston Symphony Orchestra, Symphony Hall,
    Boston, 17 Apr. 2009.

48. Lecture or public address   Begin with the speaker's name, the title of the lecture, the sponsoring organization, location, and date. If you viewed the lecture on the web, cite as you would a work from a website (see item 36). Add the label "Address" or "Lecture" at the end if it is not clear from the title.

Smith, Anna Deavere. "On the Road: A Search for American Character." National
    Endowment for the Humanities, John F. Kennedy Center for the Performing Arts,
    Washington, 6 Apr. 2015. Address.

Khosla, Raj. "Precision Agriculture and Global Food Security." *US Department of State:
    Diplomacy in Action*, 26 Mar. 2013, www.state .gov/e/stas/series/212172.htm
    .Address.

49. Musical score   Begin with the composer's name; the title of the work, italicized (unless it is named by form, number, and key); and the date of composition. For a print source, give the publisher and date. For an online source, give the title of the website, the publisher, the date, and the URL.

Beethoven, Ludwig van. Symphony no. 5 in C Minor, op. 67. 1807. *Center for
    Computer Assisted Research in the Humanities*, Stanford U, 2000, scores.ccarh.org
    /beethoven/sym/beethoven-sym5-1.pdf.

50. Sound recording   Begin with the name of the person you want to emphasize: the composer, conductor, or performer. For a long work, give the title, italicized (unless it is named by form, number, and key); the names of pertinent artists; and the orchestra and conductor. End with the manufacturer and the date.

Bizet, Georges. *Carmen*. Performances by Jennifer Larmore, Thomas Moser, Angela
  Gheorghiu, Samuel Ramey, and Bavarian State Orchestra and Chorus, conducted by
  Giuseppe Sinopoli, Warner, 1996.

Blige, Mary J. "Thriving." *Strength of a Woman*, Capitol Records, 2017.

51. Artwork, photograph, or other visual art   Begin with the artist and the title of the work, italicized. If you viewed the original work, give the date of composition followed by a comma and the location. If you viewed the work online, give the date of composition followed by a period and the website title, publisher (if any), and URL. If you viewed the work reproduced in a book, cite as a work in an anthology or a collection (item 29), giving the date of composition after the title. If the medium of composition is not apparent or is important for your work, you may include it at the end (as in the second example).

Bradford, Mark. *Let's Walk to the Middle of the Ocean*. 2015, Museum of Modern Art,
  New York.

Lindsey, Lindsay Jones. *Fibonacci Spiral*. 2012, University of Alabama, Tuscaloosa. Public
  sculpture.

Clough, Charles. *January Twenty-First*. 1988–89. *Joslyn Art Museum*, www.joslyn.org
  /collections-and-exhibitions/permanent-collections/modern-and-contemporary
  /charles-clough-january-twenty-first.

Kertész, André. *Meudon*. 1928. *Street Photography: From Atget to Cartier-Bresson*, by
  Clive Scott, Tauris, 2011, p. 61.

52. Visual such as a table, a chart, or another graphic   Cite a visual as you would a short work within a longer work. Add a descriptive label at the end if the type of visual is not clear from the title or if it is important for your work.

"Brazilian Waxing and Waning: The Economy." *The Economist*, 1 Dec. 2015, www
.economist.com/blogs/graphicdetail/2015/12/economic-backgrounder. Graph.

"Number of Measles Cases Reported by Year 2010–2019." *Centers for Disease Control and
Prevention*, 22 Feb. 2019, www.cdc.gov/measles/cases-outbreaks.html. Table.

53. Cartoon   Give the cartoonist's name; the title of the cartoon, if it has one, in quotation marks, or the label "Cartoon" without quotation marks in place of a title; and publication information. Add the label "Cartoon" at the end if it is not clear from the title. Cite an online cartoon as a work from a website (item 36).

Zyglis, Adam. "City of Light." *Buffalo News*, 8 Nov. 2015, adamzyglis.buffalonews
.com/2015/11/08/city-of-light. Cartoon.

54. Advertisement   Name the product or company being advertised and provide publication information for the source in which the advertisement appears. Add the label "Advertisement" at the end if it is not clear from the title.

AT&T. *National Geographic*, Dec. 2015, p. 14. Advertisement.

Toyota. *The Root*. Slate Group, 28 Nov. 2015, www.theroot.com. Advertisement.

55. Map   Cite a map as you would a short work within a longer work. If the map is published on its own, cite it as a book or another long work. Use the label "Map" at the end if it is not clear from the title or source information.

"Map of Sudan." *Global Citizen*, Citizens for Global Solutions, 2011, globalsolutions.org
/blog/bashir#.VthzNMfi_FI.

"Vote on Secession, 1861." *Perry-Castañeda Library Map Collection*, U of Texas at Austin,
1976, www.lib.utexas.edu/maps/atlas_texas/texas_vote_secession_1861.jpg.

Government and legal documents

56. Government document   Treat the government agency as the author, giving the name of the government followed by the name of the department and the agency, if any. For sources found on the web, follow the model for an entire website (item 35) or for a work from a website (item 36).

government   department   agency (or agencies)

United States, Department of Agriculture, Food and Nutrition Service, Child Nutrition

                                        title of work

Programs. *Eligibility Manual for School Meals: Determining and Verifying Eligibility.*

          website title   date   URL

National School Lunch Program, July 2015, www.fns.usda.gov/sites/default/files

/cn/SP40_CACFP18_SFSP20-2015a1.pdf.

Canada, Minister of Aboriginal Affairs and Northern Development. *2015–16 Report on Plans and Priorities.* Minister of Public Works and Government Services Canada, 2015.

57. Historical document   The titles of most historical documents, such as the US Constitution and the Canadian Charter of Rights and Freedoms, are neither italicized nor put in quotation marks.

Constitution of the United States. 1787. *The Charters of Freedom,* US National Archives and Records Administration, www.archives.gov/exhibits/charters.

58. Legislative act (law)   Begin with the name of the act, neither italicized nor in quotation marks. Then provide the act's Public Law number, its Statutes at Large volume and page numbers, and its date of enactment.

Electronic Freedom of Information Act Amendments of 1996. Pub. L. 104-231. 110 Stat. 3048. 2 Oct. 1996.

59. Court case   Name the first plaintiff and the first defendant. Then give the volume, name, and page number of the law report; the court name; the year of the decision; and publication information. Do not italicize the name of the case. (In the text of the paper, the name of the case is italicized; see item 18 in 50a.)

Utah v. Evans. 536 US 452. Supreme Court of the US. 2002. *Legal Information Institute*,
    Cornell U Law School, www.law.cornell.edu/supremecourt/text/536/452.

Personal communication and social media

60. Personal letter

Primak, Shoshana. Letter to the author. 6 May 2016.

61. Email message   Begin with the writer's name and the subject line. Then write "Received by," followed by the name of the recipient and the date of the message.

Thornbrugh, Caitlin. "Coates Lecture." Received by Rita Anderson, 20 Oct. 2018.

62. Text message

Wiley, Joanna. Message to the author. 4 Apr. 2019.

63. Online discussion list post   Begin with the author's name, followed by the title or subject line, in quotation marks (use the label "Online posting," with no quotation marks, if the posting has no title). Then proceed as for a work from a website (see item 36).

Griffith, Robin. "Write for the Reading Teacher." *Developing Digital Literacies*, NCTE,
    23 Oct. 2015, ncte.connectedcommunity.org/communities/community-home
    /digestviewer/viewthread? GroupId=1693&MID=24520&tab=digestviewer
    &CommunityKey= 628d2ad6-8277-4042-a376-2b370ddceabf.

64. Social media post   Begin with the writer's screen name, followed by the real name in parentheses, if both are given. For a tweet, use the entire post as a title, in quotation marks. For other media, give a title if the post has one. If it does not, use the label "Post," without quotation marks, in

place of a title. Give the date of the post, the time (if the post specifies one), and the URL.

Curiosity Rover. "Can you see me waving? How to spot #Mars in the night sky:
https://youtu.be/hv8hVvJlcJQ." *Twitter*, 5 Nov. 2015, 11:00 a.m., twitter.com
/marscuriosity/status/672859022911889408.

natgeo (National Geographic). Post. *Instagram*, 22 July 2016, www.instagram.com/p
/BIKyGHtDD4W.

50c MLA information notes (optional)

Researchers who use the MLA system of parenthetical documentation may also use information notes for one of two purposes:

1. to provide additional material that is important but might interrupt the flow of the paper
2. to refer to several sources that support a single point or to provide comments on sources

Information notes may be either footnotes or endnotes. Footnotes appear at the foot of the page; endnotes appear on a separate page at the end of the paper, just before the list of works cited. For either style, the notes are numbered consecutively throughout the paper. The text of the paper contains a raised arabic numeral that corresponds to the number of the note.

TEXT

In the past several years, employees have filed a number of lawsuits against employers because of online monitoring practices.[1]

NOTE

1. For a discussion of federal law applicable to electronic surveillance in the workplace, see Kesan 293.

51 MLA format; sample research paper

The following guidelines are consistent with advice given in the *MLA Handbook*, 8th edition (MLA, 2016), and with typical requirements for student papers. For a sample MLA research paper, see 51b.

51a MLA format

Formatting the paper: The basics

Papers written in MLA style should be formatted as follows.

Harba 1

The heading includes the [stud]ent's name, instructor's [na]me, course, and date.

Sophie Harba

Professor Baros-Moon

Engl 1101

9 November 2018

> The student's last name and the **page number** appear in the right-hand corner of every page.

What's for Dinner? Personal Choices vs. Public Health

> Center the **title**. Add no extra space above or below it, and use no quotation marks or italics.

Use Times [Ne]w Roman or [ot]her easy-to-read **font**.

Should the government enact laws to regulate healthy eating choices? Many Americans would answer an emphatic "No," arguing that what and how much we eat should be left to individual choice rather than unreasonable laws. Others might argue that it would be unreasonable for the government not to enact legislation, given the rise of chronic diseases that result from harmful diets. In this debate, both the definition of reasonable regulations and the role of government to legislate food choices are at stake. In the name of public health and safety, state governments have the responsibility to shape health policies and to regulate healthy eating choices, especially since doing so offers a potentially large social benefit for a relatively small cost.

[U]se a **1-inch** [m]argin on all [s]ides of the page, and [do]uble-space the text.

Debates surrounding the government's role in regulating food have a long history in the United States.

Formatting the paper: Other concerns

Capitalization, italics, and quotation marks   In titles of works, capitalize all words except articles (*a, an, the*), prepositions (*to, from, between,* and so on), coordinating conjunctions (*and, but, or, nor, for, so, yet*), and the *to* in infinitives — unless the word is first or last in the title or subtitle. Follow these guidelines in your paper even if the title appears in all capital or all lowercase letters in the source.

In the text of an MLA paper, when a complete sentence follows a colon, lowercase the first word following the colon.

Italicize the titles of books, journals, magazines, and other long works, such as websites. Use quotation marks around the titles of articles, short stories, poems, and other short works.

Long quotations   When a quotation is longer than four typed lines of prose or three lines of poetry, set it off from the text by indenting the entire quotation one-half inch from the left margin. Double-space the indented quotation and do not add extra space above or below it.

Do not use quotation marks when a quotation has been set off from the text by indenting. See 49b for an example.

URLs   If you need to break a URL at the end of a line in the text of a paper, break it before a period or a hyphen or before or after any other mark of punctuation. Do not add a hyphen. If you will post your project online or submit it electronically and you want your readers to click on your URLs, do not insert any line breaks.

Headings   MLA neither encourages nor discourages the use of headings and provides no guidelines for their use. If you would like to insert headings in a long essay or research paper, check first with your instructor.

Visuals   MLA classifies visuals as tables and figures (figures include graphs, charts, maps, photographs, and drawings). Label each table with an arabic numeral ("Table 1," "Table 2," and so on) and provide a clear title that identifies the subject. Capitalize as you would the title of a work (see above); do not use italics or quotation marks. Place the table number and title on separate lines above the table, flush with the left margin.

For a table that you have borrowed or adapted, give the source below the table in a note like the following:

Source: Boris Groysberg and Michael Slind, "Leadership Is a Conversation," *Harvard Business Review*, June 2012, p. 83.

Place a figure number (using the abbreviation "Fig.") and a caption below each figure, flush left. Capitalize the caption as you would a sentence; include source information following the caption. (When referring to the figure in your paper, use the abbreviation "fig." in parenthetical citations; otherwise spell out the word.) See 51b for an example of a figure in a paper.

Place visuals in the text, as close as possible to the sentences that relate to them, unless your instructor prefers that visuals appear in an appendix.

Preparing the list of works cited

Begin the list of works cited on a new page at the end of the paper. Center the title "Works Cited" about one inch from the top of the page. Double-space throughout. See the student essays in 6g and 51b for sample lists of works cited.

Alphabetizing the list   Alphabetize the list by the last names of the authors (or editors); if a work has no author or editor, alphabetize by the first word of the title other than *A*, *An*, or *The*.

If your list includes two or more works by the same author, use the author's name for the first entry only. For subsequent entries, use three hyphens followed by a period. List the titles in alphabetical order. (See item 6 in 50b.)

Indenting   Do not indent the first line of each works cited entry, but indent any additional lines one-half inch. This technique highlights the names of the authors, making it easy for readers to scan the alphabetized list. See the works cited list in 51b.

URLs and DOIs   If a URL or a DOI in a works cited entry must be divided across lines, break it before a period or a hyphen or before or after any other mark of punctuation. Do not add a hyphen. If you will post your project online or submit it electronically and you want your readers to click on your URLs, do not insert any line breaks.

51b Sample MLA research paper

On the following pages is a research paper on the topic of the role of government in legislating food choices, written by Sophie Harba, a student in a composition class. Harba's paper is documented with in-text citations and a list of works cited in MLA style. Annotations in the margins of the paper draw your attention to Harba's use of MLA style and her effective writing.

Harba 1

Sophie Harba

Professor Baros-Moon

Engl 1101

9 November 2018

What's for Dinner? Personal Choices vs. Public Health

Should the government enact laws to regulate healthy eating
choices? Many Americans would answer an emphatic "No," arguing
that what and how much we eat should be left to individual choice
rather than unreasonable laws. Others might argue that it would be
unreasonable for the government not to enact legislation, given the
rise of chronic diseases that result from harmful diets. In this debate,
both the definition of reasonable regulations and the role of government
to legislate food choices are at stake. In the name of public health
and safety, state governments have the responsibility to shape health
policies and to regulate healthy eating choices, especially since doing so
offers a potentially large social benefit for a relatively small cost.

Debates surrounding the government's role in regulating food have
a long history in the United States. According to Lorine Goodwin, a food
historian, nineteenth-century reformers who sought to purify the food
supply were called "fanatics" and "radicals" by critics who argued that
consumers should be free to buy and eat what they want (77). Thanks to
regulations, though, such as the 1906 federal Pure Food and Drug Act,
food, beverages, and medicine are largely free from toxins. In addition,
to prevent contamination and the spread of disease, meat and dairy
products are now inspected by government agents to ensure that they
meet health requirements. Such regulations can be considered reasonable
because they protect us from harm with little, if any, noticeable
consumer cost. It is not considered an unreasonable infringement on
personal choice that contaminated meat or arsenic-laced cough drops
are *un*available at our local supermarket. Rather, it is an important

Marginal annotations:
- Title is centered.
- Opening question engages readers.
- Writer highlights the research conversation.
- Thesis answers the question and presents main point.
- Signal phrase names the author. Page number is in parentheses.
- Harba provides historical background and introduces a key term, *reasonable*.
- Harba establishes common ground with the reader.

Marginal annotations indicate MLA-style formatting and effective writing.

Harba 2

government function to stop such harmful items from entering the marketplace.

Transition helps readers move from one paragraph to the next.

Even though our food meets current safety standards, there is a need for further regulation. Not all food dangers, for example, arise from obvious toxins like arsenic and *E. coli*. A diet that is low in nutritional value and high in sugars, fats, and refined grains—grains that have been processed to increase shelf life but that contain little fiber, iron, and B vitamins—can be damaging over time (United States, Dept. of Agriculture and Dept. of Health and Human Services 36). A graph from the government's *Dietary Guidelines for Americans, 2010* provides a visual representation of the American diet and how far off it is from the recommended nutritional standards (see fig. 1).

Harba uses a graph to illustrate Americans' poor nutritional choices.

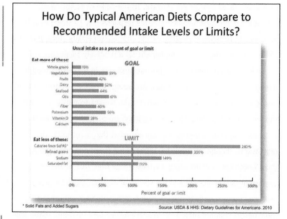

How Do Typical American Diets Compare to Recommended Intake Levels or Limits?

Usual intake as a percent of goal or limit

Eat more of these: GOAL
Whole grains   15%
Vegetables   59%
Fruits   42%
Dairy   52%
Seafood   44%
Oils   61%
Fiber   40%
Potassium   56%
Vitamin D   28%
Calcium   75%

Eat less of these: LIMIT
Calories from SoFAS*   280%
Refined grains   200%
Sodium   149%
Saturated fat   110%

0%   50%   100%   150%   200%   250%   300%
Percent of goal or limit

* Solid Fats and Added Sugars   Source: USDA & HHS: Dietary Guidelines for Americans. 2010

The visual includes a figure number, descriptive caption, and source information.

Fig. 1. This graph shows that Americans consume about three times more fats and sugars and twice as many refined grains as is recommended but only half of the recommended foods (United States, Dept. of Agriculture and Dept. of Health and Human Services, fig. 5-1).

Harba 3

Michael Pollan, who has written extensively about Americans'
unhealthy eating habits, notes that "[t]he Centers for Disease Control
estimates that fully three quarters of US health care spending goes to
treat chronic diseases, most of which are preventable and linked to diet:
heart disease, stroke, type 2 diabetes, and at least a third of all cancers."
In fact, the amount of money the United States spends to treat chronic
illnesses is increasing so rapidly that the Centers for Disease Control has
labeled chronic disease "the public health challenge of the 21st century"
(United States, Dept. of Health and Human Services 1). In fighting
this epidemic, the primary challenge is not the need to find a cure; the
challenge is to prevent chronic diseases from striking in the first place.

Legislation, however, is not a popular solution when it comes to
most Americans and the food they eat. According to a nationwide poll,
75% of Americans are opposed to laws that restrict or put limitations
on access to unhealthy foods (Neergaard and Agiesta). When New York
mayor Michael Bloomberg proposed a regulation in 2012 banning the
sale of soft drinks in servings greater than twelve ounces in restaurants
and movie theaters, he was ridiculed as "Nanny Bloomberg." In California
in 2011, legislators failed to pass a law that would impose a penny-
per-ounce tax on soda, which would have funded obesity prevention
programs. And in Mississippi, legislators passed "a ban on bans—a law
that forbids . . . local restrictions on food or drink" (Conly A23).

Why is the public largely resistant to laws that would limit
unhealthy choices or penalize those choices with so-called fat taxes?
Many consumers and civil rights advocates find such laws to be an
unreasonable restriction on individual freedom of choice. As health
policy experts Mello and others point out, opposition to food and
beverage regulation is similar to the opposition to early tobacco
legislation: the public views the issue as one of personal responsibility
rather than one requiring government intervention (2602). In other

No page
number is
available for this
web source.

Harba
emphasizes the
urgency of her
argument.

Harba treats
both sides fairly.

Harba
anticipates
objections
to her idea.
She counters
opposing views
and supports
her argument.

words, if a person eats unhealthy food and becomes ill as a result, that is his or her choice. But those who favor legislation claim that freedom of choice is a myth because of the strong influence of food and beverage industry marketing on consumers' dietary habits. According to one nonprofit health advocacy group, food and beverage companies spend roughly two billion dollars per year marketing directly to children. As a result, kids see nearly four thousand ads per year encouraging them to eat unhealthy food and drinks ("Facts"). As was the case with antismoking laws passed in recent decades, taxes and legal restrictions on junk food sales could help to counter the strong marketing messages that promote unhealthy products.

The United States has a history of state and local public health laws that have successfully promoted a particular behavior by punishing an undesirable behavior. The decline in tobacco use as a result of antismoking taxes and laws is perhaps the most obvious example. Another example is legislation requiring the use of seat belts, which have significantly reduced fatalities in car crashes. One government agency reports that seat belt use saved an average of more than fourteen thousand lives per year in the United States between 2000 and 2010 (United States, Dept. of Transportation, Natl. Highway Traffic Safety Administration 231). Perhaps seat belt laws have public support because the cost of wearing a seat belt is small, especially when compared with the benefit of saving fourteen thousand lives per year.

Laws designed to prevent chronic disease by promoting healthier food and beverage consumption also have potentially enormous benefits. To give just one example, Marion Nestle, New York University professor of nutrition and public health, notes that "a 1% reduction in intake of saturated fat across the population would prevent more than 30,000 cases of coronary heart disease annually and save more than a billion dollars in health care costs" (7). Few would argue that saving lives and dollars is not an enormous benefit. But three-quarters of

An analogy extends Harba's argument.

Harba introduces a quotation with a signal phrase and shows readers why she chose to use the source.

Americans say they would object to the costs needed to achieve this
benefit—the regulations needed to reduce saturated fat intake.

Why do so many Americans believe there is a degree of personal
choice lost when regulations such as taxes, bans, or portion limits
on unhealthy foods are proposed? Some critics of anti-junk-food laws
believe that even if state and local laws were successful in curbing
chronic diseases, they would still be unacceptable. Bioethicist David
Resnik emphasizes that such policies, despite their potential to make our
society healthier, "open the door to excessive government control over
food, which could restrict dietary choices, interfere with cultural, ethnic,
and religious traditions, and exacerbate socioeconomic inequalities" (31).
Resnik acknowledges that his argument relies on "slippery slope" thinking, but he insists that "social and political pressures" regarding food
regulation make his concerns valid (31). Yet the social and political
pressures that Resnik cites are really just the desire to improve public
health, and limiting access to unhealthy, artificial ingredients seems
a small price to pay. As legal scholars L. O. Gostin and K. G. Gostin
explain, "[I]nterventions that do not pose a truly significant burden on
individual liberty" are justified if they "go a long way towards safeguard-
ing the health and well-being of the populace" (214).

To improve public health, advocates such as Bowdoin College
philosophy professor Sarah Conly contend that it is the government's duty
to prevent people from making harmful choices whenever feasible and
whenever public benefits outweigh the costs. In response to critics who
claim that laws aimed at stopping us from eating whatever we want are an
assault on our freedom of choice, Conly offers a persuasive counterargument:

> [L]aws aren't designed for each one of us individually. Some of us
> can drive safely at 90 miles per hour, but we're bound by the same
> laws as the people who can't, because individual speeding laws aren't
> practical. Giving up a little liberty is something we agree to when we
> agree to live in a democratic society that is governed by laws. (A23)

Harba
acknowledges
critics and
counter-
arguments.

Including
the source's
credentials
makes Harba
more credible.

A signal phrase
names the
author.

Long quotation
is set off from
the text.
Quotation marks
are omitted.

Harba 6

Long quotation
is followed
with comments
that connect
the source
to Harba's
argument.

As Conly suggests, we need to change our either/or thinking (either we have complete freedom of choice *or* we have government regulations and lose our freedom) and instead need to see health as a matter of public good, not individual liberty. Proposals such as Mayor Bloomberg's that seek to limit portions of unhealthy beverages aren't about giving up liberty; they are about asking individuals to choose substantial public health benefits at a very small cost.

Conclusion
sums up Harba's
argument
and provides
closure.

Despite arguments in favor of regulating unhealthy food as a means to improve public health, public opposition has stood in the way of legislation. Americans freely eat as much unhealthy food as they want, and manufacturers and sellers of these foods have nearly unlimited freedom to promote such products and drive increased consumption, without any requirements to warn the public of potential hazards. Yet mounting scientific evidence points to unhealthy food as a significant contributing factor to chronic disease, which we know is straining our health care system, decreasing Americans' quality of life, and leading to unnecessary premature deaths. Americans must consider whether to allow the costly trend of rising chronic disease to continue in the name of personal choice or whether to support the regulatory changes and public health policies that will reverse that trend.

Harba 7

Works Cited
begins on a new
page. Heading
is centered.

Works Cited

Conly, Sarah. "Three Cheers for the Nanny State." *The New York Times*,
25 Mar. 2013, p. A23.

"The Facts on Junk Food Marketing and Kids." *Prevention Institute*, www

Access date
used for an
undated online
source.

.preventioninstitute.org/focus-areas/were-not-buying-it-get
-involved/were-not-buying-it-the-facts-on-junk-food-marketing
-and-kids. Accessed 16 Oct. 2018.

Harba 8

Goodwin, Lorine Swainston. *The Pure Food, Drink, and Drug Crusaders,*
1879–1914. McFarland, 2006.

Gostin, L. O., and K. G. Gostin. "A Broader Liberty: J. S. Mill,
Paternalism, and the Public's Health." *Public Health*, vol. 123,
no. 3, 2009, pp. 214–21, doi:10.1016/j.puhe.2008.12.024.

Mello, Michelle M., et al. "Obesity—the New Frontier of Public Health
Law." *The New England Journal of Medicine,* vol. 354, no. 24,
2006, pp. 2601–10, doi:10.1056/NEJMhpr060227.

Neergaard, Lauran, and Jennifer Agiesta. "Obesity's a Crisis but We
Want Our Junk Food, Poll Shows." *The Huffington Post,* 4 Jan.
2013, www.huffingtonpost.com/2013/01/04/obesity-junk-food
-government-intervention-poll_n_2410376.html.

Nestle, Marion. *Food Politics: How the Food Industry Influences*
Nutrition and Health. U of California P, 2013.

Pollan, Michael. "The Food Movement, Rising." *The New York Review of*
Books, 10 June 2010, www.nybooks.com/articles/2010/06/10
/food-movement-rising.

Resnik, David. "Trans Fat Bans and Human Freedom." *The American*
Journal of Bioethics, vol. 10, no. 3, Mar. 2010, pp. 27–32.

United States, Department of Agriculture and Department of Health
and Human Services. *Dietary Guidelines for Americans, 2010,*
health.gov/dietaryguidelines/dga2010/dietaryguidelines
2010.pdf.

United States, Department of Health and Human Services, Centers for
Disease Control and Prevention. *The Power of Prevention.* National
Center for Chronic Disease Prevention and Health Promotion, 2009,
www.cdc.gov/chronicdisease/pdf/2009-Power-of-Prevention.pdf.

United States, Department of Transportation, National Highway Traffic
Safety Administration. *Traffic Safety Facts 2010: A Compilation*
of Motor Vehicle Crash Data from the Fatality Analysis Reporting
System and the General Estimates System. 2010, www.nrd.nhtsa
.dot.gov/Pubs/811659.pdf.

List is
alphabetized
by authors'
last names (or
by title if no
author).

First line of
each entry is at
the left margin;
extra lines are
indented ½".

Double-
spacing is used
throughout.

The government
agency is used
as the author of
a government
document.

52 Documenting sources in APA style

In most social science classes, you will be asked to use the APA system for documenting sources, which is set forth in the *Publication Manual of the American Psychological Association*, 7th ed. (2020).

APA recommends in-text citations that refer readers to a list of references. An in-text citation gives the author of the source (often in a signal phrase), the year of publication, and often a page number in parentheses. At the end of the paper, a list of references provides publication information about the source; the list is alphabetized by authors' last names (or by titles for works with no authors). The direct link between the in-text citation and the entry in the reference list is highlighted in the following example.

IN-TEXT CITATION

Bell (2010) reported that students engaged in this kind of learning performed better on both project-based assessments and standardized tests (pp. 39–40).

ENTRY IN THE LIST OF REFERENCES

Bell, S. (2010). Project-based learning for the 21st century: Skills for the future. *The Clearing House, 83*(2), 39–43.

For a reference list that includes this entry, see 53b.

52a APA in-text citations

APA's in-text citations provide the author's last name and the year of publication, usually before the cited material, and a page number in parentheses directly after the cited material. In the following models, the elements of the in-text citation are highlighted.

NOTE: APA style requires the use of the past tense or the present perfect tense in signal phrases introducing cited material: Smith (2020) reported; Smith (2020) has argued.

List of **APA in-text citation** models

List of **APA reference list** models

List of APA reference list models (*cont.*)

1. Basic format for a quotation Ordinarily, introduce the quotation with a signal phrase that includes the author's last name followed by the year of publication in parentheses. Put the page number (preceded by "p.," or "pp." for more than one page) in parentheses after the quotation. For sources from the web without page numbers, see item 12a.

> Çubukçu (2012) argued that for a student-centered approach to work, students must maintain "ownership for their goals and activities" (p. 64).

If the author is not named in the signal phrase, place the author's name, the year, and the page number in parentheses after the quotation: (Çubukçu, 2012, p. 64). (See items 6 and 12 for citing sources that lack authors; item 12 also explains how to handle sources without dates or page numbers.)

NOTE: Do not include a month in an in-text citation, even if the entry in the reference list includes the month.

2. Basic format for a summary or a paraphrase   As for a quotation (see item 1), include the author's last name and the year either in a signal phrase introducing the material or in parentheses following it. A page number is not required for a summary or a paraphrase, but include one if it would help readers locate the information. For sources from the web without page numbers, see item 12a.

> Watson (2008) offered a case study of the Cincinnati Public Schools Virtual High School, in which students were able to engage in highly individualized instruction according to their own needs, strengths, and learning styles, using 10 teachers as support (p. 7).

> The Cincinnati Public Schools Virtual High School brought students together to engage in highly individualized instruction according to their own needs, strengths, and learning styles, using 10 teachers as support (Watson, 2008, p. 7).

3. Work with two authors   Name both authors in the signal phrase or in parentheses each time you cite the work. In the parentheses, use "&" between the authors' names; in the signal phrase, use "and."

> According to Donitsa-Schmidt and Zuzovsky (2014), "demographic growth in the school population" can lead to teacher shortages (p. 426).

> In the United States, most public school systems are struggling with teacher shortages, which are projected to worsen as the number of applicants to education schools decreases (Donitsa-Schmidt & Zuzovsky, 2014, p. 420).

4. Work with three or more authors Use the first author's name followed by "et al." (Latin for "and others") in either a signal phrase or a parenthetical citation.

> In 2013, Harper et al. studied teachers' perceptions of project-based learning (PBL) before and after participating in a PBL pilot program.

> Researchers studied teachers' perceptions of project-based learning (PBL) before and after participating in a PBL pilot program (Harper et al., 2013).

5. Work with unknown or anonymous author If the author is unknown, include the work's title (shortened if more than a few words) in the in-text citation.

> Collaboration increases significantly among students who own or have regular access to a laptop ("Tech Seeds," 2015).

In in-text citations, capitalize the first and last words of a title and subtitle, all significant words, and any words of four letters or more. For books and most stand-alone works (except websites), italicize the title; for most articles and other parts of larger works, set the title in quotation marks. In the rare case when "Anonymous" is specified as the author, treat it as if it were a real name: (Anonymous, 2011). In the list of references, also use the name Anonymous as author.

6. Organization as author If the author is an organization or a government agency, name the organization in the signal phrase or in the parentheses the first time you cite the source.

> According to the International Society for Technology in Education (2016), "student-centered learning moves students from passive receivers of information to active participants in their own discovery process" (What Is It? section).

For an organization with a long name, you may abbreviate the name of the organization in citations after the first.

FIRST CITATION   (Texas Higher Education Coordinating Board [THECB], 2012)

LATER CITATIONS   (THECB, 2012)

7. Authors with the same last name To avoid confusion, use initials with the last names in your in-text citations. If authors share the same initials, spell out each author's first name.

Research by E. Smith (2019) revealed that . . .

One 2012 study contradicted . . . (R. Smith, p. 234).

8. Two or more works by the same author in the same year In your reference list, you will use lowercase letters ("a," "b," and so on) with the year to order the entries (see item 8 in 52b). Use those same letters with the year in the in-text citation.

Research by Durgin (2013b) has yielded new findings about the role of smartphones in the classroom.

9. Two or more works in the same parentheses Put the works in the order in which they appear in the reference list, separated with semicolons: (Nazer, 2015; Serrao et al., 2014).

10. Multiple citations to the same work in one paragraph If you give an author's name in the text of your paper (not in parentheses) and you mention that source again in the text of the same paragraph, give only the author's name, not the date, in the later citation. If any subsequent reference in the same paragraph is in parentheses, include both the author and the date in the parentheses.

Bell (2010) has argued that the chief benefit of student-centered learning is that it can connect students with "real-world tasks," thus making learning more engaging as well as more comprehensive (p. 42). For example, Bell observed a group of middle-school students who wanted to build a social justice monument for their school. Students engaged in this kind of learning performed better on both project-based assessments and standardized tests (Bell, 2010).

11. Web source   Cite sources from the web as you would cite any other source, giving the author and the year when they are available.

Atkinson (2011) found that children who spent at least four hours a day engaged in online activities in an academic environment were less likely to want to play video games or watch TV after school.

Usually a page number is not available; occasionally a web source will lack an author or a date (see 12a, 12b, and 12c).

a. No page numbers   When a web source lacks stable numbered pages, include a paragraph number, section heading, or both to help readers locate the passage being cited. If a heading is long, use a shortened version of the heading in quotation marks.

If a source lacks numbered paragraphs or headings, count the paragraphs manually. When quoting audio and video sources, use a time stamp to indicate the start of the quotation.

Crush and Jayasingh (2015) pointed out that several other school districts in low-income areas had "jump-started their distance learning initiatives with available grant funds" (Funding Change section, para. 6).

b. Unknown author   If no author is named in the source, mention the title of the source in a signal phrase or give the first word or two of the title in parentheses (see also item 6). (If an organization serves as the author, see item 7.)

A student's IEP may, in fact, recommend the use of mobile technology ("Considerations," 2012).

c. Unknown date When the source does not give a date, use the abbreviation "n.d." (for "no date").

> Administrators believe 1-to-1 programs boost learner engagement (Magnus, n.d.).

12. An entire website If you mention an entire website from which you did not pull specific information, give the URL in the text of your paper but do not include it in the reference list.

> The Berkeley Center for Teaching and Learning website (https://teaching.berkeley.edu/) shares ideas for using mobile technology in the classroom.

13. Personal communication Interviews that you conduct, letters, email messages, and similar communications that would be difficult for your readers to retrieve should be cited in the text only, not in the reference list. (Use the first initial with the last name either in your text sentence or in parentheses.)

> One of Yim's colleagues has contended that the benefits of this technology for children under 12 years old are few (F. Johnson, personal communication, October 20, 2013).

14. Course materials Cite lecture notes from your instructor or your own class notes as personal communication (see item 13). If your instructor's material contains publication information, cite it as you would the appropriate source. See also item 52 in section 52b.

15. Part of a source (chapter, figure) To cite a specific part of a source, such as a whole chapter or a figure or table, identify the element in parentheses. Don't abbreviate terms such as "Figure," "Chapter," and "Section."

> The data support the finding that peer relationships are difficult to replicate in a completely online environment (Hanniman, 2010, Figure 8-3).

16. Indirect source (source quoted in another source) When a published source is quoted in a source written by someone else, cite the original source first; include "as cited in" before the author and date of the source you read. In the following example, Chow is the author of the source in the reference list; that source contains a quotation by Brailsford.

> Brailsford (1990) commended the writer and educator's "sure understanding of the thoughts of young people" (as cited in Chow, 2019, para. 9).

17. Sacred or classical text Identify the book (specifying the version or edition you used), the publication date(s), and the relevant part (chapter, verse, line).

> Peace activists have long cited the biblical prophet's vision of a world without war: "And . . . nation shall not lift up sword against nation, neither shall they learn war any more" (*Holy Bible Revised Standard Edition*, 1952/2004, Isaiah 2:4).

18. Quotation from a source without page numbers If your source does not include page numbers, include a locator—other information from the source, such as a section heading, paragraph number, figure or table number, slide number, or time stamp—to help readers find the cited passage:

> Lopez (2020) has noted that ". . ." (Symptoms section).

> Myers (2019) explained the benefits of humility (para. 5).

> The American Immigration Council has recommended that ". . ." (Slide 5).

> In a recent TED Talk, Gould (2019) argued that ". . ." (13:27).

If you shorten a long heading, place it in quotation marks: ("How to Apply" section).

52b APA list of references

As you gather sources for an assignment, you will likely find sources in print, on the web, and in other places. The information you will need for the reference list at the end of your paper will differ slightly depending on the source, but the main principles apply to all sources: identify an author, a creator, or a producer whenever possible; give a title; and provide the date on which the source was produced. In most cases, you will provide page numbers or other locator or retrieval information.

▸ List of APA reference list models, 363–364
▸ General guidelines for the reference list, 372

Section 52b provides specific requirements for and examples of many of the sources you are likely to encounter. When you cite sources, your goals are to show that the sources you've used are reliable and relevant to your work, to provide your readers with enough information so that they can find your sources easily, and to provide that information in a consistent way according to APA conventions.

In the list of references, include only sources that you have quoted, summarized, or paraphrased in your paper.

General guidelines for listing authors

The formatting of authors' names in items 1–10 applies to all sources in print and on the web—books, articles, websites, and so on. For more models of specific source types, see items 11–55.

1. Single author

author: last name + initial(s) year (book) title (book) publisher

Yanagihara, H. (2015). *A little life*. Doubleday.

2. Two to twenty authors
List up to twenty authors by last names followed by initials. Use an ampersand (&) before the name of the last author. (See items 3–5 in 52a for citing works with multiple authors in the text of your paper.)

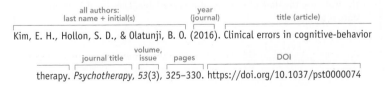

all authors: last name + initial(s) year (journal) title (article)

Kim, E. H., Hollon, S. D., & Olatunji, B. O. (2016). Clinical errors in cognitive-behavior

journal title volume, issue pages DOI

therapy. *Psychotherapy, 53*(3), 325–330. https://doi.org/10.1037/pst0000074

3. Twenty one or more authors List the first nineteen, followed by an ellipsis mark (. . .) and the last author's name. Then proceed as in item 2.

Sharon, G., Cruz, N. J., Kang, D.-W., Gandal, M. J., Wang, B., Kim, Y.-M., Zink, E. M., Casey, C. P., Taylor, B. C., Lane, C. J., Bramer, L. M., Isern, N. G., Hoyt, D. W., Noecker, C., Sweredoski, M. J., Moradian, A., Borenstein, E., Jansson, J. K., Knight, R., . . . Mazmanian, S. K.

General guidelines for the reference list

In APA style, the alphabetical list of works cited, which appears at the end of the paper, is titled "References."

Authors and dates

- Alphabetize entries in the list of references by authors' last names; if a work has no author, alphabetize it by its title.

- For all authors' names, put the last name first, followed by a comma; use initials for the first and middle names.

- With two or more authors, separate the names with commas. Include names for up to twenty authors, with an ampersand (&) before the last author's name. For twenty-one or more authors, list the first nineteen authors, three ellipsis dots, and the last author.

- If the author is a company or an organization, give the name in normal order.

- Put the date of publication immediately after the first element of the citation. Enclose the date in parentheses, followed by a period (outside the parentheses).

- Use the date as given in the publication. Generally, give the year for books and journals; the year and month for monthly magazines; and the year, month, and day for weekly magazines and for newspapers. Use the season when a magazine gives the season. For sources on the web, use the date of posting, if it is available. Use "(n.d.)" if no date is given.

→

GENERAL GUIDELINES FOR THE REFERENCE LIST (*cont.*)

Titles

- Italicize the titles and subtitles of books, journals, and other stand-alone works. If a book title contains another book title or an article title, do not italicize the internal title and do not put quotation marks around it.

- Use no italics or quotation marks for the titles of articles. If an article title contains another article title or a term usually placed in quotation marks, use quotation marks around the internal title or term. If an article title contains a title or term usually italicized, use italics for that title or term.

- For books and articles, capitalize only the first word of the title and subtitle and all proper nouns.

- For the titles of journals, magazines, and newspapers, capitalize all words of four letters or more (and all nouns, pronouns, verbs, adjectives, and adverbs of any length).

Source information

- In publishers' names, omit business designations such as Inc. or Ltd. Otherwise, write the publisher's name exactly how it appears in the source.

- For online sources, list the name of the website in the publisher position: Twitter; YouTube; U.S. Census Bureau.

- If the publisher is the same as the author, do not repeat the name in the publisher position.

- Provide locations only for works associated with a single location (such as a conference presentation).

- Include the volume and issue numbers for any journals, magazines, or other periodicals that have them. Italicize the volume number and put the issue number, not italicized, in parentheses: *26*(2).

- When an article appears on consecutive pages, provide the range of pages. When an article does not appear on consecutive pages, give all page numbers: A1, A17.

- Use "p." and "pp." before page numbers only with selections in edited books. Do not use "p." and "pp." with magazines, journals, and newspapers. →

GENERAL GUIDELINES FOR THE REFERENCE LIST (cont.)

URLs, DOIs, and other retrieval information

- For articles and books from the web, use the DOI (digital object identifier), if available. If a source does not have a DOI, give the URL. Do not insert a period after a DOI or URL.

- If a URL or DOI is long, you can create a permalink using a shortening service such as shortdoi.org or bitly.com.

- Use a retrieval date for a web source only if the content is likely to change (such as content on a website's home page or in a social media profile).

4. Organization as author

author: organization name	year	title (book)

American Psychiatric Association. (2013). *Diagnostic and statistical manual of mental*

	edition

disorders (5th ed.).

5. Unknown author   Begin the entry with the work's title.

title (article)	year + month + day (weekly publication)	magazine title

The rise of the sharing economy. (2013, March 9). *The Economist,*

volume, issue	page(s)

406(8826), 14.

6. Author using a screen name, pen name, or stage name   Use the author's real name, if known, and give the screen name or pen name in brackets exactly as it appears in the source. If only the screen name is known, begin with that name and do not use brackets. (See also items 36 and 54 on citing screen names in social media.)

If the author uses just a single name ("Sophocles") or a two-part name in which the two parts are essential ("Cardi B"), list the name with no abbreviations or changes.

7. Two or more works by the same author   Use the author's name for all entries. List the entries by year, the earliest first.

Coates, T. (2008). *The beautiful struggle*. Spiegel & Grau.

Coates, T. (2015). *Between the world and me*. Spiegel & Grau.

8. Two or more works by the same author in the same year   List the works by exact date in chronological order (the earliest first), and add the letters "a," "b," and so on after the year. Use these same letters when giving the year in the in-text citation. If the works have only a year and no exact date, or if the exact dates are identical, arrange the entries alphabetically by title.

Bower, B. (2012a, November 3). Human-Neandertal mating gets a new date. *Science News, 182*(9), 8.

Bower, B. (2012b, December 15). Families in flux. *Science News, 182*(12), 16.

9. Editor   Begin with the name of the editor or editors; place the abbreviation "Ed." (or "Eds." for more than one editor) in parentheses following the name.

editor   year   title (book)
Yeh, K.-H. (Ed.). (2019). *Asian indigenous psychologies in the global context.*

publisher
Palgrave Macmillan.

10. Translator   Begin with the name of the author. After the title, in parentheses, place the name of the translator (in normal order) and the abbreviation "Trans." (for "Translator"). Add the original date of publication at the end of the entry.

author   year   title (book)   translator   publisher

Calasso, R. (2019). *The unnamable present* (R. Dixon, Trans.). Farrar, Straus and Giroux.

original publication
information

(Original work published 2017)

Articles and other short works

▶ Citation at a glance: Online article in a journal or magazine, 378
▶ Citation at a glance: Article from a database, 379

11. Article in a journal   For an article from the web, give the DOI, if available, or include the URL for the article. If an article from a database has no DOI, do not include a URL.

a. Print

authors: last name + initial(s)   year   article title

Terry, C. P., & Terry, D. L. (2015). Cell phone-related near accidents among young

                       volume,
               journal title   issue   page(s)

drivers: Associations with mindfulness. *The Journal of Psychology, 149*(7), 665–683.

b. Web

all authors:
last name +
initial(s)   year   article title

Bruns, A. (2019). The third shift: Multiple job holding and the incarceration of

                     volume,
           journal title   issue   page(s)   DOI

women's partners. *Social Science Research, 80*(1), 202–215. http://doi.org/dfgj

all authors:
last name + initial(s) year article title

Vicary, A. M., & Larsen, A. (2018). Potential factors influencing attitudes toward veterans

who commit crimes: An experimental investigation of PTSD in the legal system.

journal title (no volume available) URL for article

Current Research in Social Psychology. https://www.uiowa.edu/crisp/sites/uiowa

.edu.crisp/files/crisp_vol_26_2.pdf

c. Database

author year article title

Maftsir, S. (2019). Emotional change: Romantic love and the university in postcolonial Egypt.

journal title volume, issue page(s) DOI

Journal of Social History, 52(3), 831–859. https://doi.org/10.1093/jsh/shx155

12. Article in a magazine If an article from the web has no DOI, use the URL for the article. If an article from a database has no DOI, do not include a URL.

a. Print

author year + month (monthly magazine) article title magazine title volume, issue page(s)

Paris, W. (2015, March/April). The new survivors. *Psychology Today, 48*(2), 66–73, 82.

b. Web

author date of posting (when available) article title

Srinivasan, D. (2019, June 4). How digital advertising markets really work.

magazine title URL for article

The American Prospect. https://prospect.org/article/how-digital-advertising

-markets-really-work

c. Database

author year + month (monthly magazine) article title

Greengard, S. (2019, August). The algorithm that changed quantum machine learning.

magazine title volume, issue page(s) DOI

Communications of the ACM, 62(8), 15–17. http://doi.org/10.1145/3339458

Citation at a glance

Online article in a journal or magazine APA

To cite an online article in a journal or magazine in APA style, include the following elements:

1 Author(s)
2 Year of publication for journal; complete date for magazine
3 Title and subtitle of article
4 Name of journal or magazine
5 Volume and issue numbers
6 DOI (digital object identifier), if article has one; otherwise, URL for article

ONLINE ARTICLE

REFERENCE LIST ENTRY FOR AN ONLINE ARTICLE IN A JOURNAL OR MAGAZINE

Jochim, A., & McGuinn, P. (2016, Fall). The politics of the Common Core assessments. *Education Next*, *16*(4). educationnext.org/the-politics-of-common-core-assessments-parcc-smarter-balanced/

For more on citing online articles in APA style, see items 11–13.

Citation at a glance

Article from a database APA

To cite an article from a database in APA style, include the following elements:

1 Author(s)
2 Year of publication for journal; complete date for magazine or newspaper
3 Title and subtitle of article
4 Name of periodical
5 Volume and issue numbers
6 Page number(s)
7 DOI (digital object identifier)

DATABASE RECORD

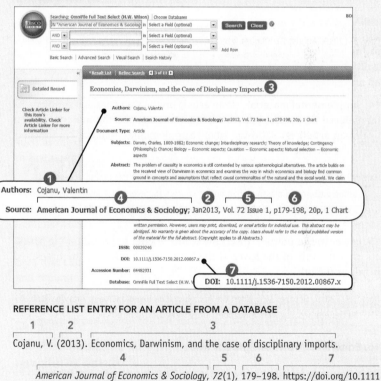

REFERENCE LIST ENTRY FOR AN ARTICLE FROM A DATABASE

1 2   3

Cojanu, V. (2013). Economics, Darwinism, and the case of disciplinary imports.

4   5 6   7

American Journal of Economics & Sociology, 72(1), 179–198. https://doi.org/10.1111

/j.1536-7150.2012.00867.x

For more on citing articles from a database in APA style, see items 11–12.

13. Article in a newspaper

a. Print

author | year + month + day | article title

Finucane, M. (2019, September 25). Americans still eating too many low-quality carbs.

newspaper title | page

The Boston Globe, B2.

b. Web

author | year + month + day | article title

Daly, J. (2019, August 2). Duquesne's med school plan part of national trend to train

newspaper title | shortened URL

more doctors. *Pittsburgh Post-Gazette*. http://bit.ly/2CbUZOX

14. Supplemental material If an article on the web contains supplemental material that is not part of the main article, cite the material as you would an article and add the label "Supplemental material" in brackets following the title.

Hansen, J. D., & Reich, J. (2015). Democratizing education? Examining access and
usage patterns in massive open online courses [Supplemental material]. *Science,
350*(6265), 1245–1248. https://doi.org/10.1126/science.aab3782

15. Letter to the editor Insert the words "Letter to the editor" in brackets after the title of the letter. If the letter has no title, use the bracketed words as the title.

Doran, K. (2019, October 11). When the homeless look like grandma or grandpa [Letter
to the editor]. *The New York Times*. https://nyti.ms/33foDOK

16. Editorial or other unsigned article

The business case for transit dollars [Editorial]. (2012, December 9). *Star Tribune*.
http://m.startribune.com/editorial-the-business-case-for-transit-dollars/182608311/

17. Review In brackets, give the type of work reviewed, the title, and the director for a film or the author for a book.

Douthat, R. (2019, October 14). A hustle gone wrong [Review of the film *Hustlers*, by L. Scafaria, Dir.]. *National Review, 71*(18), 47.

Hall, W. (2019). [Review of the book *How to change your mind: The new science of psychedelics*, by M. Pollan]. *Addiction, 114*(10), 1892–1893. https://doi.org/10.1111/add.14702

18. Published interview

author/interviewer · year + month + day · interview title

Remnick, D. (2019, July 1). Robert Caro reflects on Robert Moses, L.B.J., and his own

magazine title · shortened URL

career in nonfiction. *The New Yorker.* https://bit.ly/2Lukm3X

19. Article in a dictionary or an encyclopedia (including a wiki) When referencing a work with archived versions, like Wikipedia, use the date and URL of the archived version you read. When referencing an online, undated reference work entry, include the retrieval date.

Brue, A. W., & Wilmshurst, L. (2018). Adaptive behavior assessments. In B. B. Frey (Ed.), *The SAGE encyclopedia of educational research, measurement, and evaluation* (pp. 40–44). SAGE Publications. https://doi.org/10.4135/9781506326139.n21

Merriam-Webster. (n.d.). Adscititious. In *Merriam-Webster.com dictionary*. Retrieved September 5, 2019, from https://www.merriam-webster.com/dictionary/adscititious

20. Comment on an online article Include the first 20 words of the comment followed by the source article in brackets.

lollyl2. (2019, September 25). My husband works in IT in a major city down South. He is a permanent employee now, but for years [Comment on the article "The Google workers who voted to unionize in Pittsburgh are part of tech's huge contractor workforce"]. Slate. https://fyre.it/0RT8HmeL.4

21. Paper or poster presented at a conference (unpublished)

Wood, M. (2019, January 3–6). *The effects of an adult development course on students'*
perceptions of aging [Poster session]. Forty-First Annual National Institute on
the Teaching of Psychology, St. Pete Beach, FL, United States. https://nitop.org
/resources/Documents/2019%20Poster%20Session%20II.pdf

Books and other long works

▸ Citation at a glance: Book, 383

22. Basic format for a book

a. Print

author(s):
last name
+ initial(s)   year   book title   publisher

Southard, S. (2015). *Nagasaki: Life after nuclear war.* Viking.

b. Web (or online library) Give the URL for the page where you accessed the book.

Obama, M. (2018). *Becoming.* Crown. https://books.google.com/books?id=YbtNDwAAQBAJ

c. E-book Include the DOI or, if a DOI is not available, the URL for the page of the site from which you downloaded the book.

Coates, T.-N. (2017). *We were eight years in power: An American tragedy.* One World.
https://www.amazon.com/dp/B01MT7340D/

d. Database If the book has a DOI, include it. If not, do not list a URL or database name.

Dessler, A. E., & Parson, E. A. (2019). *The science and politics of global climate change:*
A guide to the debate (3rd ed.). Cambridge University Press.

Citation at a glance

Book APA

To cite a print book in APA style, include the following elements:

1 Author(s)
2 Year of publication
3 Title and subtitle
4 Publisher

TITLE PAGE

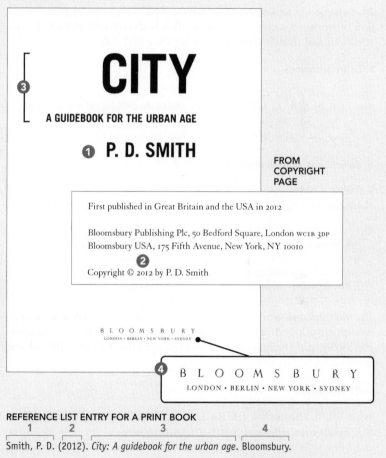

CITY

A GUIDEBOOK FOR THE URBAN AGE

❶ **P. D. SMITH**

FROM
COPYRIGHT
PAGE

First published in Great Britain and the USA in 2012

Bloomsbury Publishing Plc, 50 Bedford Square, London wc1b 3dp
Bloomsbury USA, 175 Fifth Avenue, New York, NY 10010

❷

Copyright © 2012 by P. D. Smith

B L O O M S B U R Y
LONDON · BERLIN · NEW YORK · SYDNEY

❹ B L O O M S B U R Y
LONDON · BERLIN · NEW YORK · SYDNEY

REFERENCE LIST ENTRY FOR A PRINT BOOK

1   2   3   4

Smith, P. D. (2012). *City: A guidebook for the urban age*. Bloomsbury.

For more on citing books in APA style, see items 22–26.

23. Edition other than the first Include the edition number (abbreviated) in parentheses after the title.

Harvey, P. (2013). *An introduction to Buddhism: Teachings, history, and practices*
(2nd ed.). Cambridge University Press.

24. Selection in an anthology or a collection An anthology is a collection of works on a common theme, often with different authors for the selections and usually with an editor for the entire volume.

a. Entire anthology

editor(s)   year

Amelina, A., Horvath, K., & Meeus, B. (Eds.). (2016). *An anthology of migration and*

title of anthology   publisher

social transformation: European perspectives. Springer.

b. Selection in an anthology

author of
selection   year   title of selection

Abdou, L. H. (2016). The Europeanization of immigration policies. In A. Amelina,

editors of anthology   title of anthology

K. Horvath, & B. Meeus (Eds.), *An anthology of migration and social*

page numbers
of selection   publisher

transformation: European perspectives (pp. 105–119). Springer.

25. Multivolume work If you have used only one volume of a multivolume work, indicate the volume number after the title of the complete work; if the volume has its own title, add that title after the volume number.

a. All volumes

Zeigler-Hill, V., & Shackelford, T. K. (Eds.). (2018). *The SAGE handbook of personality*
and individual differences (Vols. I–III). SAGE Publications.

b. One volume, with title

Zeigler-Hill, V., & Shackelford, T. K. (Eds.). (2018). *The SAGE handbook of personality and individual differences: Vol. II. Origins of personality and individual differences*. SAGE Publications.

26. Dictionary or other reference work

Leong, F. T. L. (Ed.). (2008). *Encyclopedia of counseling* (Vols. 1–4). SAGE Publications.

27. Dissertation

author   year   dissertation title

Bacaksizlar, N. G. (2019). *Understanding social movements through simulations of anger*

label with institution

contagion in social media [Doctoral dissertation, University of North Carolina at

specialty database

Charlotte]. ProQuest Dissertations & Theses.

28. Government document   If no author is listed, begin with the department that produced the document. Any broader organization listed can be included as the publisher of the document, as in the first example below. If a specific report number is provided, include it after the title.

author   date   document title

National Park Service. (2019, April 11). *Travel where women made history: Ordinary*

organization/website

and extraordinary places of American women. U.S. Department of the Interior.

URL

https://www.nps.gov/subjects/travelwomenshistory/index.htm

Berchick, E. R., Barnett, J. C., & Upton, R. D. (2019, September 10). *Health insurance coverage in the United States: 2018* (Report No. P60–267). U.S. Census Bureau. https://www.census.gov/library/publications/2019/demo/p60-267.html

29. Report from a private organization

Ford Foundation International Fellowships Program. (2019). *Leveraging higher education to promote social justice: Evidence from the IFP alumni tracking study.* https://p.widencdn.net/kei61u/IFP-Alumni-Tracking-Study-Report-5

30. Legal source   The title of a court case is italicized in an in-text citation, but it is not italicized in the reference list.

Sweatt v. Painter, 339 U.S. 629 (1950). http://www.law.cornell.edu/supct/html /historics/USSC_CR_0339_0629_ZS.html

31. Sacred or classical text

The Holy Bible 1611 edition King James version. (2006). Hendrickson Publishers. (Original work published 1611)

Homer. (2018). *The odyssey* (E. Wilson, Trans.). W. W. Norton & Company. (Original work published ca. 675–725 B.C.E.)

Websites and parts of websites

▶ Citation at a glance: Page from a website, page 388

32. Entire website   If you retrieved specific information from the home page of a website, include the website name, retrieval date, and URL in your reference list entry. If you mention the website in only a general way in the body of your paper, do not include it in your reference list. See item 13 in 52a.

33. Page from a website   Use one of the models below only when your source doesn't fit into any other category. The following models are for content found on an interior page of a website and not published elsewhere. The website name follows the page title unless the author and website name are the same.

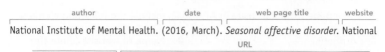

National Institute of Mental Health. (2016, March). *Seasonal affective disorder*. National
Institutes of Health. https://www.nimh.nih.gov/health/topics/seasonal-affective
-disorder/index.shtml

BBC News. (2019, October 31). *Goats help save Ronald Reagan Presidential Library*. bbc.
com/news/world-us-canada-50248549

34. Document on a website Most documents published on websites fall
into other categories, such as an article, a government document, or a
report from an organization (items 11, 28, and 29).

Tahseen, M., Ahmed, S., & Ahmed, S. (2018). *Bullying of Muslim youth: A review of
research and recommendations*. The Family and Youth Institute. http://www.thefyi
.org/wp-content/uploads/2018/10/FYI-Bullying-Report.pdf

35. Blog post Cite a blog post as you would an article in a periodical.

Fister, B. (2019, February 14). Information literacy's third wave. *Library Babel Fish*.
https://www.insidehighered.com/blogs/library-babel-fish/information
-literacy%E2%80%99s-third-wave

36. Blog comment Use a screen name if the writer's real name is not
given.

author's
screen name   date   text of comment

Mollie F. (2019, February 14). It's a daunting task, isn't it? Last year, I got a course on

                                                                        label

Scholarly Communication and Information Literacy approved for [Comment on the

                                                        blog title   URL

blog post "Information literacy's third wave"]. *Library Babel Fish*. http://disq

.us/p/1zr92uc

Citation at a glance
Page from a website APA

To cite a page from a website in APA style, include the following elements:

1 Author(s)
2 Date of publication or most recent update ("n.d." if there is no date)
3 Title of web page
4 Name of website (if not the same as the author)
5 URL of web page

PAGE FROM A WEBSITE

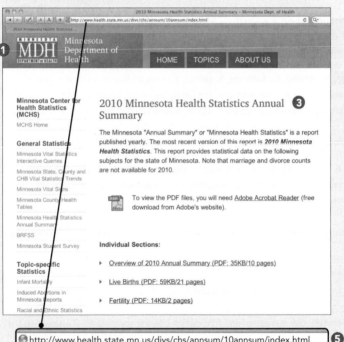

1	2	3

Minnesota Department of Health. (n.d.). *2010 Minnesota health statistics*

5

annual summary. http://www.health.state.mn.us/divs/chs/annsum

/10annsum/index.html

For more on citing documents from websites in APA style, see items 32–34.

Audio, visual, and multimedia sources

37. Podcast

Abumrad, J., & Krulwich, R. (Hosts). (2002–present). *Radiolab* [Audio podcast]. WNYC
    Studios. https://www.wnycstudios.org/podcasts/radiolab/podcasts

Longoria, J. (Host & Producer). (2019, April 19). Americanish [Audio podcast episode].
    In J. Abumrad & R. Krulwich (Hosts), *Radiolab*. WNYC Studios. https://www
    .wnycstudios.org/podcasts/radiolab/articles/americanish

38. Video or audio on the web (YouTube, TED Talk)

The New York Times. (2018, January 9). *Taking a knee and taking down a monument*
    [Video]. YouTube. https://www.youtube.com/watch?v=qY34DQCdUvQ

Wray, B. (2019, May). *How climate change affects your mental health* [Video]. TED.
    https://www.ted.com/talks/britt_wray_how_climate_change_affects_your
    _mental_health

39. Transcript of a video or an audio file

Gopnik, A. (2019, July 10). *A separate kind of intelligence* [Video transcript].
    Edge. https://www.edge.org/conversation/alison_gopnik-a-separate
    -kind-of-intelligence

40. Film (DVD, BD, or other format) If the film is a special version, like an extended cut, include that information in brackets after the title.

Cooper, S. (Director). (2015). *Black mass* [Film]. Warner Bros.

Hitchcock, A. (Director). (1959). *The essentials collection: North by northwest* [Film; special ed. on DVD]. Metro-Goldwyn-Mayer; Universal Pictures Home Entertainment.

41. TV or radio series or episode

Waller-Bridge, P., Williams, H., & Williams, J. (Executive Producers). (2016–2019). *Fleabag* [TV series]. Two Brothers Pictures; BBC.

Waller-Bridge, P. (Writer), & Bradbeer, H. (Director). (2019, March 18). The provocative request (Season 2, Episode 3) [TV series episode]. In P. Waller-Bridge, H. Williams, & J. Williams (Executive Producers), *Fleabag*. Two Brothers Pictures; BBC.

42. Music recording

Nielsen, C. (2014). *Carl Nielsen: Symphonies 1 & 4* [Album recorded by New York Philharmonic Orchestra]. Dacapo Records. (Original work published 1892–1916)

Carlile, B. (2018). The mother [Song]. On *By the way, I forgive you*. Low Country Sound; Elektra.

43. Lecture, speech, address, or recorded interview Cite the speaker or interviewee as the author.

Warren, E. (2019, September 16). *Senator Elizabeth Warren speech in Washington Square Park* [Speech video recording]. C-SPAN. https://www.c-span.org/video/?464314-1 /senator-elizabeth-warren-campaigns-york-city

44. Data set or graphic representation of data (chart, table)

Reid, L. (2019). *Smarter homes: Experiences of living in low carbon homes 2013–2018* [Data set]. UK Data Service. http://doi.org/10.5255/UKDA-SN-853485

Pew Research Center. (2018, November 15). *U.S. public is closely divided about overall health risk from food additives* [Chart]. https://www.pewresearch.org/science /2018/11/19/public-perspectives-on-food-risks/

45. Mobile app   Begin with the developer of the app, if known.

Google. (2019). *Google Earth* (Version 9.3.3) [Mobile app]. App Store. https://apps .apple.com/us/app/google-earth/id293622097

46. Video game

Firaxis Games. (2014). *Sid Meier's civilization: Beyond earth* [Video game]. Take-Two Interactive. PC.

47. Map

Desjardins, J. (2017, November 17). *Walmart nation: Mapping the largest employers in the U.S.* [Map]. Visual Capitalist. https://www.visualcapitalist.com/walmart-nation -mapping-largest-employers-u-s/

48. Advertisement

Wieden+Kennedy. (2018, September). Nike: Dream crazy [Advertisement]. https://www .wk.com/work/nike-dream-crazy/

49. Work of art or photograph

O'Keeffe, G. (1931). *Cow's skull: Red, white, and blue* [Painting]. Metropolitan Museum of Art, New York, NY, United States. https://www.metmuseum.org/art/collection /search/488694

Browne, M. (1963). *The burning monk* [Photograph]. Time. http://100photos.time.com /photos/malcolm-browne-burning-monk

50. Brochure or fact sheet

National Council of State Boards of Nursing. (2014). *A nurse's guide to professional boundaries* [Brochure]. https://www.ncsbn.org/

| | | | sheet | |
| author | date | sheet title | number | label |

World Health Organization. (2015, December). *Food safety* (No. 399) [Fact sheet].

URL

http://www.who.int/mediacentre/factsheets/fs399/en/

51. Press release

New York University. (2019, September 5). *NYU Oral Cancer Center awarded $2.5 million NIH grant to study cancer pain* [Press release]. https://www.nyu.edu/about /news-publications/news/2019/september/nyu-oral-cancer-center-awarded-- 2-5-million-nih-grant-to-study-c.html

52. Lecture notes or other course materials   Cite posted materials as you would a web document (see item 34). Cite material from your instructor that is not available to others as personal communication in the text of your paper (see item 13 in 52a).

author(s)/instructor(s)   year   course title

Chatterjee, S., Constenla, D., Kinghorn, A., & Mayora, C. (2018). *Teaching vaccine economics*

label

everywhere: Costing in vaccine planning and programming [Lecture notes and slides].

institution/website

Department of Population, Family, and Reproductive Health, Johns Hopkins University.

URL

http://ocw.jhsph.edu/index.cfm/go/viewCourse/course/TeachVaccEconCosting

/coursePage/lectureNotes/

Social media

53. Email   Email messages, letters, and other personal communication are not included in the list of references. See item 13 in 52a for citing these sources in the text of your paper.

54. Social media post   If the writer's real name and screen name are given, put the real name first, followed by the screen name in brackets. If only the screen name is known, begin with the screen name, not in brackets. For the title, include up to twenty words (including hashtags or emojis) of the title or caption. After the title, list any attachments (such as a photo or link) and the type of post in separate brackets. List the website or app in the publisher position. Include the URL for the post. Cite posts that are not accessible to all readers only in the text of your paper.

National Science Foundation [@NSF]. (2019, October 13). *Understanding how forest structure drives carbon sequestration is important for ecologists, climate modelers and forest managers, who are working on* [Thumbnail with link attached] [Tweet]. Twitter. https://twitter.com/NSF/status/1183388649263652864

Georgia Aquarium. (2019, June 25). *True love* [two hearts emoji] *Charlie and Lizzy are a bonded pair of African penguins who have been together for more than* [Image attached] [Status update]. Facebook. https://www.facebook.com/GeorgiaAquarium/photos/a.163898398123/10156900637543124/?type=3&theater

Smithsonian [@smithsonian]. (2019, October 7). *You're looking at a ureilite meteorite under a microscope. When illuminated with polarized light, they appear in dazzling colors, influenced* [Photograph]. Instagram. https://www.instagram.com/p/B3VI27yHLQG/

55. Social media profile or highlight   Because profiles are designed to change over time, include the date you viewed the webpage.

National Science Foundation [@NSF]. (n.d.). *Tweets* [Twitter profile]. Twitter. Retrieved October 15, 2019, from https://twitter.com/NSF

Smithsonian [@smithsonian]. (n.d.). *#Apollo50* [Highlight]. Instagram. Retrieved October 15, 2019, from https://www.instagram.com/stories/highlights/17902787752343364/

53 APA format; sample research paper

The guidelines in this section are consistent with advice given in the *Publication Manual of the American Psychological Association*, 7th ed. (2020), and with typical requirements for undergraduate papers.

53a APA format

Formatting the paper: The basics

A title page appears here; the full paper appears in section 53b.

All pages are numbered, starting with the title page.

1

Paper title is boldface, followed by one blank (double-spaced) line. Writer's name; department and school; course; instructor; and date follow on separate double-spaced lines.

Technology and the Shift From Teacher-Delivered to Student-Centered Learning: A Review of the Literature

April Bo Wang

Department of Education, Glen County Community College

EDU 107: Education, Technology, and Media

Dr. Julien Gomez

October 29, XXXX

2

Technology and the Shift From Teacher-Delivered to
Student-Centered Learning: A Review of the Literature

In the United States, most public school systems are struggling
with teacher shortages, which are projected to worsen as the number of
applicants to education schools decreases (Donitsa-Schmidt & Zuzovsky,
2014, p. 420). Citing federal data, *The New York Times* reported a 30%
drop in "people entering teacher preparation programs" between 2010
and 2014 (Rich, 2015, para. 10). Especially in science and math fields,

Text is set in double-spaced, easy-to-read font, such as Times New Roman. Paper has 1-inch margins on all sides of the page.

Formatting the paper: Other concerns

Capitalization, italics, and quotation marks   In headings and in titles of
works that appear in the text of the paper, capitalize all words of four
letters or more (and all nouns, pronouns, verbs, adjectives, and adverbs
of any length). Capitalize the first word following a colon in a title or a
heading. Capitalize the first word following a colon if the word begins a
complete sentence.

In the body of your paper, italicize the titles of books, journals, magazines, and other long works, including websites. Use quotation marks
around the titles of articles, short stories, and other short works named in
the body of your paper.

NOTE: APA has different requirements for titles in the reference list. See
"Preparing the list of references" later in this section.

Long quotations   When a quotation is forty or more words, indent one-
half inch from the left margin. Double-space the quotation. Do not use
quotation marks around it. (See 53b for an example.)

Footnotes   Insert footnotes using the footnote function of your word processing program. The number in the text should immediately follow a word or any mark of punctuation except a dash. The text of the footnote should be single-spaced.

Abstract and keywords   If your assignment requires an abstract—a 150-to-250-word summary paragraph—include it on a new page after the title page. Center the word "Abstract" (in bold) one inch from the top of the page. Double-space the abstract and do not indent the first line. (See the end of 53b for an example of an abstract.)

Headings   Although headings are not always necessary, their use is encouraged in the social sciences. For most undergraduate papers, one level of heading is usually sufficient. (See 53b.)

First-level headings are centered and boldface. In research papers and laboratory reports, the major headings are "Method," "Results," and "Discussion." In other types of papers, the major headings should be informative and concise, conveying the structure of the paper.

Second-level headings are left-aligned and boldface. Third-level headings are left-aligned, italic, and boldface.

In all headings, capitalize the first and last words and all words of four or more letters (and nouns, pronouns, verbs, adjectives, and adverbs of any length).

First-Level Heading Centered

Second-Level Heading Aligned Left

Third-level Heading Aligned Left

Visuals

APA classifies visuals as tables and figures (figures include graphs, charts, drawings, and photographs). Place each visual after the paragraph in which it is called out, or on the following page if it does not fit on the same page as the callout.

N

Tables Number each table (Table 1, Table 2) and provide a clear title. The label and title should appear on separate lines above the table, flush left and double-spaced. Type the table number in bold font; italicize the table title.

Table 2

Effect of Nifedipine (Procardia) on Blood Pressure in Women

If you have used data from an outside source or have taken or adapted the table from a source, give the source information in a note below the table. Begin with the word "Note," italicized and followed by a period. If you use lettered footnotes to explain specific data in the table, those footnotes begin on a new line after the source information.

Figures Like tables, number each figure in bold and include a title in italic font. If you have taken or adapted the figure from an outside source, give the source information in a note underneath the figure, starting with the word "Note" in italic and followed by a period. Use the term "From" or "Adapted from" before the source information. Notes can also give additional information or context for the figure.

Preparing the list of references

Begin your list of references on a new page at the end of the paper. Center the title "References" in bold one inch from the top of the page. Double-space throughout. For a sample reference list, see 53b.

Indenting entries Type the first line of each entry at the left margin and indent any additional lines one-half inch.

Alphabetizing the list Alphabetize the reference list by the last names of the authors (or editors) or by the first word of an organization name (if the author is an organization). When a work has no author or editor, alphabetize by the first word of the title other than "A," "An," or "The."

If your list includes two or more works by the same author, arrange the entries by year, the earliest first. If your list includes two or more works by the same author in the same year, arrange the works alphabetically by title. Add the letters "a," "b," and so on within the parentheses after the year. For journal articles, use only the year and the letter: (2012a). For articles in magazines and newspapers, use the full date and the letter in the reference list: (2012a, July 7); use only the year and the letter in the in-text citation.

Authors' names   Invert all authors' names and use initials instead of first names. Separate the names with commas. For two to twenty authors, use an ampersand (&) before the last author's name. For twenty-one or more authors, give the first nineteen authors, three ellipsis dots, and the last author (see item 3 in 52b).

Titles of books and articles   In the reference list, italicize the titles and subtitles of books and other stand-alone works. Do not italicize or use quotation marks around the titles of articles. For both books and articles, capitalize only the first word of the title and subtitle (and all proper nouns). Capitalize names of journals, magazines, and newspapers as you would normally (see 39c).

Abbreviations for page numbers   Abbreviations for "page" and "pages" ("p." and "pp.") are used before page numbers of selections in anthologies (see item 24 in 52b). Do not use "p." or "pp." before page numbers of articles in journals and magazines (see items 11 and 12 in 52b).

Breaking a URL or DOI   Do not insert any line breaks into URLs or DOIs (digital object identifier). Any line breaks that your word processor makes automatically are acceptable. Do not add a period at the end of the URL or DOI.

53b Sample APA research paper

On the following pages is a research paper on the use of educational technology in the shift to student-centered learning, written by April Wang, a student in an education class. Wang's assignment was to write a literature review paper documented with APA-style citations and references.

COURTESY APRIL BO WANG

All pages are
numbered,
starting with the
title page.

1

Paper title
is boldface,
followed by one
blank (double-
spaced) line.
Writer's name;
department and
school; course;
instructor; and
date follow
on separate
double-spaced
lines.

Technology and the Shift From Teacher-Delivered to

Student-Centered Learning: A Review of the Literature

April Bo Wang

Department of Education, Glen County Community College

EDU 107: Education, Technology, and Media

Dr. Julien Gomez

October 29, XXXX

2

Technology and the Shift From Teacher-Delivered to
Student-Centered Learning: A Review of the Literature

In the United States, most public school systems are struggling
with teacher shortages, which are projected to worsen as the number of
applicants to education schools decreases (Donitsa-Schmidt & Zuzovsky,
2014, p. 420). Citing federal data, *The New York Times* reported a 30%
drop in "people entering teacher preparation programs" between 2010
and 2014 (Rich, 2015, para. 10). Especially in science and math fields,
the teacher shortage is projected to escalate in the next 10 years
(Hutchison, 2012). In recent decades, instructors and administrators
have viewed the practice of student-centered learning as one promising
solution. Unlike traditional teacher-delivered (also called "transmissive")
instruction, student-centered learning allows students to help direct
their own education by setting their own goals and selecting appropriate resources for achieving those goals. Though student-centered
learning might once have been viewed as an experimental solution in
understaffed schools, it is gaining credibility as an effective pedagogical
practice. What is also gaining momentum is the idea that technology
might play a significant role in fostering student-centered learning. This
literature review will examine three key questions:

1. In what ways is student-centered learning effective?
2. Can educational technology help students drive their own
   learning?
3. How can public schools effectively combine teacher talent and
   educational technology?

In the face of mounting teacher shortages, public schools should
embrace educational technology that promotes student-centered learning in order to help all students become engaged and successful learners.

Sources provide background information and context.

An in-text citation includes a paragraph number or other locator for a quotation from a source without page numbers.

Wang sets up her organization by posing three questions.

Wang states her thesis.

In What Ways Is Student-Centered Learning Effective?

According to the International Society for Technology in Education (2016), "Student-centered learning moves students from passive receivers of information to active participants in their own discovery process. What students learn, how they learn it, and how their learning is assessed are all driven by each individual student's needs and abilities" (What Is It? section). The results of student-centered learning have been positive, not only for academic achievement but also for student self-esteem. In this model of instruction, the teacher acts as a facilitator, and the students actively participate in the process of learning and teaching. With guidance, students decide on the learning goals most pertinent to themselves, they devise a learning plan that will most likely help them achieve those goals, they direct themselves in carrying out that learning plan, and they assess how much they learned (Çubukçu, 2012, Introduction section). The major differences between student-centered learning and instructor-centered learning are summarized in Table 1.

Bell (2010) has argued that the chief benefit of student-centered learning is that it can connect students with "real-world tasks," thus making learning more engaging as well as more comprehensive (p. 42). For example, Bell observed a group of middle-school students who wanted to build a social justice monument for their school. They researched social justice issues, selected several to focus on, and then designed a three-dimensional playground to represent those issues. In doing so, they achieved learning goals in the areas of social studies, physics, and mathematics and practiced research and teamwork. Students engaged in this kind of learning performed better on both project-based assessments and standardized tests (Bell, 2010).

A Stanford study came to a similar conclusion; researchers examined four schools that had moved from teacher-driven instruction to student-centered learning (Friedlaender et al., 2014). The study focused on students from a mix of racial, cultural, and socioeconomic

---

Headings, centered and boldface, help readers follow the organization.

Wang uses a source to define the key term "student-centered learning."

A locator (section title) is included for a paraphrase to help readers find the source in a long article without page numbers.

A page number or other locator is not necessary for a paraphrase from a short article.

4

Table 1

Comparison of Two Approaches to Teaching and Learning

Teaching and learning period	Instructor-centered approach	Student-centered approach
Before class	• Instructor prepares lecture/instruction on new topic. • Students complete homework on previous topic.	• Students read and view new material, practice new concepts, and prepare questions ahead of class. • Instructor views student practice and questions, identifies learning opportunities.
During class	• Instructor delivers new material in a lecture or prepared discussion. • Students—unprepared—listen, watch, take notes, and try to follow along with the new material.	• Students lead discussions of the new material or practice applying the concepts or skills in an active environment. • Instructor answers student questions and provides immediate feedback.
After class	• Instructor grades homework and gives feedback about the previous lesson. • Students work independently to practice or apply the new concepts.	• Students apply concepts/skills to more complex tasks, some of their own choosing, individually and in groups. • Instructor posts additional resources to help students.

Note. Adapted from *The Flipped Class Demystified*, by New York University, n.d. (https://www.nyu.edu/faculty/teaching-and-learning-resources/instructional-technology-support/instructional-design-assessment/flipped-classes/the-flipped-class-demystified.html).

Wang creates a table to compare and contrast two key concepts for her readers.

backgrounds, with varying levels of English-language proficiency. The researchers predicted that this mix of students, representing differing levels of academic ability, would benefit from a student-centered approach. Through interviews, surveys, and classroom observations, the researchers identified key characteristics of the new student-centered learning environments at the four schools:

- teachers who prioritized building relationships with students
- support structures for teachers to improve and collaborate on instruction
- a shift in classroom activity from lectures and tests to projects and performance-based assessments (pp. 5–7)

After the schools designed their curriculum to be personalized to individual students rather than standardized across a diverse student body and to be inclusive of skills such as persistence as well as traditional academic skills, students outperformed peers on state tests and increased their rates of high school and college graduation (Friedlaender et al., 2014, p. 3).

Can Educational Technology Help Students Drive Their Own Learning?

When students engage in self-directed learning, they rely less on teachers to deliver information and require less face-to-face time with teachers. For content delivery, many school districts have begun to use educational technology resources that, in recent years, have become more available, more affordable, and easier to use. For the purposes of this paper, the term "educational technology resources" encompasses the following: distance learning, by which students learn from a remote instructor online; other online education programming such as slide shows and video or audio lectures; interactive online activities, such as quizzing or games; and the use of computers, tablets, smartphones, SMART Boards, or other such devices for coursework.

The author's name and year of publication are given in a signal phrase, so page numbers are provided at the end of the paraphrase.

6

Much like student-centered learning, the use of educational technology began in many places as a temporary measure to keep classes running despite teacher shortages. A Horn and Staker study (2011) examined the major patterns over time for students who subscribed to distance learning, for example. A decade ago, students who enrolled in distance learning often fell into one of the following categories: They lived in a rural community that had no alternative for learning; they attended a school where there were not enough qualified teachers to teach certain subjects; or they were homeschooled or homebound. But faced with tighter budgets, teacher shortages, increasingly diverse student populations, and rigorous state standards, schools recognized the need and the potential for distance learning across the board.

As the teacher shortage has intensified, educational technology resources have become more tailored to student needs and more affordable. Pens that convert handwritten notes to digital text and organize them, backpacks that charge electronic devices, and apps that create audiovisual flash cards are just a few of the more recent innovations. According to Svokos (2015), some educational technology resources entertain students while supporting student-centered learning:

> GlassLab, a nonprofit that was launched with grants from the Bill & Melinda Gates and MacArthur Foundations, creates educational games that are now being used in more than 6,000 classrooms across the country. Some of the company's games are education versions of existing ones—for example, its first release was SimCity EDU—while others are originals. Teachers get real-time updates on students' progress as well as suggestions on what subjects they need to spend more time perfecting. (5. Educational Games section)

Many of the companies behind these products offer institutional discounts to schools where such devices are used widely by students and teachers.

Wang develops her thesis.

In a signal phrase, the word "and" links the names of two authors; the date is given in parentheses.

A quotation of 40 or more words is indented without quotation marks.

A locator (section title) is used for a direct quotation from an online source with no page numbers.

Horn and Staker (2011) concluded that the chief benefit of technological learning was that it could adapt to the individual student in a way that whole-class delivery by a single teacher could not. Their study examined various schools where technology enabled student-centered learning. For example, Carpe Diem High School in Yuma, Arizona, hired only six certified subject teachers and then outfitted its classrooms with 280 computers connected to online learning programs. The programs included software that offered "continual feedback, assessment, and incremental victory in a way that a face-to-face teacher with a class of 30 students never could. After each win, students continue to move forward at their own pace" (p. 9). Students alternated between personalized 55-minute courses online and 55-minute courses with one of the six teachers. The academic outcomes were promising. Carpe Diem ranked first in its county for student math and reading scores. Similarly, Rocketship Education, a charter network that serves low-income, predominantly Latino students, created a digital learning lab, reducing the need to hire more teachers. Rocketship's academic scores ranked in the top 15 of all California low-income public schools.

Wang uses her own analysis to shape the conversation among her sources in this synthesis paragraph.

It is clear that educational technology will continue to play a role in student and school performance. Horn and Staker (2011) acknowledged that they focused on programs in which integration of educational technology led to improved student performance. In other schools, technological learning is simply distance learning—watching a remote teacher—and not student-centered learning that allows students to partner with teachers to develop enriching learning experiences. That said, many educators seem convinced that educational technology has the potential to help them transition from traditional teacher-driven learning to student-centered learning. All four schools in the Stanford study heavily relied on technology (Friedlaender et al., 2014). And indeed, Demski (2012) argued that technology is not supplemental

8

but instead is "central" to student-centered learning (p. 33). Rather than turning to a teacher as the source of information, students are sent to investigate solutions to problems by searching online, emailing experts, collaborating with one another in a wiki space, or completing online practice. Rather than turning to a teacher for the answer to a question, students are driven to perform—driven to use technology to find those answers themselves.

How Can Public Schools Effectively Combine Teacher Talent and Educational Technology?

Some researchers have expressed doubt that schools are ready for student-centered learning—or any type of instruction—that is driven by technology. In a recent survey conducted by the Nellie Mae Education Foundation, Moeller and Reitzes (2011) reported not only that many teachers lacked confidence in their ability to incorporate technology in the classroom but that 43% of polled high school students said that they lacked confidence in their technological proficiency going into college and careers. The study concluded that technology alone would not improve learning environments. Yet others argued that students adapt quickly to even unfamiliar technology and use it to further their own learning. For example, Mitra (2013) caught the attention of the education world with his study of how to educate students in the slums of India. He installed an Internet-accessible computer in a wall in a New Delhi urban slum and left it there with no instructions. Over a few months, many of the children had learned how to use the computer, how to access information over the Internet, how to interpret information, and how to communicate this information to one another. Mitra's experiment was "not about making learning happen. [It was] about letting it happen" (16:31). He concluded that in the absence of teachers, even in developing countries less inundated by technology, a tool that allowed

Wang uses a source to introduce a counterargument.

Brackets indicate Wang's change in the quoted material.

For a direct quotation from a video, a time stamp indicates the start of the quotation.

9

access to an organized database of knowledge (such as a search engine) was sufficient to provide students with a rewarding learning experience.

According to the Stanford study, however, the presence of teachers is still crucial (Friedlaender et al., 2014). Their roles will simply change from distributors of knowledge to facilitators and supporters of self-directed student-centered learning. The researchers asserted that teacher education and professional development programs can no longer prepare their teachers in a single instructional mode, such as teacher-delivered learning; they must instead equip teachers with a wide repertoire of skills to support a wide variety of student learning experiences. The Stanford study argued that since teachers would be partnering with students to shape the learning experience, rather than designing and delivering a curriculum on their own, the main job of a teacher would become relationship building. The teacher would establish a relationship with each student so that the teacher could support whatever learning the student pursues.

Many schools have already effectively paired a reduced faculty with educational technology to support successful student-centered learning. For example, Watson (2008) offered a case study of the Cincinnati Public Schools Virtual High School, which brought students together in a physical school building to work with an assortment of online learning programs. Although there were only 10 certified teachers in the building, students were able to engage in highly individualized instruction according to their own needs, strengths, and learning styles, using the 10 teachers as support (p. 7). Commonwealth Connections Academy (CCA), a public school in Pennsylvania, also brings students into a physical school building to engage in digital curriculum. However, rather than having students identify their own learning goals and design their own curriculum around those goals, CCA uses educational technology as an assessment tool to identify areas of student weakness. It then partners students with teachers to address those areas (pp. 8–9).

In a citation of a work with three or more authors, the first author's name is given followed by "et al." in parentheses or in a text sentence.

10

Conclusion

Public education faces the opportunity for a shift from the model of
teacher-delivered instruction that has characterized American public
schools since their foundation to a student-centered learning model. Not
only has student-centered learning proved effective in improving student
academic and developmental outcomes, but it can also synchronize
with technological learning for widespread adaptability across schools.
Because it relies on student direction rather than an established curriculum, student-centered learning supported by educational technology
can adapt to the different needs of individual students and a variety of
learning environments—urban and rural, well funded and underfunded.
Similarly, when student-centered learning relies on technology rather
than a corps of uniformly trained teachers, it holds promise for schools
that would otherwise suffer from a lack of human or financial resources.

The tone of the
conclusion is
objective and
presents answers
to Wang's three
organizational
questions.

11

References

List of references begins on a new page. Heading is centered and boldface.

List is alphabetized by authors' last names. All authors' names are inverted.

The first line of an entry is at the left margin; subsequent lines indent ½".

Double-spacing is used throughout.

Bell, S. (2010). Project-based learning for the 21st century: Skills for the future. *The Clearing House, 83*(2), 39–43.

Çubukçu, Z. (2012). Teachers' evaluation of student-centered learning environments. *Education, 133*(1).

Demski, J. (2012, January). This time it's personal. *THE Journal (Technological Horizons in Education), 39*(1), 32–36.

Donitsa-Schmidt, S., & Zuzovsky, R. (2014). Teacher supply and demand: The school level perspective. *American Journal of Educational Research, 2*(6), 420–429. https://doi.org/10.12691/education-2-6-14

Friedlaender, D., Burns, D., Lewis-Charp, H., Cook-Harvey, C. M., & Darling-Hammond, L. (2014). *Student-centered schools: Closing the opportunity gap* [Research brief]. Stanford Center for Opportunity Policy in Education. https://edpolicy.stanford.edu/sites/default/files/scope-pub-student-centered-research-brief.pdf

Horn, M. B., & Staker, H. (2011). *The rise of K-12 blended learning.* Innosight Institute. http://www.christenseninstitute.org/wp-content/uploads/2013/04/The-rise-of-K-12-blended-learning.pdf

Hutchison, L. F. (2012). Addressing the STEM teacher shortage in American schools: Ways to recruit and retain effective STEM teachers. *Action in Teacher Education, 34*(5/6), 541–550. https://doi.org/10.1080/01626620.2012.729483

International Society for Technology in Education. (2016). *Student-centered learning.* http://www.iste.org/connected/standards/essential-conditions/student-centered-learning

Mitra, S. (2013, February). *Build a school in the cloud* [Video]. TED. https://www.ted.com/talks/sugata_mitra_build_a_school_in_the_cloud?language=en

12

Moeller, B., & Reitzes, T. (2011, July). *Integrating technology with student-centered learning.* Nellie Mae Education Foundation. http://www.nmefoundation.org/research/personalization/integrating-technology-with-student-centered-learn

Rich, M. (2015, August 9). Teacher shortages spur a nationwide hiring scramble (credentials optional). *The New York Times.* https://nyti.ms/1WaaV7a

Svokos, A. (2015, May 7). 5 innovations from the past decade that aim to change the American classroom. *Huffpost.* https://www.huffpost.com/entry/technology-changes-classrooms_n_7190910

Watson, J. (2008, January). *Blended learning: The convergence of online and face-to-face education.* North American Council for Online Learning. http:// www.inacol.org/wp-content/uploads/2015/02/NACOL_PP-BlendedLearning-lr.pdf

Abstract and running head (for professional papers)

TECHNOLOGY AND STUDENT-CENTERED LEARNING   2

Abstract

In recent decades, instructors and administrators have viewed stu-

dent-centered learning as a promising pedagogical practice that offers

both the hope of increasing academic performance and a solution for

teacher shortages. Differing from the traditional model of instruction

in which a teacher delivers content from the front of a classroom,

student-centered learning puts the students at the center of teaching

and learning. Students set their own learning goals, select appropriate

resources, and progress at their own pace. Student-centered learning has

produced both positive results and increases in students' self-esteem.

Given the recent proliferation of technology in classrooms, school dis-

tricts are poised for success in making the shift to student-centered

learning. The question for district leaders, however, is how to effectively

balance existing teacher talent with educational technology.

Keywords: digital learning, student-centered learning, personalized

learning, education technology, transmissive, blended

For professional papers: running head (short form of the title; 50 characters or fewer) in all capital letters on every page; title "Abstract" centered and boldface.

An abstract is required for professional papers submitted for publication.

Keywords help readers search for a paper online or in a database.

Answers to Exercises

Exercise 1–2, page 11

1. b; a is too vague
2. a; b is too broad
3. a; b is a question
4. b; a is too vague
5. b; a is a statement of fact

Exercise 2–1, page 17

Topic sentence: Quilt making has served as an important means of social, political, and artistic expression for women. *Eliminate the following sentence:* They used dyed cotton fabrics much like the fabrics quilters use today; surprisingly, quilters' basic materials haven't changed that much over the years.

Exercise 5–1, page 57

logos; *ethos*; *pathos*

Exercise 8–1, page 83

Possible revisions:

a. The Prussians defeated the Saxons in 1745.
b. Ahmed, the producer, manages the entire operation.
c. The tour guides expertly paddled the sea kayaks.
d. Correct
e. The congresswoman heard the protestors' shouts as she walked up the Capitol steps.

Exercise 9–1, page 86

Possible revisions:

a. Police dogs are used for finding lost children, tracking criminals, and detecting bombs and illegal drugs.
b. Hannah told her rock-climbing partner that she bought a new harness and that she wanted to climb Otter Cliffs.

c. It is more difficult to sustain an exercise program than to start one.
d. During basic training, I was told not only what to do but also what to think.
e. Jan wanted to drive either to wine country or to Sausalito.

Exercise 10–1, page 89

Possible revisions:

a. Oranges provide more vitamin C than any other fruit.
b. The women entering the military academy can expect haircuts as short as those of the male cadets.
c. Looking out the family room window, Sarah saw that her favorite tree, which she had climbed as a child, was gone.
d. The graphic designers are interested in and knowledgeable about producing posters for the balloon race.
e. My town's high school is much larger than the neighboring town's high school.

Exercise 11–1, page 91

Possible revisions:

a. Using surgical gloves is a precaution now taken by dentists to prevent contact with patients' blood and saliva.
b. A career in medicine, which my brother is pursuing, requires at least ten years of challenging work.
c. The pharaohs had bad teeth because tiny particles of sand found their way into Egyptian bread.
d. Recurring bouts of flu caused the team to forfeit a record number of games.
e. This box contains the key to your future.

Exercise 12–1, page 94

Possible revisions:

a. The manager asked her employees to submit their reports today if they had time.

b. Many students graduate from college with debt totaling more than fifty thousand dollars.

c. It is a myth that humans use only 10 percent of their brains.

d. When she looked in the closet, Daria found the old nightgown she used to wear to sleep.

e. Not all geese fly beyond Narragansett for the winter.

Exercise 12–2, page 95

Possible revisions:

a. To complete an online purchase with a credit card, you must enter the expiration date and the security code.

b. Though Martha was only sixteen, UCLA accepted her application.

c. As I settled in the cockpit, the pounding of the engine was muffled only slightly by my helmet.

d. After studying polymer chemistry, Phuong found computer games less complex.

e. When I was a young man, my mother enrolled me in tap dance classes.

Exercise 13–1, page 97

Possible revisions:

Version 1, first person

When online dating first became available, I thought that it would simplify romance. I believed that I could type in a list of criteria—sense of humor, college education, green eyes, good job—and a database would select the perfect mate for me. I signed up for some services and filled out my profile, confident that true love was only a few mouse clicks away. As it turns out, however, virtual dating is no easier than traditional dating. I still have to contact the people I find, exchange emails and phone calls, and meet them in the real world. Although a database might

produce a list of possibilities and screen out obviously undesirable people, it can't predict chemistry. More often than not, I find that people who seem perfect online just don't click with me in person. Electronic services do help me expand my pool of potential dates, but they're no substitute for the hard work of romance.

Version 2, third person

When online dating first became available, many people thought that it would simplify romance. Hopeful singles believed that they could type in a list of criteria—sense of humor, college education, green eyes, good job—and a database would select the perfect mate. Thousands of people signed up for services and filled out their profiles, confident that true love was only a few mouse clicks away. As it turns out, however, virtual dating is no easier than traditional dating. Online daters still have to contact the people they find, exchange emails and phone calls, and meet in the real world. Although a database might produce a list of possibilities and screen out obviously undesirable people, it can't predict chemistry. More often than not, people who seem perfect online just don't click in person. Electronic services do help single people expand their pool of potential dates, but they're no substitute for the hard work of romance.

Exercise 14–1, page 101

Possible revisions:

a. The X-Men comic books and Japanese woodcuts of kabuki dancers, all part of Marlena's research project on popular culture, covered the tabletop and the chairs.

b. Our waitress, costumed in a kimono, had painted her face white and had arranged her hair in a beehive.

c. Students can apply for a spot in the leadership program, which teaches thinking and communication skills.

d. Shore houses were flooded, beaches were washed away, and Brant's Lighthouse was swallowed by the sea.

e. Laura Thackray, an engineer at Volvo, addressed women's safety needs by designing a pregnant crash-test dummy.

Exercise 14–2, page 103

Possible revisions:

a. These particles, known as "stealth liposomes," can hide in the body for a long time without detection.

b. Irena, a competitive gymnast majoring in biochemistry, intends to apply her athletic experience and her science degree to a career in sports medicine.

c. Because students, textile workers, and labor unions have loudly protested sweatshop abuses, apparel makers have been forced to examine their labor practices.

d. Developed in a European university, IRC (Internet relay chat) was created as a way for a group of graduate students to talk about projects from their dorm rooms.

e. The cafeteria's new menu, which has an international flavor, includes everything from enchiladas and pizza to pad thai and sauerbraten.

Exercise 16–1, page 110

Possible revisions:

a. Martin Luther King Jr. set a high standard for future leaders.

b. Alice has loved cooking since she could first peek over a kitchen tabletop.

c. Bloom's race for the governorship is futile.

d. A successful graphic designer must have technical knowledge and an eye for color and balance.

e. You will set up email for all employees.

Exercise 17–1, page 115

Possible revisions:

a. Dr. Geralyn Farmer is the chief surgeon at University Hospital. Dr. Paul Green is her assistant.

b. All applicants want to know how much they will earn.

c. Elementary school teachers should understand the concept of nurturing if they intend to be effective.

d. Obstetricians need to be available to their patients at all hours.

e. If we do not stop polluting our environment, we will perish.

Exercise 18–1, page 119

Possible revisions:

a. John stormed into the room like a hurricane.

b. Some people insist that they'll always be available to help, even when they haven't been before.

c. The Cubs easily beat the Mets, who were in trouble early in the game today at Wrigley Field.

d. We worked out the problems in our relationship.

e. My mother accused me of evading her questions when in fact I was just saying the first thing that came to mind.

Exercise 20–1, page 131

Possible revisions:

a. Listening to the CD her sister had sent, Mia was overcome with a mix of emotions: happiness, homesickness, and nostalgia.

b. Cortés and his soldiers were astonished when they looked down from the mountains and saw Tenochtitlán, the magnificent capital of the Aztecs.

c. Although my spoken Spanish is not very good, I can read the language with ease.

d. There are several reasons for not eating meat. One reason is that dangerous chemicals are used throughout the various stages of meat production.

e. To learn how to sculpt beauty from everyday life is my intention in studying art and archaeology.

Exercise 21–1, page 135

Possible revisions:

a. The city had one public swimming pool, which stayed packed with children all summer long.

b. The building is being renovated, so at times we have no heat, water, or electricity.

c. The view was not what the travel agent had described. Where were the rolling hills and the shimmering rivers?

d. Walker's coming-of-age novel is set against a gloomy scientific backdrop; the Earth's rotation has begun to slow down.

e. City officials had good reason to fear a major earthquake: most [*or* Most] of the business district was built on landfill.

Exercise 22–1, page 141

a. One of the main reasons for elephant poaching is the profits received from selling the ivory tusks.

b. Correct

c. A number of students in the seminar were aware of the importance of joining the discussion.

d. Batik cloth from Bali, blue and white ceramics from Delft, and a bocce ball from Turin have made Angelie's room the talk of the dorm.

e. Correct

Exercise 23–1, page 144

Possible revisions:

a. Every presidential candidate must appeal to a wide variety of ethnic and social groups to win the election.

b. If someone wants to ride David's motorcycle, they have to wear a helmet. [*or*] Anyone who wants to ride David's motorcycle has to wear a helmet.

c. The trainer motioned for all the students to move their arms in wide, slow circles.

d. Correct

e. Applicants should be bilingual if they want to qualify for this position.

Exercise 24–1, page 147

Possible revisions:

a. Some professors say that engineering students should have hands-on experience with dismantling and reassembling machines.

b. Because she had decorated her living room with posters from chamber music festivals, her date thought that she was interested in classical music. Actually she preferred rock.

c. The high school principal congratulated the seniors who were graduating later that day.

d. Marianne told Jenny, "I am worried about your mother's illness." [*or* ". . . about my mother's illness."]

e. Though Lewis cried for several minutes after scraping his knee, eventually his crying subsided.

Exercise 25–1, page 152

a. Correct [But the writer could change the end of the sentence: . . . *than he was.*]

b. Correct [But the writer could change the end of the sentence: . . . *that she was the coach.*]

c. She appreciated his telling the truth in such a difficult situation.

d. The director has asked you and me to draft a proposal for a new recycling plan.

e. Five close friends and I rented an SUV, packed it with food, and drove two hundred miles to Mardi Gras.

Exercise 26–1, page 154

a. Correct
b. The environmental policy conference featured scholars whom I had never heard of. [*or* . . . scholars I had never heard of.]
c. Correct
d. Daniel always gives a holiday donation to whoever needs it.
e. The singers whom Natalia selected for the choir attended their first rehearsal last night. [*or* The singers Natalia selected . . .]

Exercise 27–1, page 159

a. Do you expect to perform well on the nursing board exam next week?
b. With the budget deadline approaching, our office has been handling routine correspondence more slowly than we usually do.
c. Correct
d. The customer complained that he hadn't been treated nicely by the agent on the phone.
e. Of all the smart people in my family, Uncle Roberto is the cleverest [*or* most clever].

Exercise 28–1, page 165

a. The glass sculptures of the Swan Boats were prominent in the brightly lit lobby.
b. When I get the urge to exercise, I lie down until it passes.
c. Grandmother had driven our new hybrid to the sunrise church service, so we were left with the van.
d. Christos didn't know about Marlo's promotion because he never listens. He is [*or* He's] always talking.
e. A pile of dirty rags was lying at the bottom of the stairs.

Exercise 28–2, page 169

a. Correct
b. Watson and Crick discovered the mechanism that controls inheritance in all life: the workings of the DNA molecule.
c. When city planners proposed rezoning the waterfront, did they know that the mayor had promised to curb development in that neighborhood?
d. Tonight's concert begins at 9:30. If it were earlier, I'd consider going.
e. Correct

Exercise 29–1, page 172

a. A major league pitcher can throw a baseball more than ninety-five miles per hour.
b. The writing center tutor will help you revise your essay.
c. A reptile must adjust its body temperature to its environment.
d. Correct
e. My uncle, a cartoonist, could sketch a face in less than a minute.

Exercise 29–2, page 178

a. Freezing rain causes an icy glaze on trees.
b. I don't use the subway because I am claustrophobic.
c. Recently there have been a number of earthquakes in Turkey.
d. Whenever we eat at the café, we sit at a small table in the corner of the room.
e. In the 1990s, entrepreneurs created new online businesses in record numbers.

Exercise 30–1, page 183

a. The cold, impersonal atmosphere of the university was unbearable.

b. An ambulance threaded its way through police cars, fire trucks, and irate citizens.

c. Correct

d. After two broken arms, three cracked ribs, and one concussion, Ken quit the varsity football team.

e. Correct

Exercise 30–2, page 190

a. Cricket, which originated in England, is also popular in Australia, South Africa, and India.

b. At the sound of the starting pistol, the horses surged forward toward the first obstacle, a sharp incline three feet high.

c. After seeing an exhibition of Western art, Gerhard Richter escaped from East Berlin and smuggled out many of his notebooks.

d. Corrie's new wet suit has an intricate blue pattern.

e. We replaced the rickety old spiral staircase with a sturdy new ladder.

Exercise 31–1, page 194

a. Correct

b. Tricia's first artwork was a bright blue clay dolphin.

c. Some modern musicians (trumpeter Jon Hassell is an example) blend several cultural traditions into a unique sound.

d. Myra liked hot, spicy foods such as chili, kung pao chicken, and buffalo wings.

e. On the display screen was a soothing pattern of light and shadow.

Exercise 32–1, page 200

a. Correct [Either *it* or *It* is correct.]

b. If we have come to fight, we are far too few; if we have come to die, we are far too many.

c. The travel package includes a round-trip ticket to Athens, a cruise through the Cyclades, and all hotel accommodations.

d. The news article portrays the land use proposal as reckless, although 62 percent of the town's residents support it.

e. Strong black coffee will not sober you up; the truth is that time is the only way to get alcohol out of your system.

Exercise 33–1, page 204

a. Correct

b. The innovative shoe fastener was inspired by the designer's young son.

c. Each day's menu features a different European country's dish.

d. Sue worked overtime to increase her family's earnings.

e. Ms. Jacobs is unwilling to listen to students' complaints about computer failures.

Exercise 34–1, page 209

a. As for the advertisement "Sailors have more fun," if you consider chipping paint and swabbing decks fun, then you will have plenty of it.

b. Correct

c. After winning the lottery, Juanita said that she would give half the money to charity.

d. After the movie, Vicki said, "The reviewer called this flick 'trash of the first order.' I guess you can't believe everything you read."

e. Correct

Exercise 36–1, page 214

a. A client left a [*or* their] cell phone in our conference room after the meeting.

b. The films we made of Kilauea on our trip to Hawaii Volcanoes National Park illustrate a typical spatter cone eruption.

c. Correct

d. Of three engineering fields—chemical, mechanical, and materials—Keegan chose materials engineering for its application to toy manufacturing.

e. Correct

Exercise 38–1, page 223

a. The Williams sisters were the heroes of my entire high school tennis team.

b. The swiftly moving tugboat pulled alongside the barge and directed it away from the oil spill in the harbor.

c. We managed to get the most desirable seats in the theater.

d. As a livestock veterinarian, she cares for horses, donkeys, cows, and other large farm animals.

e. Roadblocks were set up along all the major highways leading out of the city.

Exercise 39–1, page 226

a. Assistant Dean Shirin Ahmadi recommended offering more world language courses.

b. Correct

c. Kalindi has an ambitious semester, studying differential calculus, classical Hebrew, brochure design, and Greek literature.

d. Lydia's aunt and uncle make modular houses as beautiful as modernist works of art.

e. We amused ourselves on the long flight by discussing how spring in Kyoto stacks up against summer in London.

Exercise 40–1, page 236

a. indefinite pronoun, verb with helping verb, preposition

b. verb, adverb, noun

c. preposition, conjunction (conjunctive adverb), pronoun

d. noun/adjective, modal verb, conjunction

e. demonstrative pronoun, verb, subordinating conjunction

Exercise 41–1, page 239

a. Complete subjects: The hills and mountains, the snow atop them; simple subjects: hills, mountains, snow

b. Complete subject: points; simple subject: points

c. Complete subject: (You)

d. Complete subject: hundreds of fireflies; simple subject: hundreds

e. Complete subject: The evidence against the defendant; simple subject: evidence

Exercise 42–1, page 251

a. so that every vote would count (adverb clause modifying *adjusted*)

b. that targets baby boomers (adjective clause modifying *campaign*)

c. After the Tambora volcano erupted in the southern Pacific in 1815 (adverb clause modifying *realized*); that it would contribute to the "year without a summer" in Europe and North America (noun clause used as direct object of *realized*)

d. that at a certain point there will be no more oil to extract from the earth (noun clause used as direct object of *implies*)

e. when you are rushing (adverb clause modifying *are overlooked*)

Exercise 43–1, page 253

a. Complex; that are ignited in dry areas (adjective clause)

b. Compound

c. Simple

d. Complex; Before we leave for the station (adverb clause)

e. Compound-complex; when you want to leave (noun clause)

Acknowledgments

Jonathan H. Adler, "Little Green Lies," *Policy Review*, Summer 1992. Copyright © 1992 by The Heritage Foundation. Used with permission.

Jennifer Alsever, "What Is Crowdsourcing?" *CBS News*, March 7, 2007. Copyright © 2007 by CBS Interactive Inc. Used with permission.

Michele Berger, "Volunteer Army," *Audubon*, November–December 2010. Copyright © National Audubon Society. Used with permission.

Eugene Boe, "Pioneers to Eternity: Norwegians on the Prairie," from *Immigrant Experience*, edited by Thomas C. Wheeler, copyright © 1971 by Penguin Random House LLC. Used by permission of Doubleday, an imprint of the Knopf Doubleday Publishing Group, a division of Penguin Random House LLC. All rights reserved.

Excerpt from "Encyclopedia of Fishing," by Dorling Kindersley. Copyright © 1994 Dorling Kindersley Limited. Reprinted by permission of DK, a division of Penguin Random House LLC.

Joshua Rothman, "What Amazon's Purchase of Whole Foods Really Means," *The New Yorker*, June 24, 2017. Copyright © 2017 by Conde Nast. Used with permission.

Anne and Jack Rudloe, "Electric Warfare: The Fish That Kill with Thunderbolts," *The Smithsonian*, vol. 24, pp. 94–105. Copyright © Jack Rudloe. Used with permission.

Betsy Taylor, "Big Box Stores are Bad for Main Street," *CQ Researcher*, November 1999. Copyright © 1999 by CQ Press, a division of Sage Publications. Used with permission.

Index

to fix run-on sentences, 133
and subordination, 102–03
Correlative conjunctions
defined, 235
parallelism with, 85–86
could, as modal verb, 164, 170, 231
could of (nonstandard), 122
council, counsel, 122
Counterarguments
addressing, 67–68, 74, 300
evaluating, 54–60
Count nouns, articles (*a, an, the*)
with, 173
Country names, abbreviations for,
216–17
couple. See Collective nouns
Credibility
assessing, 56, 58, 272
establishing, 61, 62–63, 283, 300
Critical reading. *See* Reading,
active and critical
Critical thinking
for analysis, 36–42, 49–50
about arguments, 54–60
evaluating sources, 270–76
Criticism, constructive, 29
crowd. See Collective nouns
Cumulative adjectives, no comma
with, 182–83, 192
Currency, of sources, 272

D

-d, -ed, verb ending, 160, 163–64
Dangling modifiers, 94–95
Dashes, 211
to fix run-on sentences,
133–34
data, 122
Data. *See* Facts; Statistics

Databases
articles from. *See* Article from a
database
for finding sources, 263
how-to guide, 265
Dates
in APA reference list, 372
capitalization of, 224
commas with, 189
in MLA works cited list, 321
numbers in, 218
Days of the week, capitalization
of, 224
Deadlines, planning and, 4, 256–57
Debates, entering, 258–60. *See also*
Argument papers; Research
papers; Synthesizing sources
Declarative sentences, 253
Definite article. See *the*
Definition
as paragraph strategy, 26
of words, 116
Degree of adjectives and adverbs.
See Comparative form of adjec-
tives and adverbs; Superlative
form of adjectives and adverbs
Degrees, academic, abbreviations
for, 216–17
Demonstrative pronouns, 230
Denotation (dictionary definition
of word), 116
Dependent clauses. *See* Subordinate
clauses
Description, as paragraph strategy,
22–23
Design. *See* Format; Visuals
Detail, adequate. *See* Evidence
Determiners, 172–75
Development, of ideas, 21–26, 31.
See also Evidence

A List of Charts

Revision Symbols

Boldface numbers refer to sections of the handbook.

abbr	abbreviation	37a–d	p	punctuation		
add	add needed word	10	⌃,	comma		30
adj	misuse of adjective	27	no ,	no comma		31
adv	misuse of adverb	27	;	semicolon		32a–d
agr	agreement	22, 23	:	colon		32e–g
appr	inappropriate language	17	⸍	apostrophe		33
art	article (a, an, the)	29b	" "	quotation marks		34
awk	awkward		. ?	period, question mark		35a–b
cap	capital letter	39	!	exclamation point		35c
case	pronoun case	23, 24	— ( )	dash, parentheses		36a–b
cliché	cliché	18d	[ ] . . .	brackets, ellipsis mark		36c–d
coh	coherence	2b	/	slash		36e
coord	coordination	14	¶	new paragraph		2
cs	comma splice	21	pass	ineffective passive		8
dev	inadequate development	2c	pn agr	pronoun agreement		23
dm	dangling modifier	12d	proof	proofreading problem		3e
-ed	-ed ending	28d	ref	pronoun reference		24
emph	emphasis	14	run-on	run-on sentence		21
ESL	English as a second language, multilingual	29	-s	-s ending		22a, 28c
exact	inexact language	18	sexist	sexist language		17f, 23a
frag	sentence fragment	20	shift	distracting shift		13
fs	fused sentence	21	sl	slang		17d
gl/us	see glossary of usage	19	sp	misspelled word		38a
hyph	hyphen	38b–f	sub	subordination		14
idiom	idioms	18c	sv agr	subject-verb agreement		22, 28c
inc	incomplete construction	10	t	verb tense		28f
irreg	irregular verb	28a	trans	transition needed		2b
ital	italics	37g–h	usage	see glossary of usage		19
jarg	jargon	17b	v	voice		8a
lc	lowercase	39	var	lack of variety in sentence structure		15
mix	mixed construction	11	vb	verb problem		28, 29a
mm	misplaced modifier	12a–c	w	wordy		16
mood	mood of verb	28g	//	parallelism		9
nonst	nonstandard usage	28	⌃	insert		
num	use of numbers	37e–f	#	insert space		
om	omitted word	10, 29b	⌒	close up space		

A List of Grammatical Terms

Boldface numbers refer to sections of the handbook.

Detailed Menu